Jerry Baker's

THE *New* IMPATIENT GARDENER

www.jerrybaker.com

Other Jerry Baker Books:

Jerry Baker's Supermarket Super Gardens
Jerry Baker's Dear God...Please Help It Grow!
Secrets from the Jerry Baker Test Gardens
Jerry Baker's All-American Lawns
Jerry Baker's Bug Off!
Jerry Baker's Terrific Garden Tonics!
Jerry Baker's Backyard Problem Solver
Jerry Baker's Green Grass Magic
Jerry Baker's Great Green Book of Garden Secrets
Jerry Baker's Old-Time Gardening Wisdom

Jerry Baker's Backyard Birdscaping Bonanza
Jerry Baker's Backyard Bird Feeding Bonanza
Jerry Baker's Year-Round Bloomers
Jerry Baker's Flower Garden Problem Solver
Jerry Baker's Perfect Perennials!

Healing Fixers Mixers & Elixirs
Grandma Putt's Home Health Remedies
Nature's Best Miracle Medicines
Jerry Baker's Supermarket Super Remedies
Jerry Baker's The New Healing Foods
Jerry Baker's Amazing Antidotes
Jerry Baker's Anti-Pain Plan
Jerry Baker's Oddball Ointments, Powerful Potions, and Fabulous Folk Remedies
Jerry Baker's Giant Book of Kitchen Counter Cures

Jerry Baker's Ultimate Household Tonics Book!
America's Favorite Practical Problem Solvers
Jerry Baker's Can the Clutter!
Jerry Baker's Cleaning Magic!
Jerry Baker's Homespun Magic
Grandma Putt's Old-Time Vinegar, Garlic, Baking Soda, and 101 More Problem Solvers
Jerry Baker's Supermarket Super Products!
Jerry Baker's It Pays to Be Cheap!

To order any of the above, or for more information on Jerry Baker's
amazing home, health, and garden tips, tricks, and tonics, please write to:

Jerry Baker, P.O. Box 1001
Wixom, MI 48393

Or, visit Jerry Baker online at:

www.jerrybaker.com

Jerry Baker's

THE
New
IMPATIENT
GARDENER

HOW TO GROW THE GREENEST GRASS, PRETTIEST FLOWERS, TASTIEST FRUITS AND VEGETABLES—WITHOUT A GREEN THUMB!

by Jerry Baker,
America's Master Gardener®

Published by American Master Products, Inc.

Executive Editor: Kim Adam Gasior
Managing Editor: Cheryl Winters-Tetreau
Writer: Vicki Webster
Copy Editor: Nanette Bendyna
Production Editor: Debby Duvall
Interior Design and Layout: Nancy Biltcliff
Illustrations: Craig Wilson
Cover Design: Alison McKenna
Indexer: Nan Badgett

Publisher's Cataloging-in-Publication
(Provided by Quality Books, Inc.)

Baker, Jerry.
    Jerry Baker's the new impatient gardener : how to grow the greenest grass, prettiest flowers, tastiest fruits and vegetables--without a green thumb!.
    p. cm.
    Includes index.
    ISBN 978-0-922433-03-2

    1. Gardening.   I. Title. II. Title: New impatient gardener.

SB453.B3174 2012   635
            QBI12-600033

Printed in the United States of America
2 4 6 8 10 9 7 5 3 1 hardcover

INTRODUCTION

Many years ago (more than I care to remember), I wrote a best-selling book called *The Impatient Gardener*. It was "the berries" for folks who wanted their little piece of paradise to be clean, green, and blooming to beat the band—but who didn't want to do a lot of work.

Well, since that book was published, three things have happened. The first is that I've gained plenty of hands-on experience. (Okay, I'll say it: I've grown older and wiser.) The second—judging from the mountains of mail I get—is that there are more impatient folks out there now than ever before. They want it all, and they want it now! And finally, developments in technology, plant breeding, and soil science have made it easier and faster than ever before to grow and maintain a glorious green scene. So I thought, why not put all of the stuff I've learned over the years, including my famous time- and labor-saving tips, tricks, and tonics, into one big book? That way, everyone could benefit!

Of course, wanting to have a lush lawn and glorious gardens without spending a lot of time and effort is nothing new. In fact, it's as old as the hills. In **Grandma's Grow-How**—one of the fantastic features in this book—you'll get some of my Grandma Putt's favorite nuggets of wisdom, along with her handy helpers for growing stronger, healthier plants with no muss and no fuss. Want a sneak preview? Grandma attracted beneficial insects by the bucketful—and repelled some of the most destructive insects on the planet simply by planting plenty of dill.

 My **Quick Fix** pointers show you fast, fun, and foolproof ways to prevent pest and disease problems, speed up plant growth, make fruits and vegetables ripen more quickly—and cut the time it takes to do routine chores like mowing your lawn. For instance, did you know that tomatoes will ripen as much as two weeks earlier if you simply lay aluminum foil on the ground under the plants? Amazing, but true!

 In **Take 2,** I share dozens of tips for turning would-be trash into garden-variety treasures, ranging from plant foods to pest-control aids and seed-starting pots to sprinkler testers. You'll learn how to deliver deep-down moisture to plants without the hassle (and expense) of installing a fancy maze of pipes and cables. Hint: Start saving your empty coffee cans!

 And **Help!** is just what the title implies: letters from folks like you asking for— and getting—my best advice on solving perplexing problems of all kinds. You'll get the skinny on topics like grass seed that's too pooped to participate, healthy plants that have lost their luster, and newly planted tulip bulbs that are missing in action.

 Sprinkled throughout these pages you'll see **callouts**—tiny tidbits of terrific advice that'll save you tons of time and effort in every part of your yard. Just to whet your appetite, would you believe that beating a tree in early spring with a rolled-up newspaper stimulates sap flow, which will jump-start great growth? It's true!

Finally (of course!), you'll find a whole stack of my world-famous tonics made from common products found in your local supermarket or kitchen cabinets. With these DIY fixers, you'll be able to fend off pesky pests and dastardly diseases in a jiffy, plus add lots of get-up-and-grow power to the green, green grass of home and all the other plants in your yard.

So what are you waiting for? We're in a hurry here . . . so let's get growing!

CONTENTS

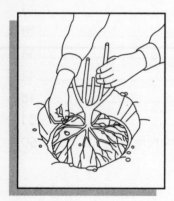

CHAPTER 9

Great Groundwork: Secrets to Green Scene Success

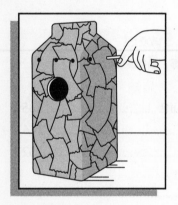

CHAPTER 10:

Timely Troubleshooting: Winning the War on Pests and Diseases

CHAPTER

1

YOUR LOVELY LAWN

Toe-Ticklin' Turf in No Time at All

Okay, I admit it: "<u>NO</u> time" is a slight exaggeration. After all, a lawn is composed of hundreds of thousands, even millions, of individual grass plants, and just like any other living thing, they need a certain amount of TLC if they're going to perform their best (assuming they even survive). But it is a fact—guaranteed—that if you follow my timely tips and simple, step-by-step instructions in this chapter, you can have the lawn of your dreams in less time and with less effort than you ever thought possible.

PLAN FOR SUCCESS

Here's a piece of advice that seems to contradict the title of this book, but take it from me, it is the key to a healthy, low-maintenance lawn: Plan before you plant. I know that when you're staring out the window at a bare plot of land or a scruffy, balding old lawn, it's mighty tempting to dive right in. Well, don't do it! If you fall for the promise of quick coverage from a bag of cheap grass seed or a "deal" on hydroseeding (a professionally applied spray-on combination of grass seed, water, fertilizer, and mulch), you'll wind up with a struggling, weedy lawn that'll give you no end of trouble.

If you'd like more incentive to invest a little time planning and caring for your lawn, consider this: Surveys of home buyers indicate that a well-maintained yard adds as much as 15 percent to the value of a house!

First Things First

Step one on the road to a lawn that's a delight and not a disgrace is to decide how you and your family (pets included) will use your lawn, how much turf you'd *like* to have, and how much you really need. For instance, if you want to host neighborhood baseball games, you'll need a lot more green space than you will if hammock-swinging is the most vigorous sport you have in mind. As you ponder the possibilities, from Ponderosa- to pocket-size, consider these factors.

Time. Decide how many hours per week you can or want to spend on lawn maintenance. If your patience for outdoor chores is short, or your work schedule does not allow time for tending as much turf as you're pining for, then consider hiring a lawn-care service.

Money. Whether you're starting a new lawn or refurbishing an existing one, you'll have to invest in seed, sod, sprigs, or plugs, as well as the tools and products it takes to care for all those tender grass plants. And remember: In most parts of the country, water will consume a major portion of your lawn-care budget and (of course) the more lawn you have to irrigate, the more cold, hard cash it will cost you.

Climate. No matter where you live, you can find grass varieties that suit your growing conditions, and it is essential that you do just that. You'll find

Here's a surefire way to achieve maximum lawn pleasure with a minimum amount of time and effort: Seek success, not perfection. If you'll settle for nothing less than turf that's as manicured as the fairways at Pebble Beach, you'll have an almost full-time job on your hands—or a humongous bill from a lawn-care service. On the other hand, if you can settle for surroundings that are a little—or a lot—more casual, you'll find your stress level falling and your lawn satisfaction flying high.

great guidance on tip-top turf selection coming up, but keep in mind the golden rule of low-maintenance lawn care: Work *with* Mother Nature, not *against* her.

Hold That Slope!

Got a steep slope that you'd like to color green? If so, you'll save yourself a whole lot of time and effort—and avert a possible mowing disaster—by planting a deep-rooted groundcover instead of turfgrass. A lot of great-looking ground-grabbers will keep the soil in place and avert the hazards of mountaineer mowing. To learn more about groundcovers (including ornamental grasses) for all sorts of situations, check out Chapter 5.

Get on Track

People may tiptoe through the tulips, but they tend to gallop over grass. Think about traffic patterns in and around your lawn and plan suitable pathways for the most frequently traveled routes. Either redirect the flow by installing a fence, hedge, or other barrier; or lay down a walkway made of stepping stones, gravel, or mulch.

Make Mowing Faster

It's no secret that mowing is the most time-consuming turf-care chore of all, but a little advance planning will translate into smooth and speedy sailing on grass-cutting days. Whether you're laying out a new lawn or revamping an existing one, keep these guidelines in mind because they'll help you get the job done in a hurry:

TAKE A HIKE

Walk around your property, visualizing yourself mowing, raking, or spreading fertilizer, and note any steep slopes where these or other routine chores would be a major pain in the grass. Dig into the soil to check the ratio of dirt to rocks. Go out after a big rain and identify spots where water lingers. There are ways to adjust your home ground to make lawn care easier, but they may take more time, effort, and cash than the end result is worth to you.

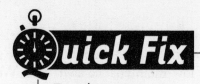

To reduce your mowing time even more, plan your lawn for straightforward movement, and skip the hassle of tugging your machine backward (or shifting into reverse). To locate places in your yard where you need to make adjustments to the shape of your lawn, try mowing the whole thing without backing up. Any areas where you can't mow while going forward are prime candidates for conversion to a garden bed or a planting of no-mow groundcovers.

🌿 Avoid sharp corners, tight circles, and fancy shapes. They'll make mowing a nightmare of twists and turns. Instead, aim for gentle corners that are greater than 90 degrees. And when you create beds for trees, shrubs, and flowers, use straight lines and soft curves.

🌿 Install mowing strips around beds and borders. These handy bits of hardscaping will eliminate your trimming chores. They let you run your mower's wheels right along the side of plantings to trim the grass without dinging the daisies or hacking the hydrangeas.

Choose the Right Stuff

Once you have a plan in mind for your own personal patch of paradise, your next step on the way to an easy-care lawn is to choose the best grass—or combination of grasses—to plant there. No matter how eager you are to start your new lawn, don't make the all-too-common mistake of running to the store and buying the first bag of grass seed you find. (That is, unless you want to spend a lot of time tending turf that's not suited to your site. And since you're reading this book, I don't think you want to do that!)

'Tis the Season

Let's start with a fundamental fact: There are basically two kinds of turfgrasses: cool-season and warm-season. So, for starters, you need to identify the basic types that will thrive in your neck of the woods.

Cool-season grasses. These are the ticket if it routinely snows during the winter where you live, and winter temperatures consistently fall below 40°F.

Warm-season grasses. These will serve you well if Jack Frost is an infrequent visitor to your home range (and snow is a real rarity), and where summer temperatures consistently climb into the 80° to 95°F range (and summer lasts from April to October).

The Tricky Transition Zone

Because lawn grasses are divided into cool-season and warm-season groups, you might think that it would be simpler to separate the zone map into two large areas, one northern and one southern. And you'd be right—that's a pretty darned reasonable way to think about turf. Except there's a part, right in the middle, known as the transition zone.

HELP!

Q I know that zoysia grass is considered a warm-season type, but here in Pennsylvania, where I live, I keep seeing ads that make it sound like the answer to a homeowner's prayers: drought-tolerant, weed-free, and needs little mowing. Is this stuff really the miracle worker it's made out to be?

A *In a word: No. My Grandma Putt taught me to be wary of things that sound too good to be true, and this is one of those things. If you live where cool-season grasses are the rule, a zoysia grass lawn is something that you (and your neighbors) will live to regret. Zoysia's ability to spread and crowd out weeds also enables it to travel across property lines and into your neighbor's bluegrass lawn. Then, when a frost hits, the zoysia turns brown, leaving dead-looking patches amid the dark green of cool-season turf around it.*

The transition zone represents parts of the country where the climate teeters back and forth between what's good for warm-season grasses and what's good for cool-season ones. Often in these areas, cool-season turf languishes in the heat of summer, while warm-season grasses are prone to winter injury. Sometimes it's just a matter of watering through the summer to help a heat-tolerant bluegrass make it in the "zone," or you may need to find a particularly cold-hardy selection of Bermuda grass. For an impatient gardener, the best approach is to look around you and see what others in your area are growing successfully, instead of puzzling over maps and the labels on bags of grass seed.

These states fall in the transition zone:

- **Arkansas**
- **Kentucky**
- **Most of Kansas**
- **North Carolina**
- **Northern Texas**
- **Oklahoma**
- **South Carolina**
- **Southern Illinois**
- **Southern Indiana**
- **Southern Missouri**
- **Tennessee**
- **Virginia**

All Turf-Care Success Is Local

Although there are only a handful of cool-season grasses and another handful of warm-season types, there are *hundreds* of improved turf varieties that have been bred to thrive in very specific kinds of growing conditions—including any that you are likely to have in your own backyard. When you're in a hurry and don't have the patience to

The hardest kind of lawn to maintain is one that's made up of only one type of grass. Mother Nature doesn't grow things that way, and neither should you—at least not if you want a lawn that's easy to live with. When you start shopping for grass seed, you'll see that most of it comes in mixes. By combining different kinds of seed, you're protecting your turf from total annihilation if one kind suffers from a pesky pest, damaging disease, or weather woe. For example, a cool-season lawn might include Kentucky bluegrass, perennial ryegrass, and creeping red fescue, while a warm-season yard could have a mixture of Bermuda, carpet, and Bahia grasses.

surf the Net or comb through books for help, follow this plan:

➤ Call your local Cooperative Extension Service. These folks are connected with your state's land-grant university and can get you the latest recommendations from their turf scientists, who are constantly turning out new, improved grass varieties.

➤ Check with your neighbors, especially if you're new to the scene and they've lived there for a while. Growing conditions can vary greatly even within a small area, and finding out what works for the folks next door can be the fastest path to lawn success.

➤ If your lawn sees a lot of rough-and-tumble action from kids and pets (or maybe grown-up touch football or badminton players), get in touch with folks who maintain the turf for local ballparks or playgrounds. Grasses that withstand the steady pounding they take in those places should work fine in your yard.

A SHINING STAR FOR SHADE

Once maligned as a pesky weed, supina bluegrass (*Poa supina*) has stepped into the spotlight as a superstar for shade. Turf scientists in Germany and at several U.S. universities have developed it into a superior turfgrass for shady, high-traffic landscapes. Supina bluegrass is fine-textured and disease-resistant with good dark green color and the ability to withstand foot traffic. The most popular named variety is 'Supra Nova.' ™

Grandma's **GROW-HOW**

In Grandma Putt's day, clover was a common ingredient in most grass-seed mixtures. In fact, it was considered the "summer savior" of green lawns when the Kentucky bluegrass fell prey to nastiness like crabgrass, mildew, or drought. Growing a little clover in your lawn is still a great way to reduce time and hassle all over your yard. Among its many pluses, clover fights off chinch bug invasions naturally and safely, draws hungry rabbits away from your flowers and vegetables, and sails right through the dog days that make most turfgrasses go belly-up.

AMERICA'S LAWN CLIMATES

Gardeners know that certain plants grow better in certain climate conditions, and they've created special zones that stretch across the country to help them keep track of winter lows and summer highs. Of course, those same standards apply to lawn grasses, but the zones aren't quite the same.

To help you figure out what kinds of turf will deliver top performance in your region, I've divided the country into six lawn zones, based on rainfall, summer heat, and winter cold. In this chart I've also listed some of the grass types that grow well there. Grasses are pretty versatile plants, and most of them are capable of growing—at least some of the time—outside the recommended boundaries. I just want to point you in the direction of the few kinds that are most likely to thrive in your yard with the least amount of time and effort on your part.

ZONE	COVERS	BEST BETS
Zone 1	Northeast Atlantic coast from southern Maine to the Middle Atlantic states; Pacific Northwest coast from Washington to northern California	• Annual and perennial ryegrasses • Bluegrass • Colonial bent grass • Tall and creeping fescues
Zone 2	Southeastern Atlantic states and west through the Deep South and Gulf states	• Bahia grass • Bermuda grass • Centipede grass • Turf-type tall fescue (northern part of zone) • Zoysia grass

ZONE	COVERS	BEST BETS
Zone 3	New England and Appalachian states, west through the Ohio Valley and Great Lakes	• Annual and perennial ryegrasses • Bluegrass • Tall and creeping fescues
Zone 4	Great Plains from central and west Texas north to the Canadian border	• Blue grama grass • Bluegrass • Buffalo grass • Tall and creeping fescues • Zoysia grass (southern plains)
Zone 5	California coast through southwestern desert	• Bermuda grass • Blue grama grass • Buffalo grass • Zoysia grass
Zone 6	Sierras, Great Basin, and Rocky Mountains	• Annual and perennial ryegrasses • Blue grama grass • Bluegrass • Buffalo grass • Tall and creeping fescues

STARTING FROM SCRATCH

I like to tell folks that starting a lawn is like baking
a cake: When you follow the recipe, use quality
ingredients, and perform all of the steps in just the
right way, you're all but guaranteed to turn out a first-
class product. Well, here's my simple, down-home
recipe for a lawn you'll be proud to call your own.

Digging up old grass
and weeds by hand
is fine, but spritz
your spade with
nonstick cooking
spray before
you start to work.
The blade will slice
right through the
vexing vegetation
like a knife
through butter.

Out With the Old

Unless you've just bought a new tract house on a lot
that's been stripped bare, you'll have to remove any
existing grass or weeds to expose the soil before you
launch your new lawn. There are several simple ways
to perform this maneuver.

Take it off the top. If your lawn is tiny—and you could use a little
exercise—grab a sharp, square-ended spade and remove the old sod by
hand. Just cut through the turf and lift it off in whatever size chunks you
can manage easily. Otherwise, rent a sod cutter from an equipment-rental
shop, and have at it. The machine will slice off the old terrible turf just

Grandma's GROW-HOW

Grandma Putt swore by compost as the ultimate
wonder drug for improving any kind of soil, and now
scientific research is proving just how miraculous
compost truly is. It's a real boon for the impatient
gardener because it not only provides nutrients
for your plants, but it also kills foul fungi and bad
bacteria while encouraging the good varieties
of both—thereby relieving you of a lot of time-
consuming work. You can buy it by the bag or the truckload at most garden
centers, or you can make your own supply, as my Grandma did, following
my easy-as-pie instructions in Chapter 9.

below the roots and leave you with a clean slate of bare ground.

Till it under. Rototilling can be a risky proposition because, rather than improving your soil, it can actually damage its structure (for the lowdown on dirt, see Chapter 9). Still, when you're in a hurry, it *is* the quickest way to bid good-bye to weeds and battered turfgrass. Just be sure to rent a tiller that has the rotating tines in the rear, behind the tires, because guiding a model with the tines in the front is like trying to control a runaway freight train! Till your lawn area to a depth of 6 to 8 inches, rake out all the old grass and weeds, then till again. Repeat the process until all the green stuff is gone.

Make a sandwich. Of all the methods I know of to prepare a plot for a new lawn—or any kind of planting, for that matter—this is the hands-down winner. You'll find the step-by-step instructions in Chapter 9, but in short, all you need to do is put down layers of newspaper, compost, and organic matter right over the existing turf. Not only does it solve your turf and weed woes with almost no effort, but it also gives your grass a good, rich starter bed that keeps improving over time, keeping your lawn green and healthy.

Quick Fix

If you choose to slice the unwanted grass cover off your lawn-to-be, you'll get a valuable bonus: a nice supply of turf slabs that you can use to fill low spots in your yard. Just pile up as many slabs as you need, upside down, sprinkling a handful of organic fertilizer or compost on each one. Then saturate the finished pile with my Super Soil Sandwich Dressing (see page 312). When the time comes to plant your brand-new lawn, you can sow seed or lay sod right on top of the pile. Over time, the old grass slabs will decompose and enrich the soil.

On the Level—More or Less

You may *think* you'd like to have a lawn that's as flat as a pancake, but take it from me, you wouldn't. What you really want is a lawn that slopes gradually away from your house on all sides. Otherwise, rainfall and water from your sprinkler will eventually find their way into your basement or, if you have no basement, into the walls and floorboards of your home, sweet home. To ensure the optimum health and well-being of your grass and your home's foundation, make sure your lawn slopes away from your house by no more than ½ inch for every foot, or roughly 2 feet for every 100 feet.

The Key to Success

Just like any other plants, the grass in your lawn can only be as healthy as the soil it's growing in. That's why I'm sharing some of my best secrets for giving your turf the best home its ever-lovin' roots could ask for—thereby saving you a lot of time and headaches down the road.

Put It to the Test

The first secret to building lawn-pleasing soil is to know what you're starting with. For just a couple of bucks, you can buy a do-it-yourself testing kit at any garden center. Don't do it! That approach is fine when you're planting a bed of annual flowers, but something as permanent (and expensive) as a new lawn deserves the red-carpet treatment. To save time and trouble later, collect a soil sample following the step-by-step directions in Chapter 9. Then send it to your local Cooperative Extension Service or a private testing lab, and request a thorough analysis. You'll get the full scoop on both major and minor nutrients, as well as soil texture, organic matter, and even the presence of toxic materials like lead.

Take 2

If you have a tiny lawn, or you just need to amend, feed, or reseed a few small areas, don't bother with a spreader. Just reach for an empty coffee can. Punch holes in the bottom, and fill the can with whatever mix you need to spread. Then put on the plastic lid, and shake-shake-shake the can as you walk along.

The Results Are In!

When your test results come back, it may show that you need to alter your soil's pH to grow the kind of grass you want. The quickest fixer-uppers are ground limestone (generally referred to as "lime") to raise the pH or sulfur to lower it. Whichever of these "wonder drugs" you use, apply it with a handheld broadcast spreader in the quantities recommended in the report.

Water, Water Everywhere

Of course, you don't really *need* a built-in irrigation system. It's perfectly possible to grow lush, green turf using only portable sprinklers or a garden hose. In fact, if you have a small lawn, or live in a place where you only have to water your grass a few times each summer during dry spells, an underground system is a waste of money. On the other hand, if you have a whole lot of grassy ground, or if summertime showers are few and far between in your neck of the woods, this marvel of modern technology is a blessing from the gods. Just keep in mind that the best time to install the equipment is *before* you plant your new lawn.

OFF TO THE RACES!

You've got your soil graded, amended, and draining like a dream. So now you're itchin' to get that new lawn up and growing! In this section, I'll walk you through the whole process of laying sod, planting plugs or sprigs, and—first off—sowing seed.

Label Lingo 101

The label on a bag of grass seed has enough confusing terms and numbers on it to make your head spin! Although they may seem like just random words and phrases, they aren't. It's important for you to understand what they mean, so you can get the best buy for your lawn and your wallet. Here's how to decipher the terminology.

Type of grass. In big letters at the top, the label should tell you whether you're holding a bag of one

If tending your yard means hitting the slopes, plant those difficult-to-maintain spots with easy-care grasses that need less mowing, watering, and fertilizing. On cool-season slopes, plant hard fescue and sheep fescue; on warm-season slopes, plant blue grama grass or buffalo grass.

species, such as red fescue or Kentucky bluegrass, or a blend of several.

Variety. In general, named varieties of grass are far superior to generic types or strains. A quality blend won't simply list, for instance, bluegrass and perennial ryegrass. It will specify, say, 'Viva' Kentucky bluegrass and 'Palmer II' perennial ryegrass.

Origin. When the quantity of a seed measures more than 5 percent of a mixture, its state or country of origin must be declared.

Germination percentage. This tells you the percentage of seed that germinates under optimal conditions. **Tip:** Steer clear of any seed that predicts less than 75 percent germination for Kentucky bluegrass and 85 percent for all other types.

Seed percentages. These numbers reveal the proportion of grass, other crop, and weed seeds by weight. So, for instance, "97 percent pure seed" on a 1-pound box means it contains 15.52 ounces of grass seed. A tiny percentage of non-grass seed finds its way into any mixture, but a good one shouldn't contain more than 0.5 percent of "other crop seed." Even weeds show up, but the proportion of weight should be less than 0.5 percent.

Inert matter. Chaff, soil, and other non-growing stuff falls into this category. It's harmless, but you sure don't want to pay good money for it! Don't buy a bag that contains more than 4 percent of it.

Noxious weeds. By law, manufacturers must 'fess up if their seed contains any notoriously bothersome weeds, such as field bindweed. In this case, the *only* number to settle for is a big, fat 0!

Test date. Fresher is better. You want a batch of seed that was tested no longer than a year ago.

FRIENDLY FUNGI

For a lawn that bugs won't want to bite, grow grass that contains the fungi known as endophytes. Found in ryegrasses and fescues, endophytes produce a substance that repels some pests and is toxic to others. Chinch bugs, sod webworms, billbugs, and armyworms are among the pests that will leave your lawn alone if it's protected by endophytes. But don't use endophyte-enhanced grasses in places where livestock will graze—they're toxic to cattle, sheep, and pregnant mares.

HOW MUCH SEED DO YOU NEED?

You might think that the more seed you sow, the thicker and lusher your lawn will be. Not so! Too many seeds in the ground will only result in too many young plants fighting for life. Many of them will die, and the survivors will be weak. This chart tells you how much seed to buy—and when you can expect to see the little seedlings start poking their heads above the soil. (Remember, though: Times will vary, depending on the weather and location.)

SEEDING RATE AND GERMINATION TIME		
GRASS TYPE	**POUNDS OF SEED PER 1,000 SQ. FT.**	**DAYS TO GERMINATION**
Bahia grass	6–10	18–28
Bent grass	½–1	6–14
Bermuda grass	1–2	10–30
Buffalo grass	2	14–30
Centipede grass	1–2	14–30
Fescue, fine	3–5	7–14
Fescue, tall	6–10	7–12
Kentucky bluegrass	1–2	6–28
Ryegrass, annual	6–8	5–10
Ryegrass, perennial	6–8	5–10

But First . . .

Before you sow your seed, you need to perform a couple of preliminary maneuvers.

Give your soil a snack. Starter fertilizer is a sort of turfgrass version of baby food that's designed to help new grass grow stronger, faster. If you've had your soil analyzed by a testing lab (see page 302), you may have been told the amount or type of starter fertilizer to use. If not, you'll find many good brands at the garden center. Just make sure the one you choose has roughly equal amounts of nitrogen, phosphorus, and potassium. Apply it according to the manufacturer's directions two or three days before seeding.

Energize your seed. Soak it for 24 hours in my Seed-Starter Tonic (below). Believe it or not, you'll speed up the germination time by about 75 percent!

Quick Fix

No matter how impatient you are to tickle your toes in your new turf, wait for a nice, calm day to do your sowing. Otherwise, before you know it, that seed will be breezin' along, blowin' in the wind!

Seed-Starter Tonic

If you presoak your grass seed in this potent potion, your lawn will be ready for its first "haircut" in no time flat!

1 gal. of weak tea water*
¼ cup of baby shampoo
1 tbsp. of Epsom salts

Mix all of the ingredients in a large container. Drop in your grass seed and put the container in the refrigerator for two days. Then strain out the seed, spread it on paper towels on your driveway to dry, and sow as usual.

* Soak a used tea bag in a solution of 1 teaspoon of dishwashing liquid and 1 gallon of warm water until the mixture is light brown.

Super Sowing in Six Simple Steps

With your soil and your seed both jump-started, you're ready for the big day. So slather on the sunscreen, grab your spreader, and get going! Speaking of spreaders, if you've got only a pint-size lawn, a handheld model will work just fine. For a bigger plot, use a rolling version. The garden center where you bought your seed may rent—or even lend—you one. Then just fill 'er up with seed and proceed as follows:

Spread seed in parallel rows.

STEP 1. Divide the seed in half, and sow the first batch in parallel rows across the seedbed.

STEP 2. Sow the second half of the seed in rows at right angles to the first. The result will be a pattern of squares, like a checkerboard.

STEP 3. Lightly rake the whole area to make sure there's ample contact between seed and soil. Go easy, though! Otherwise, you'll bury some seed so deep it'll never come up, and you'll have bare spots in your new lawn.

Lightly rake the seeded area.

STEP 4. Go over your newly seeded lawn with a water-filled roller. (The same outfits that rent spreaders may supply these dandy devices, too.) Or, if your lawn is tiny, just lightly tamp the seed with the back of your rake.

STEP 5. Apply an appropriate mulch (see "Mulch Magic" on page 18 for some good choices).

STEP 6. Last, but not least, bring on the H_2O! Either turn on your new, in-ground irrigation

Go over the seeded area with a water-filled roller.

system, crank up your portable sprinklers, or haul out the garden hose. Whichever delivery method you use, turn the nozzle to a fine spray or mist and soak the newly seeded area until the soil is moist to a depth of 6 inches. And don't guess about the distance—measure it with a ruler!

Grass germinates best and grows strongest within a certain temperature range. So in terms of your calendar this means:

- **Plant warm-season grasses in the spring, as soon as the soil temperature hits 78°F, but before it reaches 85°F.**

- **Plant cool-season grasses in late summer or fall when ground temps measure between 60° and 75°F. Or do the job between April and mid-May.**

Mulch Magic

Applying the right mulch to a newly seeded lawn is a crucial step. It helps conserve moisture in the soil; protects the small, frail seeds from harsh sun and drying winds; and helps keep weeds and bad bugs at bay. Later, as they decompose, organic mulches also provide food for young grass plants to grow on.

There are many good mulches to choose from. Like other facets of the lawn-tending game, the best one for you depends on your circumstances. Peruse the roster below, and pick the one that's right for your part of the country, your lawn's size and terrain, and your pocketbook.

Burlap, cheesecloth, or commercial mulching cloth. These are your best bets when you've seeded a steep bank. Unlike fine-textured stuff like compost or straw, they'll stay put on even the steepest slope (as long as you pin them in place, of course). The grass will grow right through any of these materials, and because they're organic, they'll break down over time, so you won't have to bother removing them.

Compost. As you might imagine if you've read the earlier parts of this chapter, compost is my favorite organic mulch. Finely screened, it makes the best nursery a baby lawn could ask for. See Quick 'n' Easy Compost (at right) for a super-simple way to start making your own supply of "black gold."

Spun-polyester row covers. These do a terrific job of protecting seeds from wind and sun, as well as insects, hungry birds, and floating weed seeds. Hold the sheets in place with pins made from old wire coat hangers, and remove the covering when the grass is 1 inch high. Row covers are expensive, but they are reusable, so after they've performed their duty, you can put them to work in your vegetable garden.

Straw. Generally inexpensive and easily available, one 60- to 80-pound bale of straw will cover a 1,000-square-foot lawn. Shake out the straw thoroughly before you spread it, then put down a layer that's no more than 1/2 inch thick. That way, it will break down quickly and you won't have to remove it once the seeds have germinated.

QUICK 'N' EASY COMPOST

Make your own compost with this no-fuss formula. Fill a large plastic garbage bag with a mixture of chopped leaves, grass clippings, and vegetable scraps. When the bag is nearly full, sprinkle a couple of quarts of water over the contents, and mix until the ingredients are moist. Tie the bag shut and leave it where the temperature will stay above 45°F for a few months. That's it!

H E L P !

Q I do a lot of woodworking, and I have a big supply of sawdust, which I used to mulch my new Kentucky bluegrass lawn. But it's been nearly three weeks now, and hardly any grass is coming up. What went wrong? And what can I do about it now?

A *This is a common problem with sawdust—and peat moss, too. Both of them tend to form a crust that's very difficult, and often impossible, for young grass to penetrate. (To an impatient gardener, that's a monumental headache!) As for what you can do: Rake up the sawdust and put it in your composting bin (see page 314). Then reseed your lawn and do those baby plants a favor: Give them a softer blanket this time.*

Water Wisely

From the time you've sown your seed until
the time the grass starts growing, you need to
keep the soil surface moist. That may mean
you'll need to water two, three, or even four
times a day. When you do that, just give it a
light misting. Don't saturate the soil, or you'll
issue an open invitation to foul fungi and
other dastardly diseases (for more on lawn
pests and diseases, see page 51). Once the
green shoots appear, start giving them more
water, less frequently. The exact timing will
vary with the weather, but my basic watering
routine is this:

Grandma's GROW-HOW

If you're like most folks I know, you've got at least a few old rulers lying around the house. Well, do what Grandma did with her old stash and "plant" them here and there in your lawn. That way, you'll know at a glance when it's time to trim your turf. (It's good to have the sticks in different places because grass grows faster in some areas of your lawn than it does in others.)

🌱 Once a day for two weeks

🌱 Every other day for two weeks

🌱 Every third day for two weeks

After that, if the grass is growing well, begin
watering it as you would a mature lawn. (You
can read all about that routine starting on
page 42.)

Hold Your Horses

No matter how impatient you are, don't rush to mow your fledgling lawn.
If you cut into those plants before they've developed a good, healthy root
system, you could kill them. At best, you'll give them a shock that will
slow their rate of growth. You could also expose the tender tissue to too
much sun, and the stems could be burned to a crisp. The right time to mow
depends on what kind of grass you've got. Cool-season types like Kentucky
bluegrass can be mowed when they're 2 1/2 inches tall. Warm-season grasses
like Bahia are ready for their first cut when they've grown 3 inches high.

The Big Day

As the old adage says, the first time's a charm—at least it should be when you're mowing your new lawn for the first time. When you get ready for that all-important rite of passage, keep these pointers in mind.

Cut high. Adjust your mower's deck to a higher-than-normal level. You want to remove no more than one-third of the grass blades' height.

Cut sharp. Make sure your mower blades have a razor-sharp edge. A ragged cut from a dull blade can be fatal to new grass.

Cut dry. Always mow young grass when the soil is on the dry side. Otherwise, you could pull the roots right out of the ground!

Starting from Sod

Although launching a lawn from sod is neither the cheapest nor the easiest way to do the job, it does have a major advantage for an impatient gardener: instant gratification. You can wake up in the morning with nothing but bare soil outside your window, and go to bed that night with the breeze wafting over fresh, beautiful turf.

Yes, But . . .

There's just one thing that's easy to overlook when you're in a hurry to green up your yard: The sodding process is not quite as instant as it appears. For starters, you need to prepare the site (or have someone else do it) exactly as you would for seed, beginning with clearing away any weeds and scruffy grass, and ending with grading the soil and installing an irrigation system if you want one.

Quick Fix

Although sod can be installed at any time the ground is not frozen solid, you'll get the best—and fastest— results if you lay your crop at the optimum time for your region. Warm-season grasses fare best when you lay the sod during either early spring or early fall. Cool-season types take hold fastest when planted in mid- to late spring, just before the temperature heads skyward.

SEED OR SOD?

If you want an instant lawn, then sod is probably the way to go—but there are factors that may make seed a better choice. This comparison of the pros and cons will help you make a sound decision.

STARTING FROM SEED	
PROS	**CONS**
It costs a whole lot less than sod, and you have a large choice of grass types.	You have a fairly small weather window for sowing (see page 18).
Seed sowing is light, easy work.	Seed is easily lost to hungry birds, heavy rain, winds, and fluctuating temperatures.
Seed will keep in its closed bag for up to a year after its testing date.	A lawn growing from seed demands almost constant care for at least the first four weeks.

STARTING FROM SOD	
PROS	**CONS**
A sodded lawn looks good right from the get-go.	Sod costs two to three times more than grass seed.
You can lay it at any time except the dead of winter.	Laying sod is hard work—a midsize lawn can require four or five people.
It stays put on a slope.	Sod must be watered upon delivery and installed within 24 hours.
It's dense enough to crowd out weed seeds before they get a toehold.	Most sod farms offer only two types of turf: one suitable for shade and one suitable for sun.

Savvy Sod-Shopping Tips

Buying sod is trickier than buying grass seed. For one thing, there are no truth-in-labeling laws for strips of sod as there are for seed. To get the best batch possible, follow these guidelines.

Find your source. Ask a good local nursery to recommend a supplier, then call and ask what kinds of grass they sell and which type or types they'd recommend for your location. (Be sure to describe your site, particularly in terms of sun and shade levels.)

Insist on fast service. Just like sweet corn, sod starts to go downhill the minute it's cut. If at all possible, find a sod farm that will cut the strips to your order and ship them to you immediately. Failing that, go with the supplier who will guarantee the freshest possible crop delivered to your doorstep at a time you'll be there to receive it. (You don't want this stuff to arrive some morning while you're at work and sit around, high and dry, until you get home that evening.)

Take a trip. Unless your source comes so highly recommended that you have no doubts about the product, pay a visit to the grower and ask to see an order that's about to go out. Make sure it's green, healthy, and free of bugs.

How Much Is Enough?

Sod comes in strips that are generally 6 to 8 feet long, 2 feet wide, and 1 to 3 inches thick, depending on the type of grass. It's sold by the square foot. To figure out how much to order for a square or rectangular lawn, simply multiply length times width. So, if your space

Quick Fix

In theory, just about any kind of grass can be grown as sod, but how well it'll perform in your yard is another story. The grasses that make the best sod are those that spread by stolons or rhizomes. Most warm-season grasses fall into this category. On the cool side of the aisle, so do bent grass and Kentucky bluegrass. On the other hand, rye and fescues tend to make terrible sod because they spread by bunching and seeding.

23

measures 30 by 40 feet, you'll need 1,200 square feet of sod. Just to be on the safe side, though, order another 10 percent so you don't run short. In this case, that would be 1,200 + 120 = 1,320 square feet total.

Tool Time

Sodding is a more tool-intensive job than seeding. Here's your must-have list:

- Sharp (and I do mean *sharp!*) knife to cut the sod.

- Wheelbarrow to haul the sod strips around. Each of these babies can weigh as much as 40 pounds, so you sure don't want to carry them!

- Piece of wood or sturdy cardboard to kneel on so you don't squish the sod you've just laid. And while you're at it, get some knee pads.

- Stakes and string to use as guidelines if your lawn doesn't have a built-in straight edge like a drive or walkway.

- Steel-headed rake to level the soil and tamp the sod into place.

- Water-filled roller to firm the sod once it's laid.

- Hose or sprinklers to keep the sod moist throughout the process.

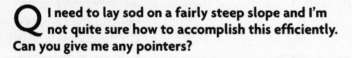

Q I need to lay sod on a fairly steep slope and I'm not quite sure how to accomplish this efficiently. Can you give me any pointers?

A I sure can! When you're dealing with any incline, lay the sod horizontally across the hill—never in the same direction as the slope. On very steep slopes, hold the sod to the soil with wooden pegs. Two pegs per strip should do the trick. Use 1- by 2-inch boards that are about 12 inches long, and pound each one 8 inches or so into the soil. That'll leave you a good handhold when you want to pull the stakes out, about 4 months later.

Savvy Sodding in Six Simple Steps

If it's at all possible, this is one job you want to do on a cool, overcast day, for two reasons: The sod will stay moist longer, and you'll stay fresh longer. And get as much help as you can—this is one labor-intensive job! Fortunately, though, it's a straightforward process. Here's all there is to it:

STEP 1. Two or three days before your sod's delivery date, apply a good dose of starter fertilizer to your soil.

Lay the first strip along a straight edge like a driveway.

STEP 2. Lay the first strip along a straight edge, like a walk or driveway, pushing the edge of the sod tightly against the hard surface. If your lawn has no straight lines, run a string across the middle, attached to a stake at either end. Then line up the sod with the string.

STEP 3. Set the remaining pieces in what bricklayers call a "staggered bond," so that the joints of one row fall in the middle of solid strips on each of the flanking rows. Push the ends of the strips together tightly, leaving no gaps where the sod could dry out. As you go along, pat down the sod with your rake to encourage good contact with the soil.

Lay sod in a staggered-bond pattern so joints don't align.

STEP 4. When you come to the end of a row—or encounter any obstacle, like a flower bed or walkway—cut the sod to fit using your ultra-sharp knife.

STEP 5. After you've arranged all of your sod strips, go back and fill the seams with

Cut sod using a sharp knife.

compost or potting soil. Don't use tiny pieces of sod, which will dry out and die, or garden soil, which could contain weed seeds.

STEP 6. Roll over your new green carpet with a roller that's filled halfway with water, working perpendicular to the sod strips.

And Then . . .

As new lawns go, sod might be low-care, but it's not *no*-care! For the first month or so, water every morning until the soil is soaked 6 to 8 inches below the surface. And every three weeks, give that turf a dose of my All-Season Green-Up Tonic (below) to encourage faster, thicker growth. Also, avoid the temptation to romp around on your new playground right away. In fact, you'll earn big-time dividends in the long run if you stay off the grass for four to six weeks. (Crucial test: When you can't lift the corners, you've got yourself a *lawn*!)

All-Season Green-Up Tonic

This bracing beverage will get your newly sodded lawn off to a sensational start—and supercharge the rest of your green scene all season long.

> 1 can of beer
> 1 cup of ammonia
> 1/2 cup of dishwashing liquid
> 1/2 cup of liquid lawn food
> 1/2 cup of molasses or corn syrup

Mix all of the ingredients together in a large bucket, and pour the mixture into a 20 gallon hose-end sprayer. Then spray your lawn (and every other green, growing thing in your yard) to the point of runoff every three weeks throughout the growing season.

Cure Bald Spots (In Your Lawn, That Is)

Brown patches can appear overnight, even on the best-tended lawns. In most cases, the only cure is to dig up the dead grass and replace it. No need to worry—it's a simple fix when you keep a stock of homegrown replacement plugs on hand. Follow these steps to make your own supply:

STEP 1. Collect a bunch of plastic flats, like the ones that many annual flowers and veggies come in. (Make sure there are holes in the bottom for drainage.)

STEP 2. Line each flat with aluminum foil, leaving about 2 inches of foil hanging out over one side. That will allow excess water to drain off and make the soil block easier to slide out later on. Also, be sure to punch holes through the foil that's on the bottom.

STEP 3. Fill each flat with potting soil or a half-and-half mixture of compost and garden soil.

STEP 4. Sprinkle grass seed on top—the same type as you've got growing in your lawn, of course—and put the flats in a bright but sheltered place. (I keep mine by the back door so I never forget to water them.)

STEP 5. Keep the soil moist until the seeds sprout; after that, just give the grass a good drink of water twice a day.

Take 2

When your garden hose springs an irreparable leak or two, don't throw it away. Instead, put it to work in one of these ways:

• Use it for trying out different shapes and sizes of planting beds. Just lay the hose out on the ground in the spot where you want a new bed, and play around with it until you get exactly the look you want.

• Cut the hose into pieces, then cut a slit down the middle of each one, and slip it over the blade of an ax, knife, or saw to protect the "business end" of the tool.

Within a couple of weeks, you'll have nice, thick blocks of turf that you can use whenever a bare spot appears in your lawn. Just slide the soil out of the flat and pop it into place, either whole or broken into pieces.

DISPATCH THATCH!

Of all the woes that can befall a lawn, thatch just might be the nastiest. Not only does it keep water, air, and nutrients from reaching the grass roots, but it also provides a dandy home for hordes of bad-guy bugs and dastardly diseases. Hint: When you walk across your lawn and it feels spongy underfoot, that's your first clue that thatch is beginning to build up. Your best plan of attack depends upon how severe the problem is.

A little thatch is actually a good thing. A layer of half an inch or so cushions the turf, guards against soil compaction, and helps conserve moisture in the soil. The trouble starts when the thatch builds up beyond that level.

How'd It Get in My Lawn?

No matter how impatient you are to attack the thatch that's in your lawn, it helps to know what caused it to get out of hand in the first place. That way, you'll be better able to keep it under control later. Any one or (more likely) a combination of these factors can lead to big trouble.

Frequent, shallow watering. It encourages both roots and organic debris to concentrate near the soil surface.

Infrequent, too-high mowing. Whether you rake up the clippings or not, this practice contributes to thatch development.

Overfeeding. This makes for overly lush growth, especially if you're using potent chemical fertilizers. In particular, supplying more nitrogen than your grass needs will quickly lead to trouble.

Herbicides, fungicides, and pesticides. They kill the earthworms and microscopic organisms that break down organic material and prevent thatch buildup.

Improper soil pH. It prevents grass from absorbing the nutrients it needs, and can also discourage the presence of earthworms.

Heavy clay. It lacks openings through which air, water, nutrients, and decomposing organisms can travel. That, in turn, means that grass roots migrate to the surface in search of sustenance, and the underground breakdown squad dies off.

Take It Off!

The right time to dethatch your lawn depends on where you live. In cool-season territory, you can do the job in spring, late summer, or early fall. For warm-season lawns, the timeline is shorter and only runs from early to midsummer. As with most lawn chores, you can choose from two modes of operation: manual and mechanical. These are the tools you'll use.

Thatching rake. This looks much like a normal rake, except that instead of tines, it has knife-like, double-ended blades. You can buy one at a garden center or hardware store, and you use it in the same way you'd use a garden rake. There's just one difference: Raking up thatch is a whole lot tougher than raking bare ground! Unless you have a teeny-tiny lawn, take my advice and go the automated route.

Dethatcher. This power tool cuts through the thatch and yanks it out of the ground. It does the job faster and with a fraction of the

WHAT IS THIS STUFF, ANYWAY?

Contrary to what many folks think, thatch is *not* a thick blanket of old grass clippings. Rather, it's a tightly woven layer of stems, roots, and crowns—both living and dead—that forms between the grass blades and the soil line. These plant parts are high in lignin, a type of organic material that breaks down more slowly than most. But in a healthy lawn, it *does* break down. (Grass clippings, on the other hand, are made up mostly of cellulose, which decomposes in a flash.)

To find out how serious the problem is, remove a slice of turf (blades, roots, and soil) using a bulb planter or sharp knife. Then examine the thatch. You'll see a layer of brownish material that resembles peat moss. If it's between 1/2 and 1 inch thick, aerating should solve the problem (see page 30). Anything thicker than that calls for full-scale dethatching.

effort required with a thatching rake. Most equipment-rental companies can supply you with a fine machine. Just one word of caution—dethatcher machines are big, heavy, and tricky to handle. If you've never used one before, have the folks at the rental place walk you through the procedure, and follow their instructions *to the letter*. And if you're not accustomed to working with power equipment of any kind, I strongly advise that you turn the task over to someone who is so you avoid injuring yourself and/or damaging your lawn.

No matter who does the "driving," it's important to get the right dethatching machine for your grass. There are two types. One has vertically rotating steel blades; it's just the ticket for thick grasses like Bermuda and zoysia. For finer-bladed grasses, such as fescue or Kentucky bluegrass, make sure you rent a wire-tined model.

Quick Fix

Dethatching your lawn is an all-but-instant way to lay out the unwelcome mat for plenty of turf-type pests, especially billbugs, chinch bugs, mole crickets, and sod webworms (for more on battling bad bugs in your lawn, see "Trouble and Woe" on page 51). Not one of them can resist the lure of that luscious layer, and once it's gone, so are they!

Give It Air

If your thatch layer is between 1/2 and 1 inch thick, aeration should send the stuff packing. This technique simply involves poking holes in the soil so that air can reach the grass roots—followed quickly by food and water. On a small lawn, or in isolated spots of a large one, you can easily do the job with a garden fork or, better yet, a hand aerator. This useful gadget has a long, tined, horizontal bar at the bottom with a handle at either end. To use it, take hold of both handles, shove the tines 6 or 8 inches into the ground, and stand on the horizontal bar. Then rock back and forth a few times to make nice, wide holes in the turf. Pull up the fork, move it along 3 inches or so, and repeat the process. When you're done, rake up any loose thatch and compost it. Then add the recommended fertilizers or amendments and water your lawn.

Bigger Guns

Larger spaces call for heavier gear. Instead of using muscle power, rent or buy a powered, walk-behind aerator that you maneuver just like a lawn mower. These dandy machines come in two types.

Open-tine or spike aerators. These simply punch holes in the soil, the same way the manually operated hand aerator does.

Core aerators. These harder workers pull out small plugs, or cores, of grass and soil and toss them onto the ground. This is a more effective procedure than mere hole punching, although, granted, it does leave your lawn littered with little bits of grassy soil. If these bother you, rake 'em up and toss 'em into the compost bin. Otherwise, just leave 'em be; they'll break down in a flash, adding valuable organic matter to the soil.

Aerating Over Easy

No matter which type of aerator you use, the basic operating procedure is the same—and it couldn't be simpler. Here's the process in four easy steps:

STEP 1. Just before you start, spray your lawn with my Aeration Tonic (below). This will leave the turf much easier to penetrate.

Aeration Tonic

This fabulous formula will help prevent soil compaction so water, nutrients, and oxygen can penetrate deep where they're needed most.

> **1 cup of beer**
> **1 cup of dishwashing liquid**

Combine the ingredients in a 20 gallon hose-end sprayer, and fill the balance of the sprayer jar with warm water. Just before you aerate, spray your lawn to the point of runoff. From then on, apply this solution once a month throughout the growing season to help keep the soil loose and fluffy.

STEP 2. Guide the aerator across your lawn, moving in parallel rows.

STEP 3. Make a second pass at a 90-degree angle to the first. Aim for 3- to 4-inch spacing between the holes.

STEP 4. Spread a ½-inch layer of compost across the lawn, and brush or rake it into the holes. That's all there is to it!

What—*Again*?

Aeration is not a one-time event—not, that is, if you want to keep your soil's channels open and your grass growing great guns. So how often should you deliver fresh air? Here's what I recommend:

- Any soil that's naturally high in clay should be aerated at least once a year.

- All lawns, even those growing in good, loose soil, benefit from an annual airing out.

- If your lawn sports a layer of thatch and you've chosen to aerate rather than dethatch, haul out your hole-puncher each spring and fall for two years in a row. After that, perform the chore once a year.

And Stay Away!

Once you've sent that thatch on its unmerry way, prevent a repeat appearance by following this routine:

- Wear aerating lawn sandals or old-fashioned golf spikes whenever

Quick Fix

You can tell at a glance when soil in a lawn is compacted just by looking at the trees growing there. If you can see surface roots on your lawn, that's a certain sign that your soil is compacted. How so? Well, normally, a tree's feeder roots roam through the top 4 to 8 inches of soil in search of air, water, and food—the same territory that grass roots call home. When that ground is compacted, the trees send their roots to the surface in their quest for oxygen—and who can blame them?

you mow your lawn. That way, you'll break up the surface-tension barrier between the soil and the blades of grass.

❧ Do your best to mow on a regular schedule and always mow at the right height for your type of grass.

❧ Apply my Thatch-Blaster Tonic (below) once a month starting in spring, as soon as temperatures stay above 50°F.

❧ Water your lawn slowly and deeply and only when it needs it.

❧ Don't overfeed, and use only the amount of fertilizer recommended for your grass variety.

❧ Just say "No!" to herbicides, pesticides, and chemical fertilizers.

❧ Apply half an inch or so of finely sifted compost in spring and fall to supply trace nutrients, improve the soil texture, and help fend off nasty turf diseases.

❧ Have your soil tested every few years, and add any soil amendments that are recommended.

Thatch-Blaster Tonic

This excellent elixir will help keep your lawn free of thatch all season long.

1 cup of beer or regular cola (not diet)
½ cup of ammonia
½ cup of dishwashing liquid

Mix all of the ingredients in a 20 gallon hose-end sprayer. Fill the balance of the sprayer jar with water, and saturate the entire turf area. Repeat once a month during the summer when the grass is actively growing.

CHOW TIME

Just like any other plants, lawn grasses require certain nutrients to help them grow strong, healthy, and better able to fend off trouble from wicked weeds, dastardly diseases, and pesky pests. Here's the lowdown on serving up the right kind of food at the right times and in the right quantities—thereby reducing your turf-tending time enormously.

The key to a healthy lawn diet is moderation. Too little or (in most cases) too much of any essential nutrient can cause your grass to look sparse, coarse, yellowish, or stunted.

The Main Course

Your lawn's smorgasbord is made up of 12 essential nutrients, but the three most important ones are nitrogen (N on the fertilizer bag), phosphorus (P), and potassium (K).

Nitrogen supplies the growing power for grass blades. When they get exactly the right amount, they develop at a steady pace into a lush, green lawn. Too little nitrogen and a lawn looks pale and sickly. Too much, and you're faced with rapid growth, delayed maturity, and weak, trouble-prone grass plants.

Phosphorus promotes the growth of strong, vigorous roots. If grass gets too little, the blades will have a reddish, purplish, or grayish cast. An overdose can interfere with the lawn's absorption of other essential elements and cause all sorts of problems.

A healthy portion of nitrogen won't cause serious harm to your turf, as a real overdose would—but it will mean you'll have to mow more often. Also, the more you feed your lawn—especially if you opt for a chemical fertilizer—the more prone it will be to thatch, soil compaction, and other forms of nastiness that you'll have to deal with. In other words, more N equals more work.

Potassium supports photosynthesis and the growth of strong plant tissue. It helps your lawn prepare for cold winters and protect itself against pathogens of all kinds. Too little potassium will cause grass to turn yellow, lose its get-up-and-grow power, and fall prey to plant diseases. Too much of the Big K interferes with the absorption of calcium and magnesium, making the grass grow poorly.

Two for the Show

Lawn fertilizers come in different formulations to meet the nutrient needs of various grass types, but every fertilizer falls into one of two categories: chemical/inorganic or natural/organic.

Chemical/inorganic fertilizers are made from synthetic substances that contain highly concentrated amounts of specific nutrients, primarily nitrogen, phosphorus, and potassium. When you apply a chemical fertilizer, you see almost instant results because the nutrients are immediately available to the grass roots. On the downside, this quick fix adds nothing to the soil itself. In fact, those potent chemicals actually destroy the beneficial organisms, including earthworms, which create the soil's natural nutrients and keep it in good shape. And, if used over time, the chemicals can build up in the soil and hinder grass growth.

Natural/organic fertilizers don't feed your grass at all. Rather, they add essential nutrients, major and minor, to the soil, where they are

Grandma's GROW-HOW

The fastest, easiest way to keep your lawn well nourished is to forget fertilizer altogether and use the method Grandma Putt used: Just spread a layer of top-quality compost across the turf twice a year, in the spring and again in the fall. If you want to try this approach, you'll need a minimum of 50 pounds of compost for each 1,000 square feet of lawn area. As for the maximum, well, the sky's the limit—there's no such thing as an overdose of black gold! You'll find everything you need to know about making and serving this miracle chow in Chapter 9.

broken down and become available to the grass plants. They also improve the structure of the soil—and thereby improve living conditions for your underground hit squad. Organic fertilizers are made of naturally occurring substances, just like the ones I use in my tonics.

Slow or Fast?

Besides the chemical/synthetic vs. natural/organic distinction, commercial fertilizers differ in how fast they release their nutrients. The distinction is:

🖝 Quick-release fertilizers start dissolving the minute they hit the ground because their ingredients (particularly nitrogen) are water-soluble. Your grass begins to feast immediately, and puts on a big growth spurt. That may sound like a dream come true for an impatient gardener, but the reality is quite the contrary: The turf will clean its plate in a flash, which means that in a month or so, you'll have to serve up more chow. And then more. And then still more.

🖝 Slow-release formulas contain nutrients that do not dissolve in water. As a result, your grass dines at a nice, leisurely pace, which means you don't have to feed it as often. Natural/organic fertilizers are, by definition, slow-release because they consist of ingredients that must be broken down by earthworms and microorganisms in the soil. But in order to make synthetic foods perform slowly, the manufacturers have to coat the chemicals with a substance that holds back their usual hair-trigger action.

Quick Fix

You can cut the amount of fertilizer you need by as much as 25 percent simply by leaving the grass clippings on your freshly mowed lawn. Furthermore, leaving those trimmings in place actually helps prevent thatch. There's just one catch: This time- and money-saving trick only works if you don't use chemical fertilizers. Studies have proven that because these potent formulas hinder the work of the underground breakdown crew (including fungi, earthworms, and beneficial bacteria), they stall the decomposition of grass clippings. The result not only robs the little plants of free food, but also contributes to thatch buildup.

❧ Bridge, a.k.a. combination, fertilizers are made from a combination of slow- and fast-acting ingredients. So you get the best of both worlds: instant gratification and longer-lasting results.

Don't Weed and Feed!

We all know that lawns have to be fed and weeds have to be controlled—but no matter how eager you are to get the job done, don't try to do both at the same time. In spite of the fact that weed-and-feed products sell like hotcakes, they're not the wonder workers they're cracked up to be. In fact, they can actually do more harm than good. That's because in order to kill weeds, you have to use so much of this double-dip stuff that you end up feeding your lawn way too much nitrogen. And that can cause big trouble! But if you try to avoid a Big N overdose by serving up less weed-and-feed, you won't put much of a dent in your unwanted-plant population.

To add insult to injury, weed-and-feed combos are expensive. A sack of a dual-action product will set you back considerably more than separate packages of commercial fertilizer and weed killer—and a *whole* lot more than the ingredients for my feeding and weed-control tonics.

Spring Wake-Up Mix

As soon as possible in the spring, issue a loud and clear wake-up call to your lawn with this marvelous mixture.

> 50 lbs. of pelletized gypsum
> 50 lbs. of pelletized lime
> 5 lbs. of bonemeal
> 2 lbs. of Epsom salts

Mix all of the ingredients in a wheelbarrow, and apply to your lawn with a broadcast spreader no more than two weeks before fertilizing. This formula will help aerate the turf, while giving it something to munch on until you start your regular feeding program.

Synchronize Your Calendars

Although all turfgrasses need to be fed in spring and fall, exactly what part of spring and fall depends on where you live:

🪱 Warm-season grasses like St. Augustine and Bermuda perform their best when they're fed in late spring and again in early fall. The reason: If you serve up the chow too early in the spring, you're likely to fill the bellies of wicked weeds. And if you wait too long in the fall, your grass won't have time to absorb all the nutrients in the food. As a result, it'll go into the winter unprepared to fend off cold-weather damage.

🪱 Cool-season grasses such as tall fescue and Kentucky bluegrass need their substantial meals in early spring and late fall. Being Johnny-on-the-spot in the spring is especially important with these

THE SECOND COURSE

If your turf starts turning yellow, suspect a lack of either iron (Fe) or magnesium (Mg). Both are key ingredients in chlorophyll (the stuff that makes your grass green). To find out for sure, have your soil tested by your Cooperative Extension Service or a professional testing lab. (For the full scoop on soil tests and building strong soil, see Chapter 9.)

Get Up and Grow Tonic

After applying my Spring Wake-Up Mix (see page 37) to your lawn, overspray it with this lively libation to kick it into high gear.

> **1 cup of ammonia**
> **1 cup of baby shampoo**
> **1 cup of regular cola (not diet)**
> **4 tbsp. of instant tea granules**

Mix all of the ingredients in a 20 gallon hose-end sprayer, and apply to the point of runoff. This tonic will get all that good stuff working to help your grass get off to a super start—so you'll enjoy the most terrific turf in town!

turf types because you want to give them their get up and grow power while the weather's still cool. If you wait too long, you'll trigger a super growth spurt just as the temperatures start to skyrocket.

Spring Start-Up

When the first balmy breezes float through the air, your lawn (like everything else in nature) wakes up rarin' to grow. That's the time to get it started on the right root with this three-step launch routine:

STEP 1. As soon as your grass starts rubbing the sleep out of its eyes, give it a dose of my Spring Wake-Up Mix (see page 37) followed immediately by a good, healthy drink of my Get Up and Grow Tonic (at left).

HELP!

Q I tried your feeding program for the first time this spring, but something went haywire—when I combined the Epsom salts with my lawn fertilizer, the mixture got all wet, and it wouldn't spread at all. What's going on here?

A I'm glad you brought this up because it's a question I hear a lot from folks who are using synthetic, slow-release fertilizers. These products work the way they do because the chemicals are coated so the nutrients are released gradually over time (see "Slow or Fast?" on page 36). And that coating can react with Epsom salts to form a damp mess that you can't get through a spreader for love nor money. My best advice: Switch to a natural/organic fertilizer. The natural ingredients team up just fine with Epsom salts—and all of my other tonic ingredients.

If you'd rather stick with a synthetic product, simply divide Steps 2 and 3 of the routine on page 40 into substeps: Spread your lawn food first, then clean your spreader to remove any fertilizer residue. Once it's clean, you can spread the Epsom salts without toil or trouble.

STEP 2. Within two weeks of serving up that dynamic duo, give your lawn its first solid meal of the season. Add 3 pounds of Epsom salts to a bag of your favorite slow-release, dry lawn food (enough for 2,500 square feet). I like to use a 20-5-10 mix. Be sure to mix the salts in well. (I pour them into the bag, close it tight, and give it a few good shakes.) Apply half of this mixture at *half* the rate recommended on the label, with your spreader set on the medium setting, moving from north to south in parallel rows across your yard. Set the other half of the mixture aside.

STEP 3. One week later, haul out the second half of the dry lawn food/Epsom salts mixture from Step 2 and pour it into your spreader. This time, apply it in rows moving from east to west. This "checkerboard" maneuver will guarantee that every square inch of turf gets fed, and you won't have any light green lines in your lawn that mark the parts you missed.

HOW DRY IT IS

Or at least it should be. If you have fertilizer left over after your last fall feeding, be sure to guard it against any dampness in your garage or workshop. If moisture seeps into the bags, it will ruin the food. Either put the sacks on boards or wooden pallets to raise them off the cold concrete floor, or tuck the bags into plastic trash cans and cover them tightly. That way, the chow will be as good as gold when it's time to dish it out in the spring.

Through the Good Old Summertime

Once you've given your lawn its hearty breakfast, it's time to begin the series of regular, light meals that will carry it through to the first cold days of fall. The best way to provide hot-weather sustenance is with my All-Season Green-Up Tonic (see page 26). Apply it every three weeks through the first hard frost, and your lawn will romp like a pup through the dog days of summer!

If the heat gets you down so much that you'd rather not fuss with mixing up tonics, then you can always substitute a good liquid lawn food or fish emulsion. Whatever you use, just remember to keep it "lite."

A Liquid Diet

With liquid fertilizers, the delivery routine is a little different than it is for dry lawn foods. For starters of course, instead of a spreader, you need to use a hose-end sprayer. Then follow this quick and easy process:

Mix ingredients thoroughly in the sprayer bottle.

STEP 1. Mix the ingredients following the directions on the package, and make sure any solids are completely dissolved before you start spraying. Otherwise, the early sprays will deliver weak doses of nitrogen, and the later ones will be too strong.

STEP 2. Start in a corner of your lawn, or along one edge if there are no corners. Then walk backward in a straight line, spraying as you go. When you reach the end, turn off the sprayer, twirl around, and walk a second line parallel to the first, spraying as you go.

Walk backward as you spray the turf.

STEP 3. Make sure you don't overlap your spray patterns. If you do, the strips that have been double-dosed will grow more quickly, and you'll wind up with a wavy-colored lawn.

Gettin' On Toward Bedtime

Your final fall feeding should be a repeat of the spring routine, only this time use a 10-10-10 dry, slow-release fertilizer instead of the 20-5-10 version you used earlier. Once again, mix 3 pounds of Epsom salts into a bag of food (enough for 2,500 square feet) and apply half of the mixture at half the recommended rate, moving

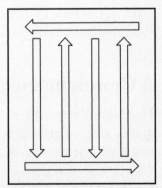

Feed your lawn in this pattern for even coverage.

from north to south across your lawn. One week later, spread the remaining food/Epsom salts mixture, going from east to west.

Then, within two days after your second feeding, serve up a season's-end drink of my Lawn-Saver Tonic (see page 53).

A lawn's water requirements vary, depending on many factors. In general, though, to stay in peak form, most turfgrasses need roughly 1 inch of water each week during the growing season, whether it's supplied by you, rainfall, or a combination of both.

TIME FOR A DRINK!

Just like every other living thing on earth, turfgrass needs water to survive. In these pages, I'll let you in on my tricks for quenching your lawn's thirst in a way that keeps it in the pink of health—and leaves you plenty of time to enjoy your gorgeous green grass.

The Root(s) of the Matter

The road to a water-thrifty lawn starts with a strong, healthy, and deep root system. Although most of a grass plant's roots grow in the top 6 to 8 inches of soil, many of those thirsty plant parts will dive a whole lot deeper if you give them half a chance. And that's one of the greatest favors you can do for your lawn and yourself. That's because the longer the roots are, the more moisture they can grab deeper in the soil, and the less water you'll have to give them. Conversely, the shorter they are, the more Johnny-on-the-spot you'll have to be with the H_2O when a dry spell hits.

A Growth Industry

Here's good news for all you impatient lawn tenders: Encouraging your grass's roots to grow down, down, down is a lot easier than you might imagine. Just keep these guidelines in mind as you tend your turf.

Cool it. On the first hot day of spring, it's mighty tempting to haul out the garden hose or crank up the sprinklers and give your lawn its first nice cool drink of the season. Well, don't do it! If the water's flowing freely early in the year, the roots will stay in the top few inches of soil. Instead, let the soil dry out some, so those underground parts will scurry down to deeper, damper territory. The moisture they find at those levels will sustain the plants when Ma Nature turns up the heat later on in the summer.

Water deeply. Whenever you water your lawn, always make sure the H_2O seeps down to the full depth of the roots. In general, that's anywhere from 6 to 18 inches (although some types, like Bermuda grass, tall fescue, and zoysia grass, can send their roots as far down as 5 feet). Shallow watering actually does more harm than good because it encourages the roots to stay in the soil's upper reaches—making for weak grass plants with a thirst that won't quit. When you water deeply, you create a reservoir that the underground legions can tap into. The more moisture they have at their disposal, the more they'll expand. And the more soil the roots occupy, the stronger and more hose-independent your lawn will be.

Take it slow and easy. Instead of serving your grass its full ration of water all at once, go at it slowly. Give it about ¼ inch of water, wait 10 minutes, then

WHEN IN DROUGHT

You can improve the water-holding power of any soil and encourage any kind of grass to grow longer, more drought-resistant roots. But the fact remains that some kinds of grass just naturally handle dry conditions better than others. Here's how the major types react when good ol' Mother Nature turns off the faucet.

WHAT DROUGHT?	WE'LL GET THROUGH THIS.	WATER NOW!
• Bermuda grass • Buffalo grass • Fine fescue • Tall fescue • Zoysia grass	• Bahia grass • Canada bluegrass • Kentucky bluegrass • Perennial ryegrass • St. Augustine grass	• Annual ryegrass • Bent grass • Centipede grass • Rough bluegrass

give it another ¼ inch. Continue this water-then-wait approach until you've applied a full inch of water. When you put in just a little water at a time, the soil absorbs it more efficiently and sends it to deeper levels.

A Grass-Roots Movement

To see how your soil stacks up, er, stacks down, in terms of grass-roots hospitality, just grab a shovel and dig up a clump of turf (don't worry: you can tuck it back in later with no harm done to the grass). Then look at the roots. What you'll want to see are plenty of nice, long roots, which means your grass is able to grab moisture from deep in the soil. But if the roots are relatively short, you have a more labor-intensive lawn. The bottom line: You'll need to water more frequently to keep your grass growing.

Wait—There's More!

Helping your grass grow long, strong roots is a crucial step in reducing your lawn's water needs (and your monthly bills). But there's a lot more you can do to curb your turf's drinking problem, beginning with these four simple maneuvers.

Sow smart. When you're starting from scratch or renovating an existing lawn, choose the most drought-resistant grasses that will thrive in your neck of the woods (see "When in Drought" on page 43).

Mow sharp. Never mow your lawn with a dull mower blade. That'll leave the grass with frayed, ragged edges that quickly release moisture into the air.

Grandma's GROW-HOW

One of the fastest ways to cut back on your watering is to do what Grandma Putt did: Add heaping helpings of organic matter to your soil. This works because soil that's made up of 3 to 5 percent organic matter retains water two to three times longer than soil that hasn't been treated to this healthiest of health foods, so bring on the compost!

Sharp cuts result in clean, even tips that hold water inside the plant, where it belongs.

Mow high. If you keep your lawn's tresses on the long side—2 inches or higher—they'll shade and cool the soil so that less moisture will be lost to evaporation.

Dispatch thatch. This nasty stuff makes it difficult—and in extreme cases, all but impossible—for water to reach the grass roots.

Care for a Drink?

There is no great skill involved in knowing when to water your lawn. When that turf is thirsty, it'll speak up loud and clear! Well, not in English, of course. Like all plants, grass communicates in sign language. Here are three signs that translate into "Please give me a drink":

> ## HOLD THE CHORES
>
> Here's a reprieve you'll be happy to have: Never aerate or dethatch your lawn in hot, sunny weather. Save those chores for cool, overcast days (preferably in spring or fall). And forget about feeding, weeding, and even battling bad bugs when the temperature skyrockets. All these chores put stress not only on you but also on your grass plants—and a stressed plant is a mighty thirsty plant.

- The grass plants turn from a healthy green color to a dull, grayish blue. At the same time, the blades curl up or fold in along the edges.

- The soil changes. Heavy soil hardens into a solid block, while lighter soils turn tan-colored and crumbly.

- When you walk across your lawn, the grass doesn't spring back. Instead, your footprints remain for a long time—often for several hours.

Want a simple and foolproof way to tell whether it's time to water your lawn? Just push a long screwdriver into the ground. If you have to struggle to get the tool 6 inches or so into the soil, it's time to turn on the sprinklers and give that turf some liquid refreshment. Now wasn't that easy?

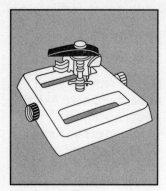

Impulse sprinkler

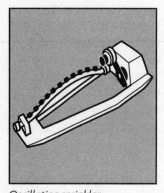

Oscillating sprinkler

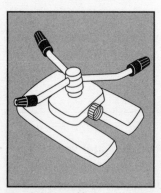

Revolving sprinkler

Serving the Drinks

A garden hose works fine for serving up my tonics or washing down a driveway, but at watering time, you need equipment with real star power—namely, a top-notch sprinkler. They come in several basic types. Each has its pros and cons, and within each type, quality varies considerably. Here's the scoop.

Impulse. These are scaled-down, domestic versions of agricultural sprinklers, and they function in the same way: As a strong jet of water shoots out from a nozzle, a spring-loaded arm whacks against that stream, shattering the water into tiny droplets and, at the same time, making the nozzle revolve in a circle. Impulse sprinklers have a good throw radius and the best uniformity of any sprinkler (including the in-ground systems).

Oscillating. This is the most popular of all sprinkler types for one reason: It delivers water in a rectangular pattern that's tailor-made for the typical suburban lawn. Unfortunately, the cheaper models drop more water on the downside of each swing as they rock back and forth. The result: mini-lakes where weeds, disease germs, and (yes) mosquitoes breed.

Revolving. These babies sport a rotating arm that spins around, shooting a cold spray of water that kids love to run through on summer afternoons. Unfortunately, although "planting" a revolving sprinkler in your lawn will make you a hero of the under-10 set, it won't do your grass much good. As with fixed sprinklers, you can expect a short throw radius and lousy uniformity. In fact, most of the water pools up around the base of the sprinkler.

Traveling. On these, the business end is a standard revolving sprinkler that's mounted on a wheeled base that moves along a hose you've laid out on the ground. It has the same low throw radius as any other revolving sprinkler, but because this sprinkler goes anywhere you send it, its spewing distance becomes a moot point. And, because most traveling sprinklers are very well made, they deliver excellent uniformity. A traveler will cost you a pretty penny, but it'll reward you with a job well done.

Going Down

Aboveground, portable sprinklers are fine if you have a small-to-middlin' lawn, or you live where rain provides most of the water your grass needs. On the other hand, if your green scene covers several acres, or you rarely see clouds from spring through fall, consider forking out for an inground irrigation system. It's not a small investment, but it could save you big bucks in water bills.

> ### SIMPLY FIXED
>
> You can't get more basic than a fixed sprinkler. These types generally have a short throw radius and poor uniformity. They're also prone to leaking around the head, which means that the ground within a couple feet of the sprinkler gets a lot more water than it should. On the plus side, they have no moving parts to break or get stuck because water simply shoots out of holes in the head.

HELP!

Q I just got a new water softener, and I'm concerned about the salt that it adds to my water. Is it true that it's harmful to grass?

A *Yep, it's true. Too much salt can make a lawn go belly-up. Fortunately, the answer to your problem couldn't be simpler: Just make sure your outdoor faucets—or the lines that run to your underground sprinklers—are not connected to the water-softener system. (Besides saving your grass, you'll save a lot of money on water-softener salt!)*

A LITTLE OFF THE TOP

On the face of it, cutting your grass seems about as straightforward as a yard chore can get. But in reality, mowing is *the* most important part of lawn care. Your timing, your technique, and even the equipment you use can spell the difference between a beautiful, healthy, trouble-free lawn and one that gives you nothing but grief. Here are my time-tested tips for trimming that turf in a way that'll keep it lush and lovely, and (believe it or not) reduce your mowing time as well as your water and fertilizer bills.

Words to Mow By

When it comes to trimming your turfgrass, the four most important words to remember are these: Mow high, mow sharp. As for the first part of that rule,

Are you tired of scraping grass clippings off your mower blades? Well, stop scraping! Instead, before you crank up the engine, just coat the underside of the mower with any of these lusty lubricants:

- **Nonstick cooking spray**
- **Household oil spray, such as WD-40®**
- **Liquid car wax**

Grass-Clipping Dissolving Tonic

If you leave your grass clippings in place (whether your mower mulches them or not), spray your turf twice a year with this timely tonic. It'll help the clippings break down more quickly and give your lawn a chance to breathe better, too.

> 1 can of beer
> 1 can of regular cola (not diet)
> 1 cup of ammonia
> 1 cup of dishwashing liquid

Mix the ingredients in a bucket and pour the solution into a 20 gallon hose-end sprayer. Then apply the solution to the point of runoff. Those clippings will decompose almost before you know it!

the classic rule of green thumb—and an easy one to remember—is to never cut more than one-third of the height of the grass at any one time. What that means in terms of actual inches depends on the type of grass and the time of year. "Mow sharp" simply means that you need to keep a razor edge on your mower blade. That way, it'll slice cleanly through the grass, leaving as little wiggle room as possible for escaping moisture and invading germs.

HOW HIGH I AM

The optimum mowing height for any lawn depends on the kind of grass and the time of year. Here's a rundown of preferences.

PREFERRED MOWING HEIGHT IN INCHES		
TYPE OF GRASS	**COOL WEATHER**	**HOT WEATHER**
Bahia grass	2	3
Bermuda grass	1/2	1
Buffalo grass	2	3
Carpet grass	1	2
Creeping bent grass	3/4	1 1/4
Fine fescue	2	2 1/2
Kentucky bluegrass	2	3
Perennial ryegrass	1 1/2	2 1/2
St. Augustine grass	2	3
Zoysia grass	1/2	1

To Everything There Is a Season

And that includes your mowing schedule. Here's my year-round routine.

Spring. Resist the temptation to rev up your mower the minute you see the first robin hopping across the lawn. Instead, let the grass grow just a little taller than one-third over the recommended height (see "How High I Am" on page 49). This way, it'll have time to wake up and gather some strength after its long winter's nap. When it's time to mow, set the mower deck to trim it back by about one-third. Then, with each trim after that, gradually lower the mower deck until you're cutting at the recommended height for your type of grass.

Summer. This is the time when your grass is most vulnerable to sunburn and water loss. So always let it grow beyond its maximum height by one-third to slow its growth, conserve moisture, and inhibit weeds. Then cut it back to its maximum, *not* minimum, height.

Fall. Aim high for your final act. To prepare your lawn for the long winter ahead, cut the grass to its maximum recommended height until it stops growing or goes dormant. Then drop the blade a notch and mow one last time.

Winter. The mower may be stored away since this is sleepy time for northern lawns, but there's no rest for you folks in the Sunbelt! Still, depending on where you live, you probably won't have to cut so often because your grass may grow more slowly. Just keep an eagle eye on it, and keep it at the recommended height for your current temperature range.

HIGH IS GOOD, BUT HIGHER ISN'T BETTER

Having delivered my mow-high lecture, I must tell you that it is possible to let your grass get too high. Turfgrasses that grow much over 3 inches tall tend to get thin and stringy; they don't form that nice, uniform look that we love in our lawns. Overly tall grass also tends to fall over and to get matted in wet weather. Then it may take it a long time to dry out, giving fungal diseases a chance to set in.

TROUBLE AND WOE

No matter how well you tend your turf, sooner or later, you're bound to encounter a problem of some kind. Well, don't fret: Here's a practical primer for solving—and preventing—various vexations ranging from pesky pests and dastardly diseases to mishaps caused by man's best friend and even wayward weeds.

Holy Moley!

Contrary to what a lot of folks think, moles are not rodents, and they do not eat grass or any other plants. Rather, moles belong to the biological order *Insectivora*, which in scientific lingo means insect eaters. Unfortunately, as they tunnel through the soil in search of dinner, they travel right through grass roots, leaving them vulnerable to drought, diseases, and other pests.

Before you launch your attack on moles, make sure they're really the culprits. Gophers make very similar tunnel systems. While moles leave simple, round piles of loose dirt at their "doors," gophers make mounds that are crescent shaped. And gophers do eat plants. In fact, they cause more trouble in flower and vegetable gardens than they do in your lawn.

Mole-Chaser Tonic

Moles will pack up and head outta Dodge (or at least out of your yard) when they get a taste of this potent potion.

> 1½ tbsp. of hot-pepper sauce
> 1 tbsp. of dishwashing liquid
> 1 tsp. of chili powder
> 1 qt. of water

Mix all of the ingredients in a bucket, and pour a little of the mixture into holes every foot or so along a mole run. The little guys will get a taste they won't soon forget!

Fortunately, there are several simple ways to say "Sayonara." Whichever one you choose, you might have to repeat it a few times, but eventually, the moles will give up and move on. First, locate the tunnel entrances, then pop one of these anti-mole tools into the hole:

🐌 A stick of Juicy Fruit® chewing gum and a partially crushed garlic clove

🐌 Several scoops of used kitty litter

🐌 A few squirts of pine-based cleaner

🐌 Half a cup or so of my Mole-Chaser Tonic (see page 51)

The one sure way to get moles out of your yard and *keep* 'em out is to banish their food supply—namely grubs (see "Insect Invaders" on page 59). Just beware that once you've sent the grubs packin', your mole problems could get worse for a while before they get better. That's because the little guys, suddenly finding themselves without their favorite food, will charge around frantically in search of dinner before they head for grubbier pastures.

Doggone Dogs

They're our best friends, all right—but it sure would be nice if they didn't leave those annoying yellow spots on the grass. (By the way, that old wives' tale that says the urine of female dogs is more potent than that of males isn't true. It causes more damage only because females tend to urinate all at once, in one spot, while males generally spray a little here

Quick Fix

It's impossible to entirely avoid dog spots on your lawn, but here are ways to minimize the damage:

• Go easy on chemical lawn food types containing highly concentrated nitrogen—a little more, courtesy of Rover doing his duty, can push grass over the edge.

• Add brewer's yeast to your pup's food. It seems to alter the chemistry of the urine, making it less damaging to turfgrass. (Check with your vet for the correct dosage.)

and a little there.) The spots are simply the result of too much of a good thing—namely, nitrogen and salts. The same brown, burned-looking patches would occur if you spilled fertilizer on the grass. If the deed has just been done, it's a snap to head off damage: Just turn on the hose, and flush the site thoroughly. After more than a day or so, though, follow this routine:

STEP 1. Lightly sprinkle gypsum over and around each spot to dissolve accumulated salts.

STEP 2. Overspray the lawn with 1 cup of baby shampoo or mild dishwashing liquid.

STEP 3. One week later, thoroughly overspray the turf with my Lawn-Saver Tonic (below).

When the burned spots have been in place for a while, you have only one choice: Dig out the damaged turf, and flush the soil with plenty of water to dilute the salts and nitrogen. Then reseed or resod the spots (better yet, also overseed your entire lawn) with fescue or perennial ryegrass.

Don't be too quick to blame Rover for damaging your lawn. Buried debris, such as rocks, wood, or even lost toys, can cause similar dead, brown spots, because they prevent the roots from reaching into the soil for life-giving moisture. The simple solution: Just get the obstacles outta there!

Lawn-Saver Tonic

When bad things happen to good grass, reach for this liquid safety net.

　　　½ **can of beer**
　　　½ **can of regular cola (not diet)**
　　　½ **cup of ammonia**

Combine the ingredients in a 20 gallon hose-end sprayer. Then saturate your turf to the point of runoff, and it should bounce right back!

Both are resistant to damage caused by dog urine. If neither of those will work where you live, at least steer clear of Bermuda grass and Kentucky bluegrass; they're the most urine-sensitive turf types of all.

Ailing Lawns

If you're cowering in fear that your lawn will fall victim to some dastardly disease, take heart: The targets of choice for turf diseases are golf courses and similar playgrounds that are highly fertilized, closely mowed, and constantly bombarded with insecticides, herbicides, and fungicides. But if you do suspect that your turf is suffering from an ailment, the fastest way—in fact, often the only way—to positively diagnose the problem is to send a "biopsy" to your local Cooperative Extension Service, or a specialist the service might recommend.

Take your sample from an area where the trouble is just starting to take hold, with about half of it healthy turf and half showing early symptoms. Dig down about 2 inches, and try to lift up a section that's roughly 1 foot square. Then pack it up carefully (ask for instructions when you call the Extension Service), and send it off to the lawn docs with a cover note telling everything you know about the problem, including these details:

❧ Age and overall appearance of the lawn

❧ Type and variety of grass

❧ Size, shape, and color of the affected areas

❧ Location of the damaged spots (e.g., along your normal mowing path, at the base of your sprinkler heads, or on a slope)

Diseases are not the only causes of lawn death. A number of environmental mishaps can—and frequently do—kill turfgrass. What appears to be an illness may be the result of one of these factors:

- **Drought**
- **Fertilizer burn**
- **Freezing**
- **Gas, oil, or chemical spills**
- **Low light**
- **Road salt damage**

Fungus-Fighter Soil Drench

Nearly all the diseases that plague turfgrass are caused by foul fungi. When they're fussing around in your soil, making a mess of your landscape, polish 'em off pronto with this potent potion.

4 garlic bulbs, crushed
1/2 cup of baking soda
1 gal. of water

Mix the ingredients in a big pot and bring the liquid to a boil. Then turn off the heat, and let the mixture cool to room temperature. Strain the liquid into a watering can, and soak the ground in the problem areas (remove any dead grass first). Go VERY slowly, so the solution penetrates deep into the soil. Then dump the strained-out garlic bits onto the soil, and work them in gently.

- Appearance of individual grass blades (e.g., streaked, spotted, wilted)

- Root condition (e.g., does the turf pull up in a mat? Have the roots rotted?)

- When the problem first appeared, and weather conditions at the time

- Recent activity in your yard, such as construction or house painting

- Your mowing, watering, and feeding routine

- Any pesticides, herbicides, and/or fertilizers you've used

Turf-Trashing Trespassers

Botanically speaking, there is no such thing as a weed. But there *is* such a thing as a plant that's growing where it's not welcome, and unlike diseases, they can—and do—show up in even the best-tended lawns. The most reliable method for whipping them depends on which kind of tenacious trespassers you're dealing with. Here are the routines I follow.

Cool-season annuals. These include chickweed, knotweed, mallow (a.k.a. cheeseweed), and shepherd's purse.

- If you live up North, avoid feeding your lawn in the spring; down South, hold the chow in the winter.

- In the North, mow high in spring and fall, so the grass can shade the soil and keep weed seeds from germinating.

- In the South, mow high in late summer to deprive seeds of light. In the fall, overseed your lawn with a cool-season grass like perennial ryegrass or Kentucky bluegrass, and mow high through the winter.

Cool-season perennials. These include broadleaf plantain, Canada thistle, clover, creeping Charlie (a.k.a. ground ivy), curly dock, and wild violet.

- Early in the season, scrape the plants out of your lawn with a metal rake.

- Immediately after that, mow your lawn to its shortest recommended height, rake up the clippings, and get rid of them fast.

HELP!

Q I've just bought an old house with a big, beautiful Kentucky bluegrass lawn. The grass is growing great, but unfortunately, so is a whole lot of crabgrass. I don't have time for much hand-weeding, and I refuse to use herbicides. Is there any other way to get rid of this ugly stuff?

A *There sure is, my friend, and it couldn't be easier! Just cover the crabgrass with either black plastic or black paper mulch (available at most garden centers), and leave it in place for 10 days. When you pull it off, that ol' crabgrass should be dead as a doornail. The bluegrass that was also covered will be yellow, but it'll green up again fast once you take the mulch away and let the sun shine in.*

Warm-season annuals. These include carpetweed, crabgrass, foxtail, goosegrass, pigweed, spurge, and yellow wood sorrel.

- Mow at the maximum recommended height, and if you've whacked off a lot of seed heads, remove the clippings.

- Avoid summer feeding, and follow my guidelines for healthy watering.

- Do everything you can to keep your lawn free of stress because these weeds *love* stressed-out turf.

- Aerate your soil, and do whatever else is necessary to reduce compaction.

Warm-season perennials. These include bindweed, chicory, dallis grass, dandelion, and yellow nut sedge.

- Dig out the clumps, toss some organic matter into the hole, and reseed.

- Mow high and avoid summertime feeding.

HIGH MOWING PAYS OFF

Simply by keeping your lawn mowed at the maximum recommended height for your type of grass, you can wipe out a lot of worrisome weeds. This easy trick works because:

• Tall grass shades and cools the soil, making it harder for weed seeds to get a toehold.

• Mowing high makes for deep-rooted, healthier grass that's better able to crowd out weeds.

• High mowing also controls low-growing troublemakers, such as crabgrass and witchgrass.

Quick Fix

When weeds are driving you to drink, don't reach for the corn liquor. Instead, run down to the garden center and buy a big sack of corn gluten meal (the same stuff that's used as filler in many dog foods). It's a highly effective preemergent herbicide for scads of troublemakers, including crabgrass, dandelions, and plantain. Unlike chemical weed killers, it won't harm the teeny life-forms that keep your soil healthy, and it's perfectly safe to use around toddlers and pets. To put this wonder "drug" to work in your yard, just apply 25 to 50 pounds per 2,500 square feet of lawn area before weeds start to sprout in the spring.

INSECT INVADERS

To hear some folks talk, you might think that every bug on earth is out gunnin' for your lawn. The fact is, though, only six kinds of insects routinely target turfgrasses throughout the country. Here's the rundown on the dirty half-dozen.

SYMPTOMS	LIKELY CULPRIT	WHAT TO DO
Round, bald spots in the turf, usually in late summer or fall.	Armyworms	• Treat your lawn with either Btk *(Bacillus thuringiensis* var. *kurstaki)* or parasitic nematodes of the species *Neoaplectana carpocapsae.* • Dig up the dead turf, and reseed the area with a grass that's resistant to armyworms.
Small, distinct circles of brown or yellowish grass; the discolored turf pulls up in a mat, and the roots are covered with a light brown powder that looks like sawdust.	Billbugs	• Release beneficial nematodes (see Chapter 10). • Improve soil drainage, control thatch, aerate the lawn regularly, and keep your soil well stocked with organic matter. • When you reseed or resod, choose billbug-resistant grass varieties.
Round, yellow patches that quickly turn brown and die.	Chinch bugs	• Control thatch, keep your lawn well watered, and avoid overfeeding, especially with nitrogen.

SYMPTOMS	LIKELY CULPRIT	WHAT TO DO
Irregular brown streaks of dead grass; chewed grass blades.	Mole crickets	• Release either Bt *(Bacillus thuringiensis)*, predatory nematodes (specifically *Steinernema scapterisci)*, a beneficial wasp by the name of *Larra bicolor*, or the Brazilian red-eyed fly, a.k.a. *Ormia depleta.* • Encourage natural enemies, including ground beetles, assassin bugs, toads, snakes, raccoons, foxes, and birds (see Chapter 10).
Small dead patches (1 to 2 inches in diameter) in early spring, which by summer develop into *big* dead patches; small, white moths rise up in clouds in front of your lawn mower.	Sod webworms	• Walk around your yard in aerating spiked lawn sandals or old-fashioned golf spikes to puncture the thatch layer. • Apply Btk (*Bacillus thuringiensis* var. *kurstaki*). • Encourage natural enemies, especially birds and spined soldier beetles.
Irregular, brown patches that look burned; if you tug on one of the dead clumps, it'll come right up like a piece of loose carpet, often exposing the grubs.	White grubs	• For short-term relief, drench your turf with beneficial nematodes. • If the grubs are Japanese beetle larvae, treat your lawn with milky spore disease *(Bacillus popilliae)*, according to the package.

YOU CAN'T FOOL MOTHER NATURE

But you can save your lawn from the challenges she sends your way. Here's a rundown of fast and easy tips for coping with her lightning-quick curveballs.

Drought Defense

We all know that prolonged dry spells seem to be hitting more of the country every year, and lasting longer than they used to. The time to start guarding your grass from drought is before Ma Nature turns off the faucets. Follow the watering and mowing guidelines earlier in this chapter, and for good measure, in spring and fall top your lawn with a 1/2- to 1-inch layer of compost. That security blanket will conserve precious moisture—besides feeding your grass, killing disease germs, and discouraging weeds from sprouting.

Many pests and diseases strike turf while it's under stress from extended periods of heat, drought, or excessive moisture. But symptoms generally don't appear until the weather has returned to normal. Once it does, keep an eagle eye out for signs of trouble so you can jump into action fast.

High and Dry

When a prolonged dry spell does hit, follow this plan of action (or, in some cases, non-action) to help your lawn survive.

Spread the wealth (again). If you're fortunate enough to have some warning that a hot, dry period is looming in the not-too-distant future, give your lawn extra protection by applying another 1/2-inch layer of compost. (This should be in addition to the layer you spread earlier in the spring.)

Hold the chow. Feeding your lawn during drought will only add to its stress level. And stressed-out grass is a sitting duck for pests, diseases, and weeds.

Declare a truce. Speaking of pests, diseases, and weeds, if they do show up, just ignore them until cooler, wetter weather arrives. Believe it or not, engaging in battle now will only make things worse!

Keep watering. Continue your normal watering routine for as long as your City Fathers and Mothers allow. And be sure to perform this chore early in the morning, so as little H_2O as possible is lost to evaporation. Whatever you do, don't water in the evening because grass that stays wet after dark—especially on a hot night—is fair prey for foul fungi.

Enough, Already!

Sometimes, an impatient lawn keeper's biggest weather woe isn't rain that doesn't come—it's rain that just won't quit! Well, you can't make the clouds dry up, but you can help your lawn rebound once the blue skies return. For starters, while the rain is falling and until the ground dries out later, declare your turf off-limits to nonessential foot traffic. Romping on sopping-wet grass will put your soil on the road to compaction—fast! Then once any surface water has drained away, follow this three-step plan to put your soil (and, therefore, your grass) on the road to recovery:

Grandma's
GROW-HOW

Whenever a drought strikes, take a tip from Grandma Putt and stay off the lawn as much as possible—regardless of whether you're still able to water, or you've had to let the grass go dormant. Otherwise, the added trauma of foot traffic and other activity just may put that turf over the edge, and it'll never come back to life. As Grandma Putt used to say, "When in doubt, sit it out!"

STEP 1. Shove the tines of a garden fork deep into the soil, and vigorously move it back and forth a few times to enlarge the holes. This will help the water that's lingering under the soil surface to percolate downward.

STEP 2. Apply gypsum at a rate of 50 pounds per 2,500 square feet of lawn area. This will loosen the soil to encourage better drainage. It works almost like an army of little rototillers—but without the damage rototilling can do to the soil structure.

STEP 3. One week after you apply the gypsum, follow up by applying a premium, natural, organic fertilizer applied at the recommended rate.

Get Ready for Winter

With just a little preparation in the fall, you can head off a whole lot of springtime headaches. Here's your season-ending to-do list.

Keep mowing. Throughout the fall, keep cutting your grass to its maximum recommended height until it stops growing or goes dormant. Then drop the blade a notch and mow one last time.

Give it a bedtime bath. Before the temperature falls to 50°F, give your lawn a final wash-down with my Fall Cleanup Tonic (below). How come? Because a lawn that goes to bed clean in the fall is more likely to wake up healthy in the spring!

Fall Cleanup Tonic

Fend off snow mold, foul fungi, and other wild and woolly wintertime nasties with this excellent elixir.

> **1 cup of antiseptic mouthwash**
> **1 cup of baby shampoo**
> **1 cup of chamomile tea**
> **1 cup of tobacco tea***
> **Warm water**

Mix the mouthwash, shampoo, and chamomile and tobacco teas in a bucket, then add 2 cups of the mixture to a 20 gallon hose-end sprayer, filling the balance of the jar with warm water. Overspray your turf when the temperature is above 50°F. Follow up with your regular fall lawn feeding.

* To make tobacco tea, place half a handful of chewing tobacco in an old nylon stocking and soak it in a gallon of hot water until the mixture is dark brown. Pour the liquid into a glass container with a tight-fitting lid for storage.

Give it a good supper. Feed your lawn according my directions in "Gettin' On Toward Bedtime" on page 41.

Protect your borders. Before the first snow flies, liberally spread a 5-foot band of gypsum over the turf along roadsides, walkways, or any other surfaces that could be hit by salt from your town's de-icing trucks. Then mix 1 cup of dishwashing liquid and ½ cup each of ammonia and beer in a 20 gallon hose-end sprayer, and apply the solution over the gypsum to the point of runoff. Your soil and grass should sail through the winter in fine shape.

Hold the Salt!

Where your roadside grass is concerned, you have to take whatever the highway department dishes out (unless you've got a *lot* of clout at City Hall). But in the rest of your yard, you don't have to put up with one iota of salt damage. The next time you wake up to an ice-covered patio, walkway, or driveway, reach for one of these kinder, gentler helpers:

- If you simply want to turn the ice into a nonslip surface, cover it with cinders, sand, or wood ashes.

- To melt the ice, use alfalfa meal or a pet-safe commercial de-icer. These critter-friendly formulas are also harmless to grass, landscape plants, and wooden surfaces like decks and porches.

- When you need to clear a walkway or driveway on the double, fire up a propane weed torch and take aim. But first, make sure that you have a place for the melted ice to drain; otherwise, you'll just be moving your problem from one spot to another!

Quick Fix

Salt damage isn't a problem in warm regions, but there is one winter nuisance: While cool-season grasses stay green until the snow flies, warm-season types turn brown at the first touch of frost. The simple solution: Overseed in October with annual ryegrass. It'll take off in a flash, stay green all winter, then fade away just as your warm-season turf is gearing up for a new season in the sun.

CHAPTER
2

TIP-TOP TREES AND SUPER SHRUBS

Woody Wonders on the Double

Don't get me wrong: There is no way on God's green earth that you or I—or anyone else—can make a tree or shrub grow as quickly as turfgrass or flowers. But I do have secrets that will reduce the time and effort it takes to care for these woody wonders, and I'll share them with you here. And for those times when you're <u>REALLY</u> eager to see results, I'll clue you in on some of the best, ultra-fast-growing varieties available.

In addition to heading off major trouble, finding and planting trees and shrubs that are well suited to their sites will save you a lot of time on routine maintenance chores like pruning, feeding, and watering.

PLANNING MAKES PERFECT

Just as we saw with lawn care in Chapter 1, the surest way to save time and trouble with the trees and shrubs in your yard is to plan before you plant. That's true of every green, growing addition you make to your landscape, but it's even more important with trees and large shrubs, simply because they're so big. If you make a hasty decision, it could wind up causing enough trouble to rile up even the most patient gardener on the planet! So you should start your plan for quick success by deciding what purpose(s) you want trees and shrubs to serve in your yard.

What's the Use?

Besides adding a jolt of seasonal color with their festive spring flowers or Technicolor™ autumn leaves, trees and shrubs can perform a lot of purely practical feats around the old homestead.

Cut your energy costs. Carefully chosen and strategically placed deciduous trees and large shrubs offer cooling shade in the summer, and then conveniently shed their leaves in fall, so that sunlight can filter through all winter long—just when you need it most.

Hold your soil in place. Trees' and shrubs' extensive root systems grab the ground, so the soil is less likely to wash away when a big storm hits, or when the rain just won't stop.

Fight your pest-control battles. Trees and shrubs offer food and shelter for birds and other critters, which, in turn, feast on destructive (and disease-spreading) insects—and give you hours of viewing pleasure to boot.

Boost your property value. Handsome, healthy, and well-placed trees and shrubs can increase your home's sticker price considerably—just ask any real estate agent!

Speaking of Property Values

Whether you're planning to sell your house soon, or you're simply in a hurry to make your yard into a more attractive and pleasant place to be, trees and shrubs can help you accomplish your mission. After all, no one likes to look out at a bare yard. So here are just some of the ways both kinds of these

PLANT A GREEN SCREEN

Does your home turf get too much wind to suit you (and your tender plants)? Then give your yard some shelter with this simple trick: Plant a row or (better yet) two rows of evergreen trees on the windward side of your lot. Then set a row of flowering shrubs or small flowering trees along the side of the windbreak closest to the house. Any white or light-colored blooms sparkle like stars when they're backed up by an evergreen screen!

woody plants can give you (and your landscape) dramatic results in fairly short order.

Make it homey. Even a medium-size yard can feel empty and bleak if the whole thing is just grassy lawn. But add a few trees or shrubs, and you've turned that space into a warm, welcoming retreat.

Divide and conquer. By planting trees and shrubs in the right spots, you can make separate outdoor "rooms" in your yard—say, for instance, a vegetable garden, a badminton court, or a playground for children and pets.

Fast-growing trees and shrubs are a godsend for hiding things you'd just as soon not look at, such as a busy road, the neighbors' back porch, or your own laundry line.

Frame a view. You know how a picture frame draws your eye into a painting? Well, trees and shrubs can do the same thing in a landscape, directing your gaze toward a beautiful scene like your prized flower garden, or a range of hills in the distance.

Put it in the spotlight. If you want to call attention to something in your landscape, like the entrance to your driveway, just flank it with a couple of especially eye-catching trees or shrubs. Never again will your guests miss the turn and go flying on by! Just one note of caution: Make sure you position

Grandma's GROW-HOW

Hundreds of shrubs and small trees have white or pale-toned flowers that glow against an evergreen windbreak. Here's a handful of Grandma's favorites:

Bridalwreath spirea (*Spiraea prunifolia*)

Japanese tree lilac (*Syringa reticulata*)

Sweet azalea (*Rhododendron aborescens*)

Tea viburnum (*Viburnum setigerum*)

White fringe tree (*Chionanthus virginicus*)

the plants in such a way that you can see over or around them as you pull out of your driveway—and oncoming drivers can see you!

Honey, I Shrunk the House

Did you know that you can use trees to visually alter the size of your house or your yard? It's true! Landscape designers do it all the time; they call it "refining the sense of scale." Here's how it works:

- If a house is tall and rather intimidating, large trees planted close by will make it look less imposing and more welcoming. (Bear in mind, though, that "close" is relative. Never plant a tree where its branches will overhang your roof; in most instances, that means keeping a tree at least 25 feet away.)

- On the other hand, to make a small house appear a little larger and more substantial, you should choose trees that barely reach the roofline.

- When you want to make a big yard seem cozier and more intimate, set large trees at the far edges of the property.

- Conversely, small trees viewed from a distance fool the eye into thinking they are quite far away, indeed—thereby making a small yard feel much more spacious than it really is.

Quick Fix

One of an impatient gardener's worst nightmares is a hillside where grass washes away in any big rainstorm. The quick and easy answer: Cover that meandering ground with fast-growing, spreading shrubs. Aboveground, their branches and leaves slow down pelting raindrops, thereby preventing soil erosion. Belowground, the dense root systems knit together quickly to hold the soil firmly in place. Lots of shrubs work wonders on slope patrol, but to get the biggest time-saving bang for your buck, go with evergreens that are native to your area— they'll need the least amount of maintenance. You'll find many excellent evergreen choices at a local nursery that specializes in native plants.

Now You See It . . .

Now you don't. You say you'd like to block a busy road from view when you're sitting on your patio—without hiding the beautiful scenery on the other side? No problem! Just use this simple fool-the-eye trick:

STEP 1. Get an 8-foot-long strip of wood, and mark it at 1-foot increments.

STEP 2. Stand on your patio, looking at the offending road.

STEP 3. Have a helper stand at the edge of your yard, in front of the road, holding the wooden strip upright on the ground.

STEP 4. At the spot where you no longer see the road above the strip, note the measurement.

STEP 5. Plant a hedge of fast-growing trees or shrubs that will reach the measured height at maturity, and they'll easily block the undesirable view.

The secret of this trick lies in the fact that your eye sees objects grow smaller as you move away from them. You'll be surprised at how low your green screen can be to banish that eyesore—and, therefore, how quickly you'll get the results you want.

Just bear in mind that the operative words in Step 5 are "at maturity." If you plant trees or shrubs that are the right height now, you'll have to do a lot of pruning in years to come.

PUT 'EM ON GUARD DUTY

When I was growing up, folks didn't have fancy burglar-alarm systems in their houses (at least nobody in our neighborhood did!). Instead, they used shrubs to ensure the safety of their homes and gardens, and you can, too. Just install thickets of thorny, prickly shrubs in strategic places—such as under windows or just outside a fence. They'll deter all kinds of unwelcome visitors, including burglars, roving dogs, and even deer. Good choices for this task include barberry (*Berberis thunbergii*), crown of thorns (*Euphorbia milii*), firethorns (*Pyracantha*), hollies (*Ilex*), thorny elaeagnus (*Elaeagnus pungens*), and many kinds of roses, especially old-time species. (For the full scoop on roses, see Chapter 4.)

CHOOSE HAPPY CAMPERS

We all know that avoiding trouble is a lot easier
and less time-consuming than coping with it
after it strikes. And you can head off a whole lot
of problems in your yard simply by selecting the
right plants and putting them in the right places.
Here are some of my best secrets for choosing trees
and shrubs that will live happily ever after in your
landscape—with the least amount of care from you.

**With trees and shrubs,
fertility, drainage,
and pH are all crucial
to success. So make
sure you have your
soil tested. And don't
use a do-it-yourself
kit—get a thorough
analysis from a
professional testing
laboratory.**

Do Your Homework

No matter how impatient you are to start putting
woody plants to work in your yard, do yourself a
favor: Before you even begin perusing catalogs or landscaping books
(with all those pretty pictures leading you into temptation), follow this
foolproof trouble-avoidance plan.

Study your site carefully. Consider prevailing winds, temperature ranges,
and humidity levels, as well as the amount of sunlight the plant will get.
A tree or shrub that's out of its comfort range in any of these conditions
is a prime target for pests and diseases.

Consider the mission. For instance, do you want a big, leafy canopy to
shade your hammock on hot summer days? A privacy screen for your
swimming pool? A windbreak to shield your house from winter gales and

Humidity is an important consideration when you're choosing trees and
shrubs. Fortunately, it's a snap to determine the level in your yard. Just look
at the weeds that are growing there. Common lamb's-quarters and pigweeds
grow best in high humidity, while common purslane thrives in dry conditions.

high heating bills? Or simply a frilly fountain of pastel flowers to dress up your yard in the springtime?

Get help. Trees and shrubs can be big financial investments—particularly when you consider the frustration and heartbreak of losing one or more to problems you could have prevented. Unless you're absolutely certain about which plants will thrive in your yard and perform the work you have in mind, consult a professional arborist. (You'll find them listed in the Yellow Pages.) Or get in touch with your local Audubon Society or Nature Conservancy office, and ask their plant experts to recommend trees and shrubs that are native to your area and your site's growing conditions. You just might learn that the answer to your prayers is a plant you didn't even know existed!

THE SPEED DEMONS

Over the past few years, breeding fast-growing trees and shrubs has become a big-time business. A quick Internet search will bring up dozens of nurseries that specialize in woody plants with ultra-rapid growth rates. Here's just a small sampling of what you can expect to find.

SPEED DEMON	ANNUAL GROWTH RATE (FT.)	MATURE HEIGHT & WIDTH (FT.)
EVERGREEN TREES		
Cryptomeria Radicans (*Cryptomeria japonica* var. *sinensis*) Zones 5–9	3–5	H: 30–40 W: 15–20
Leyland cypress (x *Cupressocyparis leylandii*) Zones 6–10	3–5	H: 40–60 W: 8–12
Thuja 'Green Giant' (*Thuja standishii* x *plicata*) Zones 5–9	3–5	H: 20–40 W: 8–12

DECIDUOUS TREES		
Royal Empress tree (*Paulownia*) Zones 5–11	15	H: 40–50 W: 30–40
Wax myrtle (*Myrica cerifera*) Zones 7–11	3–5	H: 15–20 W: 10–15
Willow hybrid (*Salix* 'Willow hybrid') Zones 4–9	6–10	H: 35–45 when in rows, 50–75 alone W: 20–30
EVERGREEN SHRUBS		
American boxwood (*Buxus sempervirens*) Zones 5–9	1–2	H: 10–12 W: 8–10
Soft Touch holly (*Ilex crenata* 'Soft Touch') Zones 5–9	1	H: 2–3 W: 2
Variegated privet (*Ligustrum sinense*) Zones 7–10	2–3	H: 6–8 W: 6–8
DECIDUOUS SHRUBS		
Burning bush (*Euonymus alatus*) Zones 4–8	2–3	H: 4–8 W: 4–8
Lynwood Gold forsythia (*Forsythia* x *intermedia* 'Lynwood Gold') Zones 4–8	2–4	H: 8–10 W: 8–10
Redtwig dogwood (*Cornus alba* 'Elegantissima') Zones 2–9	1–2	H: 6–8 W: 6–8

H E L P !

Q I'm planning on planting trees in my yard, but when I got some advice from my neighbors, they used terms I've never heard before. Can you tell me what the difference is between *evergreen* and *deciduous*—and what in heaven's name does *semi-evergreen* mean?

A *Evergreen plants are the ones that hold on to their leaves or needles all year long, while deciduous trees and shrubs drop their leaves each fall and grow new ones each spring. Semi-evergreen plants keep their leaves into winter before shedding them. In cold climates, the leaves may last only until midwinter, while in warmer areas, they can stay almost until spring.*

Coming to Terms with Trees and Shrubs

Before we go any further, let me clear up a common misunderstanding about woody plants. Technically, the only difference between trees and shrubs is that trees have a single trunk, and shrubs have multiple woody stems. Many people assume that shrubs have to be a certain size—usually somewhere between 4 and 8 feet tall—and that trees are considerably taller than that. In fact, shrubs can range from less than 12 inches tall all the way up to more than 15 feet high. As for trees, there are plenty that naturally grow only a few feet tall, and plant breeders are continually developing new small cultivars. That means you're sure to find a tree or shrub that's just the right size to fit every part of your yard—or even grow happily ever after in a container on your deck or patio.

Shape Up!

Trees and shrubs grow in half a dozen general shapes. Your best choices depend upon the functions you want the plants to perform in your landscape, the size of your yard, and—of course—personal preference. These are the basic forms.

Columnar or fastigiate. Their branches tend to grow up, rather than out, so they have a narrow outline that makes them perfect for tight spots. Fastigiate beech (*Fagus sylvatica* 'Fastigiata') is one tree example. On the shrub side, 'Helmond Pillar' barberry (*Berberis thunbergii* 'Helmond Pillar') is a good example.

Horizontal, a.k.a. spreading. The branches grow straight out from the main stem, so the plant has a broad-spreading outline. Two good examples are common flowering dogwood (*Cornus florida*) and doublefile viburnum (*Viburnum plicatum* f. *tomentosum*).

Pyramidal. This is the classic, triangular Christmas-tree outline. It's the most common shape for pines, spruces, and many other evergreen trees.

Rounded. Think of a tree a child would draw: a straight, upright trunk topped with a globe-shaped mop of green. Crabapples and maples have this shape. Many shrubs do, too, including hydrangeas and mugo pine.

Vase-shaped. These plants have a sort of a V- or upside-down triangular shape. Hybrid elms usually grow in this form.

Weeping. Instead of growing upward or outward, the branches of weeping trees and shrubs hang downward. Weeping willow is the best-known example, but there are many others.

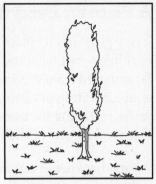

Columnar trees and shrubs are good for tight spots.

Horizontal trees and shrubs spread out and need plenty of space.

Rounded trees fit nicely into many landscape styles.

A Place for Everything

Every plant has its place in Mother Nature's scheme of things—but for some trees, that place needs to be far removed from driveways, swimming pools, and outdoor seating or dining areas. To be specific, when you're searching for trees for such areas, avoid those that produce any of the following potential hazards.

Be careful where you plant trees or bushes that produce soft or gooey fruits. They can make messy splotches on your car, paved surfaces, and outdoor furniture (not to mention the soles of your shoes).

Roots that spread out and upward. They could grow right through your pavement or into the sides of your pool! Instead, look for trees with roots that go straight down. There are many beautiful choices, including black locust, linden, and pin oak, to name just a few. On the other hand, er, root, California fuchsia, poplar, and willows will buckle your pavement and clog your water pipes in no time flat.

Nuts. They'll put dings in your car and (whoops!) act like marbles under your feet. They'll also attract droves of squirrels, which, besides eating the nuts, will rob your bird feeders, munch on your bulbs, and help themselves to any other plants that happen to strike their fancy.

An unpleasant aroma. Whatever you do, steer clear of any tree or shrub with *foetida*, *foetidus*, *foetidum*, *foetidissima*, or *foetidissimum* in its botanical

Grandma's **GROW-HOW**

If you live in a region where winter is serious business, as Grandma Putt did, do yourself a favor and give the cold shoulder to trees with weak, brittle wood that snaps easily under snow and ice loads. Prime examples are box elder, cottonwood, silver maple, and Siberian elm. Likewise, if your area tends to get severe thunderstorms, be wary of oaks, tulip trees, hickories, and pines, as well as silver, sugar, and Norway maples. All of these are major lightning magnets.

name. The word—in whichever form it's used—means foul-smelling or stinky. With some plants, the common name is a dead giveaway. For instance, who would ever think of planting smelly shepherd's tree (*Boscia foetida*) or stinking juniper (*Juniperus foetidissima*)? In other cases, the common name doesn't even give you a clue that you might be stumbling into aromatic trouble. Two cases in point: tree of a thousand stars (*Serissa foetida*) and false mastic (*Sideroxylon foetidissimum*).

A-Shopping We Will Go

When you're shopping for trees or shrubs—especially if you're in a hurry to get on with the planting process—there are so many factors to consider that it's nearly impossible to remember them all. And overlooking any one of them could result in big (and possibly expensive) problems in the future. So to avoid trouble, make a photocopy of this list, take it with you on shopping day, and check it against the label on every plant that strikes your fancy. Yes, that may try your patience, but it can help you avoid a lot of trouble (and possibly expense) down the road! Here's your tree and shrub shopping checklist:

🌿 How tall will the plant grow?

🌿 How far will it spread when it reaches maturity?

🌿 What is its shape and form?

Take 2

Besides looking great all year round, evergreens like pine, spruce, and hemlock can make your pest- and disease-control efforts faster and easier. When the trees shed their needles, just gather them up and use them as mulch for tender fruits, flowers, and vegetables. That scratchy blanket will fend off slugs and other soft-bodied crawlers and keep any low-growing leaves and fruit off the ground, away from soilborne pests and diseases.

But that's not all! Evergreen needles are also just the ticket for lowering your soil's pH and adding valuable organic matter at the same time.

- Do the roots run deep or stay close to the surface?

- How much sun does it need?

- How dense will the shade be five years from now?

- How fast does it grow?

- What can you expect in terms of fall color?

- What will the plant look like in winter?

- Last, but far from least, is it well suited to your climate and the growing conditions in your yard?

Shop for Comfort

Pollen allergies can turn even the most ardent plant lover into an impatient gardener in the blink of an eye. If you're among the 38 percent of the population that suffers from allergies, I know a quick and easy way to cut back on your sneezin' and wheezin'—plant only female trees and shrubs. ("*Huh*?" I hear you saying.) Here's the deal: Many trees and shrubs are *dioecious*, which means that each individual plant is either male or female. In order to reproduce their kind, the males release huge amounts of pollen into the air. When a female of the same species is close by, her flowers snag most of those particles. But when your yard (or, your whole neighborhood) is an old boys' network, the pollen just floats around—until it reaches your sinuses.

So do yourself a favor: When you're shopping for woody plants, tell the folks at the garden center that you want a female. And don't let anyone sell

Quick Fix

You say you've got your heart set on a plant that simply won't survive in your growing conditions, or even your climate? Well, don't fret. Mother Nature has graced the earth with small versions of many trees and shrubs, and plant breeders have developed a whole lot more. These tiny treasures thrive in containers, which makes it a snap for you to give them any kind of soil their little roots desire—and whisk them to shelter from cold winds or blistering sun.

you a so-called "seedless" variety. These are actually male clones, and although they don't produce seeds, fruits, or flowers, they still produce plenty of pollen.

Caution: Danger Ahead

When you're shopping for trees and shrubs, remember this: That cute little number in its neat little pot may be perfect right now, but within a few years, your instant gratification might turn into a nightmare. That plant could grow into a rampaging monster that will send its roots through your driveway, drop its leaves into your gutters, block light from reaching your house and garden, and who knows what else! At the very least, a woody plant that's too big for its site will require constant pruning to keep it in bounds. So always buy a tree or shrub that will be the height and width you want when it reaches maturity, *not* when you see it at the garden center. This is one time when what may appear to be the slow route really is a quick fix!

INTO THE GROUND!

Well, you've done your homework and shopped carefully. You're all set and ready to get growing. But don't let your impatience get the upper hand—there's still one more crucial step remaining: planting your trees or shrubs so they get off to the healthiest possible start in life. Here's how to go about it, while getting the job done right.

YANKEES, REJOICE!

Some of the easiest tiny shrubs to grow in containers are gardenias, jasmine, angel's trumpet, and oleander. These fragrant flowering beauties are too tender to survive even a mild northern winter. But they take to potted plant life like ducks to water, and they're delighted to spend the winter indoors in a sunny window. Just beware that oleander is highly poisonous, so give it a pass if you have pets or small children.

No matter how impatient you are to have a big tree in your yard, your best bet is to plant young trees that are less than 8 feet tall. Besides being easier to handle than larger trees, they settle in more quickly and usually don't need to be staked.

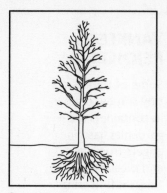

Bare-root tree

Balled-and-burlapped tree

Container-grown tree

High Time

The time for planting a tree or shrub depends on how the plant has been grown and packaged for delivery. There are three possibilities.

Bare-root. This is the way they'll arrive if you've ordered them from a catalog. They're grown in a nursery field, then dug up, cleaned of soil, and shipped to garden centers, or directly to mail-order buyers. These must be planted when the plants are dormant, in either early spring or late fall.

Balled-and-burlapped (a.k.a. B-and-B). These are dug from a nursery field with as much soil as possible around the roots, then quickly wrapped in burlap and tied with twine. They can be planted any time the ground isn't frozen, except on the hottest days of summer.

Container-grown. Trees and shrubs that have started life in pots can be planted any time the ground isn't frozen. Still, I've found that they settle in fastest and best when you plant them in spring or fall, when the weather won't make heavy demands on them. A word of caution: When you buy a woody plant in a container, make sure it was actually *grown* in that pot. Some less than top-notch nurseries sell *containerized* shrubs and very small trees. These have been dug up bare-root, then stuck in containers (sometimes with the roots chopped to fit) and put out for sale. That's a shocking experience for the plants and a risky proposition for you. If you have any doubts, have a nursery salesperson pull it partway out of the pot. If you see a tangled mass of roots filling the container, you're good to go. Otherwise, walk away.

The Question of Packaging

It goes without saying (I hope!) that before you puddle in a bare-root tree or shrub, you should remove and discard the package it came in. Container-grown and balled-and-burlapped plants require slightly different treatments. Here's all you need to know:

- If you've purchased a balled-and-burlapped tree or shrub, there is no need to remove the wrapping; like any other organic material, it will decompose over time, enriching the soil in the process. (Just make absolutely certain that the wrapping is genuine burlap, and not a synthetic material, which you *will* have to remove.) Likewise, it's fine to leave natural twine in place, but be sure to cut away any nylon cord or plastic strapping to prevent it from strangling the plant as it grows.

- To remove a container-grown plant from its pot, invert it and tap the sides to loosen the roots. Then hold your hands over the soil, and squeeze

> ### BARE-ROOT PRELIMINARIES
>
> Bare-root plants take off faster when you use a simple preplanting procedure called "puddling in." Just mix soil and water in a bucket or tub until it reaches the consistency of gravy. Swish the roots around in the mixture for a minute or two, then let them soak in it for a few hours (but no longer than overnight). This will get the fine root hairs moist and plumped up, so they'll be all ready to grow when you cover them with soil.

Grandma's GROW-HOW

Whenever I plant a tree or shrub, I use an old trick Grandma Putt and her pals used to speed up the get-up-and-grow process: I line the planting hole with baking potatoes. The taters help in two ways: They hold in moisture that helps the young plants' roots get a good start in life. Then later on, as the spuds decay, they provide valuable nutrients for the tree or shrub to grow on.

Woody Plant Booster Mix

This healthful breakfast supplies just enough nutrients to get your young trees and shrubs off to a good start without encouraging their roots to hang around the home hole too long.

4 lbs. of compost
2 lbs. of gypsum
1 lb. of dry dog food*
1 lb. of dry oatmeal
1 lb. of Epsom salts

Mix all of the ingredients together in a tub or wheelbarrow. Then work a handful or two of the mixture into the planting hole of each tree or shrub. After planting, sprinkle another handful over the soil before you water.

* Use a low-priced supermarket brand that contains corn gluten, a filler that's lacking in premium pet foods.

or push from the bottom. If the root-ball doesn't slide out easily, set the container on the ground, and use a knife or tin snips to cut down the sides. But whatever you do, no matter how impatient you are, don't yank the plant out by its top—that could cause severe damage!

The Up-to-Date Planting Process

Tree experts used to recommend planting trees and shrubs in the same kinds of holes you'd prepare for prize perennials—that is, filled to the brim with organic matter and various soil amendments. Well, I have good news for all of you impatient gardeners: That's not so anymore. That kind of coddling actually does more harm than good because it encourages the plant's roots to stay in the soft, lush confines of the hole. And for a tree or shrub to thrive, it needs to send its roots many feet beyond the hole, into whatever soil happens to be there. Here's the modern approach to getting woody plants—both deciduous and evergreen—started out on the right root:

STEP 1. Thoroughly water the roots of your tree or shrub (or puddle in bare-root plants, as described on page 79).

STEP 2. Dig a hole that's wide enough to accommodate the roots without bending or circling, and just deep enough to set the plant at the same depth it was growing before, either in its pot or in the ground at the nursery. Use a shovel to make jagged slices into the sides of the hole; this will ensure that the roots can more easily penetrate the soil. Then work a handful or two of my Woody Plant Booster Mix (at left) into the bottom of the hole.

STEP 3. Set the tree or shrub into the hole so the beginning of the trunk—the spot where the bark turns lighter—is above the soil surface. (In the case of a grafted plant, such as a dwarf fruit tree, you want the graft union to be above ground level.) If the root-ball is wrapped in burlap, cut off any fabric or twine that sticks above ground level; otherwise, it will wick moisture away from the roots. With a container-grown or bare-root plant, gently spread out the outer roots, but keep your hands off the central taproot; you don't want to disturb it! Then dribble about a quart of my Terrific Tree and Shrub Transplanting Tonic onto the roots (see page 82). It will help reduce the stress of planting, thus ensuring a healthier start in life.

Quick Fix

When you need to determine the right planting depth for a tree or shrub, don't hoist it into and out of the hole. Instead, stand a strip of wood up against the plant, and mark the spot where the trunk begins (or the graft union in the case of a dwarf fruit tree). Then, as you fill the hole with soil, use your marked stick as your measuring tool. This way, you'll save time and prevent damaging the tree—and your back!

STEP 4. Refill the planting hole about halfway, firming the soil with your foot as you go, to eliminate air pockets. Flood the hole to the top with water, wait for it to sink in, and finish refilling the hole with soil.

STEP 5. Use any leftover soil to form a raised ring around the edge of the planting hole. This will make a basin that directs water down to the roots, instead of letting it run off elsewhere. Water again for about five minutes with your hose nozzle on moderately low pressure.

Terrific Tree and Shrub Transplanting Tonic

Whether you're setting a new tree or shrub into the ground or moving an older one to a new location, it's a stressful experience for the plant. But you can ease that strain by serving up a healthy dose of this soothing potion.

⅓ cup of hydrogen peroxide
¼ cup of baby shampoo
¼ cup of instant tea granules
¼ cup of whiskey
2 tbsp. of fish emulsion
1 gal. of warm water

Mix all of the ingredients in a bucket. Then after you've set your tree or shrub into its planting hole, pour about a quart of the solution onto and over the roots. Store the leftover solution in a clearly marked container with a tight-fitting lid until you need it again.

STEP 6. Finish up by spreading several inches of organic mulch, such as compost or shredded bark, within the basin that you've made around the root zone. But be sure to keep the mulch about 6 inches away from the trunk (or the base of a shrub) to protect it from both dampness and pests.

Tough Love for Trees

Like elaborate hole preparation, tree staking is another time-honored custom that's recently undergone a change in thinking. We now know that young trees develop stronger root systems and sturdier, more resilient trunks when they're allowed to grow unencumbered by straps and stakes. However, if a young tree simply can't stand on its own, you will need to stake it, following this procedure:

⌁ When the root-ball is in the planting hole, but before you replace any soil, drive in two suitably sized posts, one on either side of the hole and well clear of any roots. (Either metal or wooden posts will do just fine.)

❧ Fasten the tree to the posts with soft cloth, broad strips of rubber, or lengths of strong panty hose. *Never* use cord or wire, even if it's cushioned by pieces of rubber hose—it can girdle the bark. And make sure the straps are loose enough so the trunk has room to move 2 inches in every direction.

❧ Check on the tree from time to time to be sure the straps haven't shifted and are digging into its tender trunk.

❧ Remove the ties and posts within six months to one year after planting.

Water to Grow On

Like any other young plants, newly planted trees and shrubs need a lot more water than their older counterparts. Here's my rule of thumb for supplying this life-giving elixir.

Trees. For the first three years or so, water deeply and thoroughly once a week (that is, unless the rain clouds are serving up a steady supply of moisture). Don't have the patience to stand there with a hose for half an hour or more? Then lay a soaker hose in a circle around the tree at the far edge of the branches, turn on the water, and let it drip for an hour or two. After the first few years, you should only have to water during prolonged dry spells.

Take 2

If you don't have a soaker hose, don't run out and buy one. You have two ways to turn trash into deep-watering treasure for those baby roots:

• Grab an old garden hose and, using a hammer and nail, poke holes in the sides at roughly 1-inch intervals. Then lay the hose on the ground around the plant.

• Gather up some 1-gallon milk jugs, and poke small holes in the sides, about an inch above the bottom. Set the jugs all around the root zones of your plants, and fill each container with water. It'll seep out at a slow, easy pace.

Shrubs. Water daily for the first three or four days (again, a soaker hose is your best and least labor-intensive option for delivering deep-down moisture). Following that, shrubs differ greatly in their need for liquid replenishment, so ask for guidance at the nursery where you bought them, or check a comprehensive book on the care of woody plants.

TENDER LOVING TREE AND SHRUB CARE

If you've chosen trees and shrubs that are truly well suited to your site, you can heave a big sigh of relief. That's because in the years to come, those plants should require very little in the way of maintenance. But of course, like any living things, they will need *some* basic care. In this section, you'll find a collection of helpful hints for keeping your woody wonders in tip-top shape with the least amount of time and effort.

This old-time trick may sound a bit kooky, but it really works! Around mid-April, before you feed your trees, simply beat the trunk of each one with a long, soft twig or a rolled-up newspaper. This will stimulate sap flow, so the tree can more effectively absorb the nutrients in the fertilizer.

Your Fast Feeding Routine

Like all plants, trees and shrubs need nourishment to survive. Follow this simple routine each spring to keep yours hale and hearty: Start by scattering handfuls of a well-balanced organic fertilizer (10-10-10 is ideal) around the base of each plant. If your soil tends to be acidic (that's common in the eastern half of the country), add a dusting of lime to help keep the pH near neutral. Finish up with 1/4 cup of Epsom salts for every 3 feet of plant height. Sprinkle it on the ground in a ring around the plant, out at the tips of the farthest branches. Then every three weeks during the growing season, apply my All-Season Green-Up Tonic while you're spraying the rest of your yard. (You'll find the recipe on page 26.)

Pruning Shrubs

Unlike trees, most shrubs do need to be pruned on a regular basis, but the process is a lot faster and simpler than some folks make it out to be. Here's all you need to remember.

Evergreen shrubs. If you've chosen the right plants for your site (where have you heard that phrase before?), the only pruning required should be to lop off damaged branches, those that stick out in awkward directions, or those that are dragging on the ground.

Spring-flowering shrubs. Prune the plants just *after* they've finished blooming. This will give them nearly an entire year to develop new bud-bearing branches.

Summer-flowering shrubs. These plants flower only on "new" wood, which means stems that are produced in the current growing season. Butterfly bush and chastetree are two common examples. In early spring, give them a hard

Quick Fix

For the biggest, showiest hydrangeas in town, just give your plants an occasional drink of baking soda dissolved in water. You don't need to worry about precise measurements, but I use about 2 teaspoons of soda per gallon of H_2O. And, by the way, begonias, geraniums, and any other flowers that prefer alkaline soil enjoy this treatment, too!

trim—cutting all the way back to a foot or so above the ground—and they'll reward you with showers of flowers (and butterflies) that'll lighten up the dog days of summer.

Don't Look a Gift Shrub in the Mouth

Have you inherited an old, ill-chosen shrub that's outgrown its site? Well, don't despair, and don't call a crew to come and dig it out—you've got almost-instant gratification staring you right in the face! Without investing much time at all, you can give that old veteran a new lease on life. How? With a process called renewal pruning. Just grab your pruning saw or your loppers (depending upon the thickness of the stems), and proceed as follows: Every year for three years running, cut out one-third of the branches close to the ground. By the second spring, you'll already see plenty of new growth beginning to reach for its place in the sun. By the third (and final) rejuvenation pruning, you'll be taking out the last of the old wood, and bingo—you'll have a vigorous new shrub. **Note:** After each renewal pruning, give the old-timer a nice drink of my Shrub Rejuvenation Potion (below).

Shrub Rejuvenation Potion

This elixir is just what old shrubs need to get them started on their way to a robust new life in a hurry!

> 1 can of beer
> 1 cup of ammonia
> ½ cup of dishwashing liquid
> ½ cup of molasses

Mix all of the ingredients in a 20 gallon hose-end sprayer. Then after each renewal pruning, drench your shrubs thoroughly to the point of runoff, including the undersides of the leaves. But don't stop there—it's a great spring perk-me-up for young, healthy shrubs (and trees), too!

ⓗⓔⓛⓟ!

Q I know shrubs need regular trimming, but what about my newly planted trees? Do I need to prune them from time to time, or can I leave them alone to do their own thing?

A *A whole lot of people ask me that question. And the answer is: maybe yes and maybe no. That's because many trees actually grow better if you just let them get on with life as they know it. Of course, you will need to give your young trees occasional haircuts if you want to encourage a strong branching pattern or a particular shape. In most cases, though, the only parts that really need to be removed are twiggy "suckers" that sprout from the base, branches that cross or grow very close together, and limbs that have been damaged by bad weather or disease (see "The Pruning Process," Parts 1 and 2, starting on page 88).*

Hedge Your Bets

I'm the first one to admit that maintaining a neat-looking evergreen hedge can be way too time-consuming for an impatient gardener to bother with. But it doesn't have to be. Just give it a trim three or four times a summer, using either manual or electric hedge shears. When you're done, rake up the trimmings, and either toss 'em into the compost bin, or bury them in a flower or garden bed, where they'll break down and enrich the soil over time. Or, if the shrubs have sharp needles, gather them up in a bucket, and sprinkle them on the soil around any plants that are plagued by slugs or other soft-bodied pests. The prickly mulch will keep these marauders from moving in.

When you trim a hedge, always keep it wider at the bottom than it is at the top, so that sunlight can reach the lowest branches. Otherwise, the foliage will die out around the bottom, and you'll have a ratty-looking row of scraggly plants.

Trimming Better Electrically

There are no two ways about it: You'll get your hedge-pruning chores done much faster if you use electric trimmers rather than manually operated versions. To achieve the best results, follow these guidelines:

- Plug the trimmer into an extension cord that's long enough to give you plenty of slack as you move upward, downward, and side to side.

- Start trimming from the bottom. Hold the trimmer with two hands and place it at the base of the hedge, slowly moving it upward. How deeply you trim depends on how narrow you want your hedge to be.

- When you reach the top, hold the trimmer straight out from your body. To make a simple squared-off top, just move the trimmer across it from side to side. For rounded edges, start about 2 inches from the top and move the trimmer inward as you go up to the top. Repeat until you have a nice smooth, rounded shape.

> **Quick Fix**
>
> You don't have to spend hours trimming your hedges to get them all neatly lined up at the same height. Just do what the pros do: Make a trimming guide by sticking two stakes in the ground at either end of the hedge. Then run a string tightly between the stakes, making sure that the string is level from one end to the other (use a carpenter's level to get it just right). Then, just guide your clippers along the string. You'll get perfect results every time—guaranteed!

The Pruning Process, Part 1

Removing big, heavy tree limbs can be a risky proposition, especially if you need to stand on a ladder to do the job—and your patience for such chores is short to begin with. In those circumstances, have a professional arborist do the work. On the other hand, pruning off lower, lighter limbs is a simple three-step process. Just grab a pruning saw and proceed as follows:

STEP 1. On the underside of the limb, about 10 inches from the main trunk, make a cut that's one-third to one-half of the way through the branch. This cut will prevent the bark from ripping all the way down the tree when the limb falls off.

STEP 2. Remove the limb by cutting into it from the top a few inches beyond where you made the first cut.

STEP 3. Cut all the way through the remaining stump, just outside the branch collar (the point where the limb and trunk join), about ¹⁄₂ inch from the main trunk. Make sure you don't scrape or cut the trunk's bark in the process—that would make the tree vulnerable to infection.

The Pruning Process, Part 2

Trimming off smaller branches from trees or shrubs is a piece of cake—simply use your loppers for limbs that are 1 to 2 inches in diameter. For thinner branches, all you need is a sturdy pair of hand pruners. Then follow these guidelines:

🍃 Make sure the branch is all the way back in the jaw of your loppers or pruners, and the rounded, sharp blade is on the bottom.

🍃 Cut at a 45-degree angle just above an outside-facing bud.

🍃 *Never* cut straight across a dormant bud, or the top wood will die back and kill it.

🍃 If you're pruning out dead wood in a shrub, cut the branches flush to the ground.

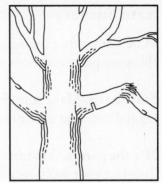

Make your first cut on the underside of the limb.

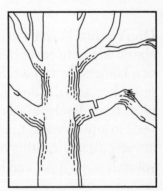

Cut from the top to remove the limb.

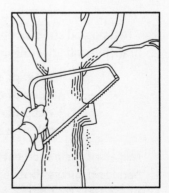

Carefully cut through the stump about ¹⁄₂ inch from the trunk.

Safe Surgery

Whether you're pruning vigorous, young plants or reviving an old-timer, these simple precautions will help head off trouble.

Stay sharp. Make sure the tools you use are razor-sharp. Dull blades make ragged cuts that can usher in pests and diseases.

Nix the germs. Anytime you're removing dead, dying, or diseased tissue, disinfect your tools between cuts to avoid spreading the germs. Either rubbing alcohol or a solution of 1 part household bleach to 3 parts water will do the trick. Then follow up by spraying the wounds with my Tree Wound Sterilizer Tonic (below).

Don't paint. When you cut off a limb or the bark gets damaged, ignore the classic advice to cover the wounds with either a commercial wound paint or a homemade sealant. Modern science has discovered that the cover-up procedure actually does more harm than good. Not only does it prevent the plant from developing a calloused wood that keeps out bacteria, but it also seals in any bacteria, fungi, or decay that may be getting a foothold—and attracts disease-causing organisms that feed on the wound paint. So save yourself some time, and leave those cuts for Mother Nature to heal.

Tree Wound Sterilizer Tonic

Anytime you cut diseased tissue from a tree or shrub, or just prune healthy branches, kill lingering germs in the wood with this powerful potion.

¼ **cup of ammonia**
¼ **cup of antiseptic mouthwash**
¼ **cup of dishwashing liquid**
1 **gal. of warm water**

Mix all of the ingredients together in a bucket. Pour the solution into a handheld sprayer bottle, and drench the spots where you've recently pruned the tree or shrub.

A Bit Off the Base

Some shrubs, called basal growers, have a great many stems that spring up out of the soil. To keep these plants neat and clean, you need to clip those stems off at ground level at least every other year. The most popular basal growers are mock orange and oakleaf hydrangea. The cast also includes autumn elaeagnus, drooping leucothoe, flowering quince, and gray dogwood.

TROUBLESHOOTING TREES AND SHRUBS

Even the best-tended trees and shrubs can fall victim to trouble every now and then—but they're not the disaster magnets that some folks make them out to be. In this section, I'll clue you in on fast and easy ways to battle pests, diseases, and other woody plant mishaps.

Golden Rules for Good Health

You may not be able to prevent problems entirely, but you can keep them—and therefore your plant-tending time—to a minimum by following this simple formula.

Go native. Trees and shrubs that are native to your region are much less susceptible to pests and diseases than any plant that's been brought in from somewhere else—even if the newcomer is a variety that can perform in your growing conditions. Don't worry: It won't take you much time to find top performers. Nowadays, in every part of the country, there are nurseries that specialize in trees and shrubs that grow, or once grew, naturally in that area. To find a native plant nursery near you, just crank up your favorite Internet search engine and type in "native plants."

When the leaves of a healthy tree suddenly turn yellow, but the veins stay green—a common occurrence, especially in oaks—it usually signals an iron deficiency. Apply liquid iron at the rate recommended on the label. Repeat the process in six weeks, and your tree should green up, pronto.

Ask for help. Do whatever you can to entice predators that feast on pest insects. There are many, and you can read all about them in Chapter 10.

Keep it clean. We all know the old saying that cleanliness is next to godliness. Well, that's especially true in your yard and garden. So every time you go out into your yard, take along a bag and a pair of pruners. Pick up debris as soon as you see it. And when you spot leaves or twigs that just don't look right somehow, clip them off and toss them in the bag. Both pests and diseases thrive in litter and weakened tissue of all kinds.

The Unwanted List

Although my "Golden Rules for Good Health" (see page 91) will go a long way toward guarding your trees and shrubs from multilegged marauders, it pays to have this collection of timely tricks up your sleeve. That way, if trouble does come knocking at your door, you can say, loud and clear, "Go away—*now!*"

AVOID TROUBLE— THE EASY WAY

Plant hardiness zone numbers are based on the coldest temperature in an average winter. And heat zone numbers are based on the hottest temperature in an average summer. So don't take chances. When you choose your trees and shrubs (or any other kinds of plants), go with ones that are hardy to at least one zone colder and one zone hotter than yours. That way, you won't have to panic when the weatherman says, "We're in for a real record-setter today, folks!"

Bagworms. These pests roam every place east of the Rocky Mountains, and any tree or shrub is fair game. As the name implies, bagworms live, feed, and breed inside bags they make by weaving leaf strips together. You have three excellent good-riddance options, depending on your timing:

➤ Before the eggs hatch (generally in May and June), cut the bags off the plants, and drop them into a bucket of water laced with soap or alcohol. The operative word is "cut." If you pull on the silk bands that hold the bags to the plant, you're likely to damage or even break the branch—the silk is that *strong*!

🥬 No longer than two weeks after the larvae have hatched, while they're still young and tender, spray the plant with Btk (see page 58).

🥬 Once the worms are bigger and tougher, release beneficial nematodes, which will go right into the bags after their prey. (Read the label carefully to make sure you're getting the right species.)

After you've sent parasitic nematodes charging after your tree or shrub borers, don't scrape the gummy stuff off the bark! It'll help seal the openings and prevent other pests and disease organisms from moving in.

Borers. If your tree or shrub appears weak and branches are dying back starting 5 to 10 feet above the ground, then borers may be hard at work. You might also see holes in the bark, surrounded by rings of what looks like gummy sawdust; on poplars or birches, the bark may look roughened or bumpy.

The culprits are the larvae of several species of clearwing moths. They eat through the bark and wood of many kinds of trees, leaving them less resistant to heat and drought and making them prime targets for diseases. The classic response to a borer invasion is to insert a crochet hook into each hole and stir it around to kill the pests. A neater alternative is to get some parasitic nematodes and a garden syringe, and squirt the good guys into each hole, following the directions on the package. It's quick and easy and should take care of the problem lickety-split.

Quick Fix

If you have a wood-burning fireplace, then you've got a super-simple way to keep borers out of your trees and shrubs. Just mix your wood ashes with enough water to make a paste, and spread it on the trunks up to a height of 2 feet or so. (The simplest and most effective way to do the job is to put on rubber gloves and slap the stuff on by hand.) Both female moths and newly hatched larvae hate the stuff, so they'll seek lodging elsewhere.

Gypsy moths. As with many pests, it's the larvae (hairy, red-and-blue-spotted caterpillars) that do the dirty work—and plenty of it! They generally appear in midspring or early summer, and when there are large numbers of them, they can strip a tree bare of its leaves in no time flat. Any tree or shrub is fair game, but oaks and aspens are special favorites. Your action plan depends on when you first spot the culprits:

🌿 To nip trouble in the bud, check your trees for mahogany-colored pupae beginning in midsummer (they're usually in cracks in the bark of the trunk). From July onward, watch for egg cases stuck to the bark. They're about 1 inch long and look like little suede pouches. When you spot either form of these menaces in the making, scrape it off the tree pronto, and drop it into a bucket of soapy water.

🌿 Later in the summer, catch the future mothers (small, tan-colored moths) by wrapping a band of cardboard around the trunk and coating it with Tanglefoot® or a spray adhesive. Just make sure to keep the trap free of twigs, leaves, or (yuck) dead bug bodies that the moths could otherwise use as bridges.

HELP!

Q I came back from my summer vacation to find gypsy moth larvae hatching all over the place. How can I get rid of them all and protect my trees?

A *For each tree, get a strip of burlap about 1 foot wide and long enough to wrap around the trunk with a few inches of overlap. Tape the top edge of the burlap onto the tree to keep it in place, and tie a piece of twine around the strip at about the middle, and coat it with petroleum jelly. Then remove the tape, and fold the upper half of the burlap down over the twine so that it covers the lower half of the burlap. As the caterpillars mosey on up the trunk, they'll get stuck in the jelly-filled fold. Check the traps every day, and either squash the varmints or scrape them off into a bucket of soapy water.*

Doggone Ants!

Ants don't damage trees or shrubs—they improve growing conditions for all plants. Besides breaking down organic matter into soil-building humus, they dig literally thousands of miles of little underground tunnels, which allow free passage for water, nutrients, and earthworms. Ants also wage war on termites, and they prey on some of the peskiest pests around, including mealybugs, scale insects, cockroaches, and (for all you cotton farmers out there) boll weevils. The problem comes when they start "farming" sap-sucking insects like aphids in your trees to ensure a steady supply of the honeydew the little monsters produce.

We'll get into more aphid battle tactics in Chapter 10, but the good news is that if you can keep the ants out of your tree for just a couple of months, other good-guy bugs will take over and your aphid woes will be history—with no effort from you. Here's how to lock the gate to the old corral in three easy steps:

STEP 1. If necessary, prune your tree so that only the trunk is in contact with the ground.

STEP 2. Wrap a band of carpet tape or double-sided masking tape around the trunk. The tape won't harm the tree, but it will trap the ants as they try to scamper up it. Be sure to inspect the tape every few days, and remove any twigs, leaves, or other "bridges" that appear.

STEP 3. For added protection, sprinkle bonemeal or diatomaceous earth liberally around the trunk. Ants won't dare to cross the scratchy stuff.

Grandma's GROW-HOW

My Grandma Putt always looked for the good in everybody—even garden-variety mischief makers like chipmunks and voles. She never chased these little fur balls out of her yard because both of them eat loads of voracious pests. She figured a few missing flower buds or a little chewed bark was a small price to pay for freedom from creepy crawlers.

Lethal Weapon Tonic

If ants have turned your favorite tree into an aphid ranch, don't pull any punches. Reach for your trusty hose-end sprayer, and load it with this magic bullet.

    3 tbsp. of garlic and onion juice*
    3 tbsp. of skim milk
    2 tbsp. of baby shampoo
    1 tsp. of hot-pepper sauce
    1 gal. of water

Mix all of the ingredients in a bucket, and pour the solution into a 20 gallon hose-end sprayer. Then spray your tree every 10 days until the aphids are lyin' 6 feet under on Boot Hill.

* To make garlic and onion juice, put 2 garlic cloves, 2 medium onions, and 3 cups of water in a blender, and puree. Strain out the solids, and pour the remaining liquid into a jar. Bury the solids in your garden to repel aphids and other pesky pests.

What do you do about ants that are already up in the branches, or on their way up the trunk? Simple: Spray the tree with my Lethal Weapon Tonic (above). It'll wipe out the aphids and their midget minders at the same time.

To get rid of an ant colony for good, sprinkle instant grits on top of the anthill. The worker ants will carry the grains into the nest, where they and the queen will have a feast. The grains will swell up inside their bodies, and that'll be all she wrote!

Deer Me!

After years of practice, I've come up with a lot of tricks for keeping these beautiful, brown-eyed bruisers away from my trees and shrubs. But I have to admit that the only surefire way to keep them out of your yard is to put up a fence. Or, better yet, two fences that are at least 5 feet high and 4 feet apart. The reason: Deer can jump high, and they can jump far, but they can't do both at the same time. So use that deficiency to your advantage if you can.

Smelly substances like deodorant soap, unwashed socks, and human hair are classic deer deterrents, and for good reason: They work well—that is, as long as you keep the scent from washing away in rain or snow. Here's how to do exactly that:

STEP 1. Tuck your deterrent of choice into an old panty hose toe or a mesh onion bag, and tie the pouch closed with a string.

STEP 2. Poke a hole in the bottom of a 12-ounce foam or waxed-paper drink cup.

STEP 3. Tuck the pouch into the cup, pull the string through the hole, and tie it into a loop. Then fasten the loop to a tree or shrub branch, and you're good to go. Your smell emitters should keep their deer-chasing power for about a year, right through rain, sleet, snow, or dark of night!

PLANT A LIVING FENCE

If you lack the time, the inclination, or the budget to corral your yard with any artificial barrier, plant shrubs the deer don't like. Unless they're really hungry, they'll probably go elsewhere. Good plant choices include barberries (*Berberis*), box elder (*Acer negundo*), butterfly bush (*Buddleia davidii*), hollies (*Ilex*), junipers (*Juniperus*), and mountain laurel (*Kalmia latifolia*).

Quick Fix

In early spring, buck deer love to use trees as scratching posts to scrape the velvet off their new antlers—scraping off the tree bark in the process. This can stunt the tree's growth or even kill it, depending on the severity of the damage. So to keep your trees from going bald, get some plastic-mesh construction fencing and wrap it loosely around the trunk of each tree to a height of 4 feet or so. The dear deer will go elsewhere for their head rubs.

Mosey On, Mice!

Although mice can sink their little choppers into woody plants at any time of the year, most mouse-inflicted damage to trees and shrubs occurs between October and April, when the tiny terrors move into mole runs or tunnels, unseen, through the snow. They may also spend the winter in mulch that you've spread around your shrubs to protect them from cold-weather damage. These simple measures will go a long way toward protecting your woody plants from mini-marauders:

➤ Before winter sets in, wrap the trunks of your shrubs (or young trees) loosely in aluminum foil to a height of 18 inches to 2 feet. The glittering, rattling surface will send the little gnawers looking elsewhere for food!

➤ If aluminum foil isn't your idea of pleasing garden decor, guard your shrubs with a mini-fence. Just circle your shrub bed, or the root zone of each plant, with fine-mesh wire that extends 3 to 4 inches above the ground and 6 to 8 inches below. Then, for added protection, spray the

Hot-Pepper Spray

Here I come to save the day! To keep mice and other small varmints from nibbling your young trees and shrubs to nubs, give 'em a taste of this highly effective repellent

> **2 tbsp. of cayenne pepper**
> **2 tbsp. of hot-pepper sauce**
> **2 tbsp. of Murphy® Oil Soap**
> **1 qt. of warm water**

Mix all of the ingredients together in a bucket, then pour the solution into a handheld sprayer bottle. Drench all young tree and shrub trunks with it in late fall, and repeat every few weeks, if the weather is rainy, to keep the scent fresh.

entire area with my Hot-Pepper Spray (at left)—it'll make the mice take off for cooler pastures, pronto.

☙ When you mulch your trees and shrubs, keep the material at least 6 inches away from the plants' trunks. That way, you'll deprive mice of one of their favorite hiding places.

☙ Wait until the ground has frozen solid before you mulch your plants for the winter. Then, even if mice snuggle down in the cozy blanket, they won't be able to tunnel into the soil.

When They're Under the Weather

Like any other plants, trees and shrubs can fall victim to diseases that affect their roots, stems, leaves, and/or flowers. The good news (I know I sound like a broken record when I say this) is that if you choose the right plants for your growing conditions and tend them well, you stand a very good chance of keeping them out of sick bay. The not-so-good news—especially for an impatient gardener—is that tree and shrub diseases can be the very dickens to diagnose. For one thing, a great many of them cause almost identical-looking symptoms. For another, what appears to be disease damage is often the dirty work of tiny pests. And sometimes the culprit is neither pests nor disease germs, but cultural problems (see "The Great Pretenders" on page 101).

Take 2

In every part of the country, somebody's trash is just waiting for you to claim it for planting treasure (a.k.a. organic mulch). Here are some nutritious and good-looking mulches that might be waiting for you, just a phone call away:

• Chopped tobacco stalks

• Cocoa bean shells*

• Cottonseed hulls

• Ground corncobs

• Ground oyster shells

• Peanut shells

• Pecan shells

• Pine needles

• Seaweed

• Shredded oak leaves

Steer clear of cocoa shell mulch if you have a dog on the scene. Chocolate in any form is toxic to canines.

So do yourself a favor: The minute you spot trouble, either call a professional arborist to come out for a look-see, or clip off some of the afflicted plant parts and send or take them to your local Cooperative Extension office. They should be able to solve the mystery lickety-split and advise you on your best and fastest options.

Rain, Rain, Come Again— Please!

Although mature trees and large shrubs can usually get along fine without watering, even they get thirsty when a prolonged dry spell hits—as many of you may have learned the hard way during the droughts of recent years. If you're setting out to replace trees or shrubs that you've lost, look for the most drought-tolerant varieties you can find, and (yep, I'm going to say it again) make sure the plants you choose are well suited to the growing conditions in your yard. Then do everything you can to encourage the plants to develop strong, deep root systems. To do that, simply follow these guidelines:

Quick Fix

When I was a lad, all of our neighbors collected rain in barrels, then dished the water out to their plants when the clouds closed up shop. Like a lot of other old-time ideas, this one is staging a big-time comeback. Of course, unless you have either an enormous number of barrels or a tiny yard, you won't accumulate enough rain to get your whole landscape through a dry spell. But most likely, your wet savings account will help you save more than a few trees and shrubs.

- When you plant your trees or shrubs, do *not* add any amendments to the planting hole. Rich soil will discourage the roots from reaching out and down, where they need to go to find water.

- Anytime you have to irrigate, supply the water slowly and deeply. Shallow watering will do much more harm than good because it only encourages roots to stay near the soil surface.

- After you've watered, spread an organic mulch around the root zone to help hold in the moisture in the soil.

THE GREAT PRETENDERS

When you see signs of trouble on your trees or shrubs, don't be too quick to pin the blame on pests or diseases. Those symptoms could be the result of cultural problems. Here are some conditions to watch for, and what to do about them.

SYMPTOM	LIKELY CAUSE	WHAT TO DO
Branches dying; leaves mottled, turning silvery, speckled white, or tan	Air or ground pollution, or damage from road salt	• Avoid using salt to melt snow and ice (see page 63 for plant-friendly alternatives). • Feed the plant and water it thoroughly, or replace it with a more salt-resistant variety.
Wilted, scorched, or dropping leaves	Too little water is reaching the roots	• Soak the soil slowly and thoroughly from the trunk to the far edges of the canopy. • Mulch with compost or well-cured manure.
General decline in vigor and appearance	Soil may be compacted by foot or vehicle traffic	• Reroute traffic (erect a barrier around the root zone if necessary). • Work compost into the soil as far as you can without disturbing the roots, then add organic mulch.
Leaves turning brown or wilting; top branches dying; general decline in appearance and vigor	Poor drainage	• If the plant is small enough, move it to a better-draining site. • Improve the drainage. (This may take a lot of time and effort, and help from a landscaping pro.)
Older, lower leaves turning yellow and maybe dropping; overall growth slow and spindly	Nitrogen deficiency	• Work compost and a high-nitrogen substance like bloodmeal or fish meal into the soil. • Avoid low-nitrogen mulches like bark or wood chips.

When the Winter Winds Do Blow

If you live in an area where winter is serious business, then even the sturdiest trees and shrubs will benefit from a little extra TLC when the temperatures begin to drop. The good news is that as long as you've provided good, regular care throughout the growing season, this simple routine should keep your woody pals safe and sound till spring— without trying your patience:

✿ Before the temperature falls to 50°F, give your trees, shrubs, and all the other plants in your yard (including turfgrass) a good, thorough wash-down with my Fall Cleanup Tonic (see page 62). Plants that go to bed clean are more likely to wake up healthy in the spring!

✿ Before winter sets in, apply a thick coat of an antidesiccant spray (available at garden centers) to all of your evergreen trees and shrubs to guard against drying winter winds. It can help reduce moisture loss by up to 50 percent. Most sprays won't last through the winter, however, so be sure to repeat the process in early February if you can.

✿ Give evergreen shrubs and small trees coats of burlap to protect them from drying winter winds. Just wrap the fabric around the plant, and tie it on with twine. Whatever you do, don't wrap your plants in plastic. It cuts off air circulation, and on a sunny winter day, it will retain the heat—acting much like an oven—and literally bake your shrubs.

✿ To guard a hedge or a row of shrubs, pound stakes into the ground at each side, and stretch a burlap screen across from end to end. **Note:** Depending on the length of the planting, you may also need to insert stakes in the middle of the row as well as along the sides.

EVERGREEN SUNSCREEN

Besides being vulnerable to cold winds, young evergreens, like yews, arborvitae, and hemlocks, are prone to sunburn in the winter. To protect them, pound three or four stakes into the ground around each plant (make sure they're at least 6 inches taller than the plant), about 2 feet out from the branch tips. Then set a piece of garden lattice on top and attach it to the stakes with wire ties.

Winter-Weather Warning

For us humans, a crisp, sunny winter day can be heaven on earth. But for a young tree, it's just the opposite. When the sun's warmth hits the southwest side of the trunk, the tree's growth cells spring into action. Then when the sun sets and the temperature plummets, the cells rupture and the bark splits wide open. It's a condition known as sunscald, and it plagues young, thin-barked trees, especially ashes, lindens, maples, oaks, willows, and nearly all fruit trees. In most parts of the country, the prime danger period is January and February.

Besides acting as sunscreens, trunk protectors will also fend off mice, voles, and rabbits—a young tree's most fearsome wintertime foes.

Fortunately, there's a simple way to protect your newly planted treasures: Either use commercial tree wrap that you can buy at any garden center, or make your own "armor" using 4-inch-diameter plastic drainpipe. Just cut a 2-foot piece for each tree, slit it down the side, and slip it around the tree base. (Be careful you don't ding the bark in the process!) Whether you use pipe or wrapping, remove it in early spring, when the wild temperature swings even out. Otherwise, it will give pesky pests a cozy place to hide. **Note:** Sunscald will pose less of a risk as your tree matures and develops thicker bark and larger branches that (even without leaves) can help shade the trunk.

Grandma's **GROW-HOW**

Grandma Putt lived in the cold, gusty North, where wintertime temperatures routinely plunged well below zero. If that sounds a lot like your home, sweet home, too, you need to give your small trees some extra TLC going into winter. It's a snap if you use this super-simple trick Grandma came up with to guard her little woodies from snow and ice damage: Just surround each tree with tomato cages, line them with newspaper, and fill 'em up with leaves or straw. Your little treasures will be snug as bugs in a rug all winter long!

CHAPTER
3

FABULOUS FLOWERS
Annual and Perennial Pleasures—Pronto!

I just can't imagine life without flowers, and I'll bet
you can't either. A garden filled with a colorful mix of
annuals, perennials, and bulbs is the best perker-upper
a person could ask for. And if you use the tips, tricks,
and tonics I've laid out in this chapter, you can
produce a flowery paradise in the blink of an eye.
In these pages, I'll also clue you in on my super
secrets for keeping the show on the road with the
least amount of time, effort, and money.

Can't decide on a color
scheme for your new
garden? Just find some
patterned fabric that
you like—say, a quilt,
a favorite dress, or a
piece of upholstery
material. Then plan
your flower garden to
feature those colors.

SETTING THE STAGE

No matter how eager you may be to get your
floral show started, before you run out and buy
seeds or plants, it's important to (you guessed
it) do some planning first. While it is true that
flowers can transform a ho-hum yard into a
neighborhood blockbuster, you need to direct the
action. That job begins with deciding what role(s)
you want beautiful bloomers to perform in your
landscape. It continues with choosing the right
plants to play the parts while basking in whatever
growing conditions you can give them. Just a
small investment of time at this stage can save you
a lot of time and trouble down the road.

Pretty Is as Pretty Does

If you think of flowers as just pretty faces, think again: Flowering plants of all kinds can help solve some of your most challenging yard dilemmas. So before you start considering color schemes, bed shapes, or even your growing conditions, sit down and ponder some of the important work a new garden or two might perform in your landscape—even through the long, dark days of winter. Here are a few possibilities.

Reduce your mowing chores. If you'd like to cut back on the time you spend mowing, simply decide how much lawn you're ready to dispense with. Replace it with whatever flowering plants please you and suit your growing conditions.

"Furnish" problem spots. If your yard has areas where grass simply refuses to grow, don't let it get you down. Think of it as a chance to add color and scent to your yard, while bypassing the time-consuming fuss of trying to improve your soil.

Help avoid trouble. Flowering plants provide food and homes for hordes of beneficial insects, which in turn pollinate fruits and vegetables and gobble up bad bugs that are gunnin' for your trees, shrubs, flowers, veggies, and turfgrass.

Screen a view—fast. Maybe the biggest thorn in your side is an eyesore—perhaps your garbage cans, the road in front of

Quick Fix

When you want privacy on the double, reach for any—or better yet, a combination—of these rapid growers. They'll give you a 5- to 6-foot screen almost before you know it!

Annuals

- Cannas (*Canna*)
- Dahlias (*Dahlia*)
- Flowering tobacco (*Nicotiana sylvestris*)
- Love-lies-bleeding (*Amaranthus caudatus*)
- Spider flower (*Cleome hassleriana*)

Perennials

- Boltonia (*Boltonia asteroides*)
- Common rose mallow (*Hibiscus moscheutos*)
- Cut-leaved coneflower (*Rudbeckia laciniata*)
- Joe Pye weed (*Eupatorium fistulosum*)
- Queen of the prairie (*Filipendula rubra*)

your house, or the old cars in your neighbors' driveway. A dense hedge of evergreen trees or shrubs can cover it up eventually, but even the fastest-growing ones take some time to mature. So go for the quick fix: Plant a border of tall, bushy annuals or perennials to fill in while the slower-growing evergreens mature.

How Color Works

We're all aware that color preference is a highly subjective matter. But as designers know, there are some hard-and-fast rules of physics that influence the way our eyes (and, therefore, our minds and spirits) perceive color. Cool tones—the colors of water—such as blue, violet, purple, mauve, and green make you feel calm and relaxed. They're ideal for a garden that's meant for quiet de-stressing time (or for a sea lover living in a landlocked area).

On the other hand, warm, fiery hues like red, orange, bright yellow, and hot pink project energy and excitement. They also attract hummingbirds by the score, so they're the backbone of any bird lover's garden.

Keep in mind that a garden featuring one or two flower colors (especially white or pastels), plus green foliage, looks more spacious than one with a Joseph's-coat mixture of shades. A pale palette also lends an air of peace and restfulness to any space. If you have little time to enjoy your garden during daylight hours, plant white flowers and foliage with white markings. They hold their own long after dusk.

Grandma's GROW-HOW

Grandma Putt loved posies all right, but she taught me early on that leaves are just as important when it comes to creating a flower garden that looks great all season long. So when you're planning your showcase, search out plants with colorful foliage—red, orange, yellow, blue, purple, or silver—as well as green leaves that are marked with white, silver, cream, or gold. When you mix these in with the more common green-leaved flowers, their foliage adds zip that you can count on from earliest spring to the first frost in the fall. Talk about putting plants to work!

ALLURING ANNUALS

We've covered the basics of the fine (and fun) art of planning your garden. Now, let's take a look at some of the fabulous flowers you can plant there. We'll start with annuals—not because they come first in the alphabet, but because they're the greatest gifts an impatient gardener could ever ask for. In fact, they come close to performing miracles right before your eyes. You simply bring home a cell pack or two from the garden center, put them in the ground, and within days—sometimes overnight—you've got paradise on your doorstep! Here are some terrific tips that will help you make the most of these treasures.

Want to jazz up your yard with a new color scheme? Before you spend a lot of time and money on perennials, plant annuals in the shades you're contemplating. If you like the look, replace the annuals with perennials in the same colors. If not, try a different combo next year.

Get Up and Grow!

When you don't want to spend time tucking plants into the ground, your route to fast results lies with easygoing annuals that prefer to start life right in the garden. They're just the ticket for impatient gardeners—simply sow

Here's a fast, no-muss, no-fuss way to sow annual flower and vegetable seeds. Just empty a packet of gelatin—either flavored or unflavored—into a bowl. Add warm water, little by little, stirring as you go, until you've got a thick slush. Mix in your seeds, and pour the goop into a plastic squirt bottle (a clean mustard or ketchup container is perfect). Then squeeze the mixture onto your prepared garden bed or indoor seed-starting flat. Later on, when the seedlings emerge, you can thin them out to the right distance. (For the whole nine yards on starting seeds indoors, see Chapter 6.)

seeds in the spring, and they'll get up and grow in no time at all. These are some of my favorites:

- Annual baby's breath (*Gypsophila elegans*)

- Annual poppy (*Papaver*)

- Annual sweet pea (*Lathyrus odoratus*)

- Bachelor's buttons (*Centaurea cyanus*)

- China pink (*Dianthus chinensis*)

- Cosmos (*Cosmos bipinnatus*)

- Four o'clocks (*Mirabilis jalapa*)

- Larkspur (*Consolida ajacis*)

- Moss rose (*Portulaca grandiflora*)

- Zinnia (*Zinnia elegans*)

Tops for Transplants

On the other hand, many popular annuals start out slowly from seed. Unless you live in a warm climate, you'll get the show on the road faster if you start with transplants (either homegrown or store-bought). These are some good transplant candidates:

- Browallia (*Browallia speciosa*)

- Canterbury bells (*Campanula medium*)

- English daisy (*Bellis perennis*)

- Floss flower (*Ageratum houstonianum*)

- Gloriosa daisy (*Rudbeckia hirta* var. *pulcherrima*)

- Heliotrope (*Heliotropium arborescens*)

These slowpokes take 12 weeks or more from seed to transplant time. So don't even think of starting them from seed—buy these seedlings at the garden center:

- **Gerberas (*Gerbera*)**

- **Madagascar periwinkle (*Catharanthus roseus*)**

- **Petunias (*Petunia*)**

- **Tuberous begonias (*Begonia* x *tuberhybrida*)**

- **Twining snapdragons (*Asarina*)**

- **Verbena (*Verbena* x *hybrida*)**

- **Wax begonias (*Begonia* x *semperflorens- cultorum*)**

- Impatiens (*Impatiens*)

- Joseph's coat (*Alternanthera ficoidea*)

- Lisianthus (*Eustoma*)

- Lobelia (*Lobelia erinus*)

Sow, Sow, Sow Your Seeds

The instructions on the seed packets will tell you the best time to sow your particular annuals, and the procedure couldn't be simpler. Once you've prepared the planting bed, make shallow furrows in the soil with a hoe, trowel, or your fingers. Then set in the seeds, and cover them with either compost or commercial potting mix. That way, the little sprouts will have an easy time pushing themselves up toward the sun. (For everything you need to know about preparing a planting bed, including my recipe for whipping up a Super Soil Sandwich, see Chapter 9.)

Just to Be Sure

Taking a few basic precautions will help ensure that your seeds grow into healthy, young seedlings.

Watch the depth. Some seeds need light to germinate—so press them into the soil just enough to keep them from blowing away. Others must be completely covered. The depth varies, but my rule of thumb is to set a seed into the ground at a depth that's equal to two times its diameter. (Seed packets and catalog descriptions will provide you with your plants' particular preferences.)

Grandma's GROW-HOW

Whenever Grandma Putt bought young annual plants, she always avoided any with big, beautiful blooms, and you should, too. You might think that they'd take off and fill up your flower bed in the blink of an eye. But chances are, they'll just sit there for a *long* time. That's because churning out flowers takes a lot of energy, leaving the plants with no steam to put down new roots in your garden. So do yourself a favor: Look for transplants that have good, healthy roots and few, if any, flowers.

Give them a hand (maybe). Some seeds, including morning glory, moonflower, and annual sweet pea, have thick coatings that are all but impossible for a growing tip to break through without help. Your job is simply to soak the seeds in weak tea for 24 hours before you plant (48 hours in the case of sweet pea).

Water carefully. A strong blast of water can wash seeds away, so use a fine mist from your hose nozzle or watering can. If you expect heavy rain, protect the seedbed by driving some stakes into the soil around it and draping a sheet of plastic on top. Just remember to remove the plastic when the sun comes out again.

It can be the very dickens to tell the difference between direct-sown seedlings and newly sprouted weeds. But there's a simple way to keep your treasures safe. Every time you sow seeds in your garden, save a few of each kind and sow them in labeled containers. Then when it's time to weed, take a pot of each type with you for plant ID. You'll never pull up a baby flower by mistake!

Flower Garden Soil Booster

Before you sow your seeds or set your transplants into the ground, perk up the soil with this energizing elixir. (This recipe makes enough to cover about 100 square feet of garden area.)

> **1 can of beer**
> **1 cup of antiseptic mouthwash**
> **1 cup of dishwashing liquid**
> **1 cup of regular cola (not diet)**
> **¼ tsp. of instant tea granules**

Mix all of the ingredients in a bucket, and pour the solution into a 20 gallon hose-end sprayer. Overspray the soil in your garden to the point of runoff (or just until small puddles start to form). Let it sit at least two weeks, then plant your seeds or set in your transplants.

Keep the Color on Parade

While it is true that annuals can give you nonstop color from spring till fall, you do need to lend a hand to keep the show going. That's because in most cases, once an annual plant has produced a good crop of flowers, and they've set seed for the next generation, that's all she wrote. From the plant's perspective, it has accomplished its mission in life. That's particularly true of species and old-time varieties (a.k.a. heirloom flowers).

If you want to enjoy flowers all season long, your mission is to remove the flowers before they set seed—a process called deadheading. The more you clip, the more blooms the plant will churn out. Most annuals will keep right on going until frost bowls 'em over. So get out there and clip away! But don't think of it as a chore. Instead, think of it as a chance to fill your house with flowers all summer long—and have plenty left over to share with friends and neighbors.

Perennial Annuals

Botanically speaking, an annual is a plant that sprouts, grows, flowers, sets seed, and dies in a single season. But that doesn't mean all annuals are one-year wonders. Many of them come back year after year from their own self-sown seed—thereby relieving you of the time and effort it takes to plant them every spring. Better yet, when you're in a hurry to get the seasonal show on the road, self-sown seeds will sprout and grow a whole lot faster than ones that you sow yourself. There's nothing second-best about these beauties, either. In fact, they have some of the prettiest flowers in all creation.

> **PROLIFIC PERFORMERS**
>
> These are some of the most delightful self-sowing annuals I know of:
>
> - California poppy (*Eschscholzia californica*)
>
> - Corn poppy (*Papaver rhoeas*)
>
> - Cosmos (*Cosmos bipinnatus*)
>
> - Larkspur (*Consolida ajacis*)
>
> - Love-in-a-mist (*Nigella damascena*)
>
> - Shoo-fly plant (*Nicandra physalodes*)
>
> - Spider flower (*Cleome hassleriana*)
>
> - Sweet alyssum (*Lobularia maritima*)

To Tell the Truth . . .

When most of us think of our favorite annuals, petunias, impatiens, and geraniums *(Pelargonium)* rank high on the list. But did you know that they're not true annuals but are actually tender perennials? That means they return year after year in mild climates, but they can't survive freezing temperatures. Now comes the good news: Even if you live in the cold, snowy North, these sensitive beauties can give you perennial pleasure, too. All you need to do is give them shelter for the winter. There are two ways to go about it. Either bring whole plants indoors, and keep them in a bright, cool spot (55° to 65°F), or take stem cuttings in late summer and root them, following the simple directions in "The Kindest Cut of All" on page 128. Then when the weather warms up, return them to your garden—after you harden them off, of course (see "Kindergarten, Seedling Style" on page 208).

Save the Leftovers

It makes good sense (and cents) to save any leftover seeds for next year. They should perform just as well, too: Most annual flower and vegetable seeds remain viable for two to three years. But in order for the seeds to

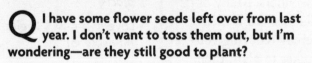

Q I have some flower seeds left over from last year. I don't want to toss them out, but I'm wondering—are they still good to plant?

A I can't answer that question, but you can. Just pour the seeds into a glass of water. The ones that float on the surface are nonstarters, so throw 'em into the compost bin. The seeds that sink stand a good chance of growing up sleek and sassy. You'll need to plant them soon, though, because they'll have soaked up water, and they'll be sprouting before you can say, "Everybody out of the pool!"

germinate, they need to be stored properly. Here's the simple three-step process:

STEP 1. Get a container of powdered milk and some glass jars with tight-fitting lids (one jar per type of seed).

STEP 2. In each jar, put 1 part seed to 1 part powdered milk.

STEP 3. Seal the jars very tightly, and stash them in the refrigerator (not the freezer). The milk will keep the seeds dry and fresh all winter long. Then come spring, they'll be rarin' to grow!

Containers to the Rescue

An easy way to add color to your landscape is to plant your annual flowers in containers rather than directly into the ground. This gives you a lot of flexibility because you can move the containers around to suit your needs. And container plants aren't just for decks and patios. One ideal location for container annuals is beneath a tree. As you may have already discovered, it can be very hard to grow grass under a tree because most turfgrasses need plenty of sunshine to thrive. Growing shade-loving flowers solves the low-light problem, but a couple of challenges remain: For one thing, the tree's roots make digging all but impossible. They also drink up most of the available moisture, and quenching your plants' thirst can become a full-time job. The simple solution: Set big containers under those leafy branches, and fill them with showy, shade-loving annuals like begonias, impatiens, or coleus. And the larger the pot, the less often you'll have to water.

Take 2

When you reach the end of a roll of aluminum foil, plastic wrap, or wax paper, don't throw it away! Those handy tubes make terrific seed-starting pots. Cut them into sections about 3 inches long, then wrap foil or plastic wrap around the outside of each piece to keep the cardboard from falling apart when it gets wet. Stand the little pots on a waterproof tray, then add seed-starting mix and sow your seeds. Come transplant time, remove the outer covering, and plant your seedlings, pots and all.

A container garden can also turn a boring sidewalk or set of stairs into a passageway to paradise. But remember: People and pets will be moving through this narrow Eden on a regular basis. The designers' rule of thumb says that a walk or stairway leading to a house should measure at least 4 feet across—the minimum space needed for two or three people to walk comfortably, side by side. But if you're not blessed with that much room, don't worry. Just allow as much space as possible, and take these basic precautions.

Avoid fragile containers. Save your favorite ceramic and terra-cotta pots for less exposed sites. Instead, use containers made of unbreakable materials like wood, stone, metal, and sturdy plastic. And steer clear of narrow, top-heavy shapes that can tip easily.

> ## TOO DARN HOT!
>
> When a plant's roots are sitting high and dry in a pot, warm weather can dehydrate them in no time flat. So if summers get steamy where you live, take extra precautions when you pot up your posies by setting each container inside a bigger one. Then fill the space in between the two pots with peat moss. The insulation will reduce heat stress on the roots, and keep your flowers in fine fettle all summer long.

Keep plants low. When space is tight, use compact, low-growing plants. They're far less likely to be damaged or to fall over than taller ones are, and low plants will keep the walkway from feeling closed-in.

Keep pots heavy. Lightweight containers can topple over easily when they're bumped. So choose the biggest, heaviest containers your space and budget will allow. Then increase stability and conserve potting mix by filling the bottom 8 inches or so with rocks. (After you've set the pots in place, of course!) Just one word of caution: Use this trick only with annuals and shallow-rooted perennials. Trees, shrubs, and deep-rooted perennials need all the root space they can get. (For more on growing all kinds of plants in containers, see Chapter 9.)

Fasten them down. If your containers rest on a wooden structure, nail or screw them to the surface. And when you fasten planters to railings, position them so that they hang on the outside of the traffic area.

Ah, Freedom!

The bigger your containers are, the less frequently you'll have to water them—but it is a fact of life that all potted plants need more water than their in-ground counterparts. If you want to cut your irrigation time to a minimum, use the self-watering pots that are sold in catalogs and garden centers.

Make sure the cord you use for your irrigation system is all cotton; if it's made of synthetic fiber, it won't absorb moisture.

On the other hand, if you simply want to keep your potted garden well moistened while you go on vacation, it's simple—and cheaper—to set up your own automatic irrigation system. Here's how it works:

- Before you put each plant into its pot, run a piece of thick cotton cord or clothesline through the drainage hole and into the pot, leaving a long piece outside.

- Then before you go away, fill a large container with water, and set the end of the cord into it. The longer you plan to be gone, the bigger your water container will need to be. Play it safe, though, and give the system a trial run before you take off.

- When departure time rolls around, leave your plants with at least 30 to 50 percent more water than they drank in the trial. That way, the roots will have enough to satisfy their thirst even if a heat wave strikes or you get delayed in your travels.

Quick Fix

It's important to keep the load light when your containers sit on a deck, porch, or balcony. To reduce both weight and the amount of planting mix you'll have to buy, fill the pot about one-third to halfway with light, bulky material like empty beer or soda cans, plastic pots, or chunks of plastic foam. Just one word of caution: If you use packing "peanuts," make sure they're not the kind made from cornstarch, which will soon dissolve and make your plants drop right to the bottom of the pot!

Press the liner into the basket.

Gently insert the roots from the outside of the basket.

Set in the remaining plants.

Color on High

To a lot of folks (yours truly included) nothing says "summer" like hanging baskets spilling over with colorful annuals. You can find great-looking baskets made of plastic, wood, rattan, and terra-cotta. But my favorite is the kind made of openwork metal and fitted with a liner that holds the soil, but also allows you to plant right through it—thereby giving you a fabulous floral sphere. The inner holder may be made of plastic, sphagnum moss, or a moss substitute like coir fiber. A 16-inch basket will accommodate about 18 transplants. Good plant choices include petunias, ivy-leaved geraniums, impatiens, and (in the edible department) strawberries and 'Tumbler' tomatoes. Here's the simple process:

STEP 1. Press the liner into place. If you're using moss, soak it in warm water before pressing it into the basket.

STEP 2. Cut a 3-inch slit in the side for each plant. Gently insert the roots through the opening.

STEP 3. Pour in enough planting mix to reach just below the rim of the pot.

STEP 4. Set in the remaining plants.

STEP 5. Water thoroughly, and hang up the basket. Once the basket is hung, you can water it easily with a watering wand that fastens into the end of a garden hose. Or you can cover the soil with ice cubes, piled to the rim of the container, and let them melt.

PERFECTLY PLEASING PERENNIALS

When it comes to diversity of color, form, fragrance, and size—not to mention sheer beauty—nothing on God's green earth can equal perennials. They range in stature from ground-hugging dianthus to towering delphiniums; they come in every color from pure white to almost black; and they thrive in every condition from damp, shady woodlands to parched deserts. Best of all, they come back year after year with just a little TLC from you.

Here's a super money-saving tip: Buy potted perennials at end-of-the-season sales, then bring them home and divide them before planting. By the next season, you'll have two, three, four, or even more great-looking plants for less than the regular price of one!

Lasting Impressions

Although it's true that perennials come back year in and year out, many of the most beautiful ones (peonies and poppies, for instance) bloom for only a few weeks out of the growing season. But that doesn't mean the show has to stop. With the right plant choices—and these simple tips—you can create a garden that looks lush and lovely all year round!

Look for fabulous foliage. The focus doesn't have to be only on the flashy flowers. Dozens of perennials, including hostas, artemisias, peonies, yuccas,

Grandma's GROW-HOW

If you spend a lot of time away from home in the summer, ignore all the advice you hear about producing nonstop blooms in your perennial garden. Instead, do what Grandma Putt did when she had a big summer vacation planned: Focus your efforts on the times when you *are* at home. Pairing spring-blooming and fall-blooming plants in the same bed gives you a glorious show at the beginning and end of the growing season, when you and your family will be around to enjoy it.

Fabulous Foliage Formula

Perennials with superstar foliage, like yuccas, hostas, and bearded irises, deserve a little extra-special TLC. So feed them this sweet treat every three weeks. They'll reward you with big, bright, shiny leaves all through the growing season.

> **1 can of beer**
> **$^{1}/_{2}$ cup of ammonia**
> **$^{1}/_{2}$ cup of fish emulsion**
> **$^{1}/_{4}$ cup of blackstrap molasses**
> **$^{1}/_{4}$ cup of instant tea granules**

Mix all of the ingredients together in a 20 gallon hose-end sprayer and apply until the mixture starts running off the leaves. **Note:** If your plants are in bloom, aim the spray carefully so that it touches only the foliage, *not* the flowers.

and lamb's ears, have leaves that are every bit as striking as their flowers (sometimes more so). Some even have evergreen foliage. These winners include bergenias, Christmas roses, and barrenworts.

Consider the seeds. Include perennials with interesting seed heads that last into the winter. Purple coneflowers and Siberian irises are two. Besides looking pretty, many seed heads provide food for birds.

Vary bloom times. To double—or even triple—your flower display in the same amount of space, look for perennials with varieties that bloom at different times. Peonies, for instance, come in "early," "midseason," and "late" varieties. When the early ones are finishing, the midseason ones are just getting started, and the later ones are waiting in the wings. Planting some of each type can extend your total blooming period from just two weeks up to eight weeks or even longer! Irises, astilbes, asters, and daylilies also offer this season-extending option.

Prolong the Pleasure

Here are two more tricks to keep your perennial beds looking better, longer.

Pinch them back. This performs the same function that deadheading does for annuals: It makes the plant produce more blossoms. With perennials, though, the technique is slightly different. When individual flowers start to fade, look for tiny buds in the leaf axils (the point where a leaf joins the stem). Then pinch or cut off the growth just above those joints. Before you know it, new blooms will appear. Prime candidates for this treatment include balloon flower, peach-leaved bellflower, phlox, pincushion flower, and Shasta daisy. Of course, this process will take a little bit of time on your part, but your reward will be perennials that bloom for weeks—or even months—longer than they normally would.

Shear them off. Giving bushy perennials a haircut is a great way to keep them shipshape all summer long. They'll bounce back with handsome, compact mounds of foliage, and many will send up another round of flowers to boot. The process is quick and easy: After the main flush of flowers has faded, just grab your pruners or hedge shears and trim the plants down to 2 or 3 inches above the ground. This shearing technique works like a dream with many plants, including candytuft, columbines, hardy geraniums, lady's mantle, pinks, and spiderworts.

Quick Fix

The quickest, easiest way to fill your garden with color all summer long—and then some—is to plant a variety of these perennial winners. They all bloom for months on end:

- Anise hyssop (*Agastache foeniculum*)
- Balloon flower (*Platycodon grandiflorus*)
- Blanket flower (*Gaillardia x grandiflora*)
- 'Butterfly Blue' pincushion flower (*Scabiosa* 'Butterfly Blue')
- Catmints (*Nepeta*)
- Coreopsis (*Coreopsis*)
- Gaura (*Gaura lindheimeri*)
- 'Goldsturm' black-eyed Susan (*Rudbeckia fulgida* 'Goldsturm')
- 'Happy Returns' daylily (*Hemerocallis* 'Happy Returns')
- Jupiter's beard (*Centranthus ruber*)

An Impatient Gardener's Wish List

To have a beautiful garden while devoting the least amount of time to its health and well-being, you need to keep maintenance needs firmly in mind at plant-shopping time. Here are a half-dozen traits that make for an easy-care perennial:

- Lives longer than four years

- Can go at least three years before needing to be divided

- Doesn't need daily deadheading

- Doesn't need staking or support

- Is not prone to pests or diseases

- Is vigorous without being invasive (through either creeping roots or rampant self-sowing)

'Goldsturm' black-eyed Susan and 'Autumn Joy' sedum are two easy-to-please perennials that meet the criteria at left. Read catalog descriptions and garden books to learn about other varieties that have at least four of the six traits listed. Your time will be well spent!

Drought on the Land

Of all the plant-selection questions I hear, the most frequent involves drought resistance. People are trying to cut back on the water they use without sacrificing a beautiful flower garden. The good news is that you can find plenty of gorgeous perennials that need very little moisture. Here are some characteristics that indicate a definite lack of thirst:

- Deep roots that resent being transplanted—peonies, for instance

- Fleshy, thickened roots that hold moisture—like daylilies

- Silver or gray leaves with waxy or hairy coverings—such as lavenders and dusty miller

- Thin or narrow leaves—for example, yuccas and many ornamental grasses

- Fleshy leaves and stems—such as sedums and hardy cacti

DIFFICULT DUTY

As we've discussed before in this book, if you look around, you can find plants that are suited to any kinds of growing conditions you've got. Here's a sampling of perennials that will rise to the challenge and thrive in the most demanding areas of your yard.

SHADE	HOT SUN	WET SOIL
• Bleeding hearts (*Dicentra*) • Creeping phlox (*Phlox stolonifera*) • Foamflowers (*Tiarella*) • Lady's mantle (*Alchemilla mollis*)	• Basket of gold (*Aurinia saxatilis*) • Blue false indigo (*Baptisia australis*) • Coral bells (*Heuchera sanguinea*)	• Astilbes (*Astilbe*) • Bergenia (*Bergenia cordifolia*) • Japanese iris (*Iris ensata*) • Lobelias (*Lobelia*)

Just keep in mind that even the most drought-tolerant plants need a steady supply of water while their root systems are forming. The amount varies, but in most cases, it's about an inch of water a week, either from your hose or from Mother Nature's rain clouds.

Plant Those Plants!

You can plant potted perennials pretty much any time the ground isn't frozen, but in most areas, early spring and early fall are ideal. How do you decide between the two? Just follow these guidelines.

Fall. This is the time to plant if you can expect a long, warm autumn, followed by a hard, freezing winter.

Spring. Opt for this time of year if your area tends to see a lot of alternating freezing and thawing in winter.

Whichever season you choose, the first step on the road to quick success is to ease the plant out of its pot in just the right way. And it's as easy as 1, 2, 3:

STEP 1. Water thoroughly, or soak the whole pot in water for 30 minutes before transplanting. This will help the roots hold together and come out of the pot more easily.

STEP 2. Slip one hand over the top of the pot, so the base of the plant is between your fingers.

STEP 3. Tip the pot over onto that hand, then use your other hand to slide off the pot. If it doesn't come loose right away, tap it gently on a table. Whatever you do, don't tug on the stems, or you'll end up with a torn plant in your hands!

TOUGH LOVE

I've found over the years that sometimes, perennial transplants need what seems like tough treatment. When you unpot the plants, if the roots are circling or matted, use an old kitchen knife to cut slits 1 inch deep every 3 to 4 inches around the root-ball, from the top down to the base. If the roots are really tangled, slice off the whole bottom inch or two from the root-ball. Cutting the roots encourages them to branch out into the soil for water and food.

Transplant Tonic

This fabulous formula is perfect for getting perennials and all sorts of other transplants off to a super-fast start!

> ½ can of beer
> 1 tbsp. of ammonia
> 1 tbsp. of baby shampoo
> 1 tbsp. of instant tea granules
> 1 gal. of water

Mix all of the ingredients together in a small bucket. Use 1 cup of the tonic for each planting hole at transplant time.

In We Go!

No matter what time of year you set your perennials into the ground, try to perform the procedure on a cloudy day, so the plants won't be stressed out by the hot sun. If that's not possible, do the job as early in the morning as you can, before Ol' Sol starts heating up. Then follow this five-step process:

STEP 1. Dig a hole slightly larger than the width of the pot.

STEP 2. Remove the plant from its pot, and use your fingers to loosen the soil on the sides of the root-ball.

STEP 3. Place the plant in the hole, and half-fill around the roots with the soil you removed to make the hole.

STEP 4. Add enough water to make a "soup," then let the water soak in for a few minutes. (This important step settles the soil and eliminates air pockets, which can damage developing roots.)

STEP 5. Finish filling the hole with soil, and water again generously. Then stand back and watch your perennials take off!

The Bare-Root Routine

When you buy perennials by mail, they're shipped when they're dormant, and what you get will be a tangled mass of roots topped by a small

Dig a hole that's slightly larger than the pot.

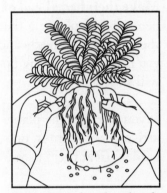

Loosen the soil on the sides of the root-ball.

Set the plant into the hole, and fill it halfway with soil.

tuft of foliage. Fortunately, it doesn't matter how much foliage perennials have; it's the roots that count. These plants may look downright scary, but give them a good start, and they'll be up and running in no time flat. Here's all you need to remember to do so.

Don't fret about timing. Reputable mail-order nurseries will ship bare-root perennials at the best time for planting in your area. North of Zone 6, that's early spring; in warmer areas, it's fall. In either case, the idea is to give the new plants a generous period of mild, moist weather so they can send out a good root system before summer's heat encourages a lot of leafy growth.

Make their bed ahead of time. The key to successfully growing bare-root perennials is planting them as soon as possible. So it's smart to make sure their new bed is ready and waiting well before they arrive. Otherwise, you'll be rushed to dig up a new area—and both you and your new plants will suffer!

If you can't get the plants into the ground within three days after they arrive, plant them in pots. Then, when you're ready to put them in your garden, treat them as you would any other potted perennial.

Root-Revival Tonic

Get your bare-root perennials rarin' to grow with an overnight bath in this powerful potion. (It's just the ticket for bare-root roses, too!)

> 1/4 cup of brewed tea
> 1 tbsp. of dishwashing liquid
> 1 tbsp. of Epsom salts
> 1 gal. of water

Mix all of the ingredients in a bucket or tub, insert your plants' roots, and let them soak for up to 24 hours. This will revive any dried-out underparts, so all systems will be ready for liftoff!

Get 'Em Growing

When your bare-root babies arrive, carefully remove the wrappings and packing material. Examine the plants thoroughly, then follow these five simple steps:

STEP 1. Start by clipping off any broken or discolored roots cleanly with sharp shears, then soak the remaining roots in my Root-Revival Tonic (at left) for up to 24 hours before planting.

STEP 2. Dig a planting hole that's large enough to hold all the roots without bending them.

STEP 3. If the plant has a great many roots, use some of the soil that you removed from the ground to make a mound in the center of the hole. The top of the mound should be close to the level of the surrounding soil, so the plant's crown will be at the right level after planting (see "Just My Depth!" on page 126). Carefully spread the roots as evenly as you can over the mound, then fill in around the roots with the remaining soil.

STEP 4. If the plant has one main root, hold the crown at the correct level with one hand (or have a helper hold it), while you fill in around the root with the soil you removed from the hole.

STEP 5. After planting, firm the soil around the crown using your hands or a hoe, then water the plant generously.

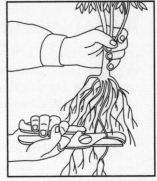

Clip off broken or discolored roots.

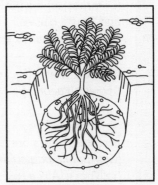

Dig a hole that can accommodate the roots without bending them.

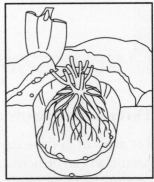

If the plant has a lot of roots, build a mound in the center of the hole.

JUST MY DEPTH!

A key part of getting any perennial off to a fast start and a long, healthy life is planting it at just the right depth. But you don't have to spend time memorizing complicated depth charts. Just follow these simple guidelines for beautiful blooms year after year.

PERENNIALS	PLANTING GUIDELINES
Most common perennials, including carnations (*Dianthus*), phlox (*Phlox*), and Shasta daisies (*Chrysanthemum* x *superbum*)	These plants have a fibrous (many-branched) root system. Put the crown (the point where the stems and roots join) just at or a smidge above the soil surface.
Bleeding hearts (*Dicentra*), peonies (*Paeonia*)	Plant them deep enough so the tips of the new eyes (buds) are about 2 inches below ground level.
Perennial baby's breath (*Gypsophila paniculata*), hollyhock (*Alcea rosea*)	These perennials have long taproots, so plant them with the crown just below ground level.
Bearded iris (*Iris* bearded hybrids)	Set the thick rhizomes (the fat, horizontal stems, a.k.a. rootstock, from which the plants grow) flush with the soil surface because they need the kiss of the sun to thrive.

Perennials to Sow and Grow

For many of us these days, filling up even a midsize bed with potted perennials can be hard on the budget. Fortunately, a lot of great-looking perennials are super-easy to grow from seed. Start them indoors in late winter or early spring according to the directions in Chapter 6, or outdoors in late spring or early summer (see "Sow, Sow, Sow Your Seeds" on page 109). Any of these accommodating customers will take off with the speed of a southbound freight train, filling your beds with beauty in almost no time at all:

- Asters (*Aster*)

- Black-eyed Susans (*Rudbeckia*)

- Blanket flower (*Gaillardia* x *grandiflora*)

- Hollyhock (*Alcea rosea*)

- Lupine (*Lupinus*)

- Shasta daisy (*Chrysanthemum* x *superbum*)

These perennial seeds all need a taste of winter weather (either real or manufactured) before they spring to life:

- **Anemones (Anemone)**

- **Bleeding hearts (Dicentra)**

- **Columbines (Aquilegia)**

- **False indigos (Baptisia)**

- **Goatsbeard (Aruncus dioicus)**

- **Lady's mantle (Alchemilla mollis)**

Prenatal Care

Not all perennial seeds are as easygoing as the ones listed above. Some need a period of cool, moist conditions, just like they'd get outdoors during the winter, before they'll germinate. There are two simple ways to satisfy this craving. One is to sow the seeds in pots in late summer or early fall, then leave the pots outside in a sheltered spot over the winter. (A cold frame is ideal; otherwise, set them in a basement window well or against the foundation of your house.) They'll be adequately protected as they go through the usual freezing and thawing cycles, then sprout in spring when the mild and sunny weather returns.

Your other option is to mix the seeds with a small handful of moistened vermiculite and put it all in a sealed plastic bag in your refrigerator for 8 to 12 weeks. Then sow the seed-and-vermiculite mixture indoors according to the directions in Chapter 6.

Setting Out Seedlings

When it's time to get your seedlings up and growing in the garden, first harden them off according to the instructions in "Kindergarten, Seedling

Style" (see page 208). Then 24 hours before transplanting them, water the little plants thoroughly. Use a trowel to dig a small hole for each seedling. Set the tiny tyke into the hole, gently firm the soil around the roots, and pinch off the top to encourage branching and flowering. Finally, water thoroughly, and give each plant a good dose of my Transplant Tonic on page 122.

The Kindest Cut of All

Granted, starting perennials from cuttings won't give you the instant gratification you'd get if you bought plants at your local garden center, but the process couldn't be simpler. And to my way of thinking, it's worth every bit of time and effort, even if money is no object. That's because when you root cuttings that came from the gardens of people you love, or from special, old-time plants you can't find in commercial markets, you produce far more than a pretty garden—you create a beautiful living scrapbook!

STAKE EARLY, NOT OFTEN

Once your tall perennials are in the ground, don't wait to stake them until the plants are falling over in summer. Instead, set out your stakes and supports in early spring, just when the new growth appears. As the plants grow up, the leaves will quickly cover the structures. It's the fastest, easiest way to keep all of your perennials growing on the up-and-up!

Before you begin your project, buy a bag of sterilized rooting medium made especially for starting cuttings and a rooting hormone that contains a fungicide (thereby heading off trouble from soilborne fungi that can kill your future plants). Then follow this routine:

STEP 1. Gather your cuttings in the morning, when the plants are full of moisture. (And make sure the plants you choose are strong and healthy—otherwise, you'll just be importing trouble to your garden!) Using a clean, sharp knife or clippers, snip off stem tips 4 to 6 inches below their topmost leaves. Stick them in a jar of water that you've brought along, or wrap them loosely in wet paper towels, and tuck them into a plastic bag as you go.

STEP 2. When you're back inside, cut each stem about ¼ inch below a node (the place where a leaf or pair of leaves meets the stem). Then pinch off the lower leaves so the bottom third to half of the cutting stem is bare. Keep the upper leaves in place, but pinch off any buds or flowers. That way, all the shoot's energy will be directed toward forming roots.

STEP 3. Dip the bottom of each cutting into the rooting hormone, then tuck the bottom third to half of the stem into the rooting medium. With a spoon or the eraser end of a pencil, press the rooting medium firmly around the cutting. Water lightly, then wrap each pot or flat with a plastic bag to keep the humidity high, or put them all into an old aquarium covered with plastic, or a clear, plastic storage box with a lid. Then put your plant incubator in a warm, bright place.

STEP 4. When you see new shoots forming (usually within three to five weeks), it means the roots are starting to grow, too. Wait a week or so, then start leaving the plastic covers off for several hours each day. Come spring, harden off your babies as you would any other newborn plants (see "Kindergarten, Seedling Style" on page 208).

HELP!

Q A friend gave me some cuttings from her prized perennials, and I rooted them in trays. They had tiny roots, and they seemed to be doing just fine. Then this morning, when I went to check on them, the stems were all turning dark at the base! What's going on?

A *What's going on is an infection called black leg of cuttings, which is caused by water- and soilborne fungi. It strikes before or shortly after roots start to form. There is no cure, so if all the cuttings in a tray are turning color, you'll have to kiss 'em good-bye and start over. But if the nasty stuff hasn't spread through a whole tray, there is hope. Just mix up a half-and-half solution of hydrogen peroxide and water, and saturate the rooting mix in the flat. If you're lucky, that'll kill off any lingering fungi, and your babies will be saved.*

Divide to Multiply

Most perennials need to be divided every three to five years—you'll know it's time when you see what I call the "doughnut syndrome." That's a ring of healthy growth surrounding a dead-looking center. (Of course, you don't need to wait until the dreaded doughnut appears; you can divide a mature, healthy perennial anytime it's beginning to outgrow its place in the bed, or if you simply want to increase your supply of plants.) As for timing, you want to divide spring-blooming plants in fall, and fall-blooming plants in spring. As usual, though, there are a couple of exceptions to this rule. Both Oriental poppies and bearded iris fare best when you divide them in mid- to late summer.

No matter what your reason is for dividing your perennials, it's a simple procedure. Here's all you need to do: A day or two before you set to work, thoroughly soak the ground around the clump, and cut back any top growth to about 6 inches above the ground. This will make the divisions less likely to wilt before you replant them.

The next day, dig up the plant, and toss the old, dead center growth into your compost bin. Cut the remaining, healthy part into several sections, making sure each piece has three to five "eyes," or buds, and a good supply of roots. Then plant the divisions wherever you want them in your garden. If you have more than you need, share your bounty with friends, neighbors, or your local community garden.

NIX THE DIVISION

If you'd just as soon not fuss with dividing and moving plants, you're in luck. A lot of great-looking perennials grow from long, thick, carrot-like taproots, or have extra-deep, wide-spreading root systems, and they'd rather be left alone. These are some of the most reluctant travelers:

- Balloon flower (*Platycodon grandiflorus*)

- Bugbanes (*Cimicifuga*)

- Butterfly weed (*Asclepias tuberosa*)

- False indigos (*Baptisia*)

- Gas plant (*Dictamnus albus*)

- Goatsbeards (*Aruncus*)

- Peonies (*Paeonia*)

Grandma's
GROW-HOW

Grandma Putt was a whiz at dividing perennials. She had three simple secrets: First, whatever tool you use for the job, make sure it has a razor-sharp blade that will slice through the roots neatly. Dull blades make ragged cuts, which can usher in pests and diseases.

Second, wipe your blade between cuts with a solution of 1 part household bleach to 3 parts water. Impatient gardeners may be tempted to skip this crucial step, but it's needed to keep your divisions free of any disease germs in the soil.

And third, before you plant your new sections, toss a handful of dry oatmeal and one of human hair into each hole. It'll help the youngsters get off to a stronger, healthier start.

BULBS: PACKAGED TO GROW

To my way of thinking, bulbs are one of the greatest gifts an impatient gardener could ask for. They're literally wrapped-up packages of leaves and flowers, all ready to burst into bloom. And, because all the food they need is stored inside, they grow like lightning when conditions are right—and breeze through trying times (such as dry spells) when they're dormant. In other words, bulbs are about as foolproof as living things can be. Still, to get the best these beautiful bloomers can offer, it helps to have a few tricks up your sleeve.

My all-time favorite bulb-planting tool is a planter bit. It looks like a huge drill bit, and it fits any $3/8$-inch or larger electric drill. This bit makes a perfect 3-inch-round hole so quickly, you won't believe it! Planter bits are available from garden catalogs and on the Internet.

What's in a Name?

Technically speaking, a bulb is a swollen, underground stem with a bud in the center; wrapped around it are scale-like leaf bases that are chock-full of food. Tulips, daffodils, lilies, and onions are true bulbs. However, folks who sell or write about bulbs generally include the following three other plants that behave the same way but are not *really* bulbs.

Corms. Similar to bulbs, corms carry the bud on top instead of the bottom. Every year, the old corm withers away, and a new one takes its place. Gladioli and crocuses are examples of corms.

Tuberous roots. These are exactly what their name implies: swollen roots. In order to produce a plant, the root must have a piece of stem and at least one bud attached. Dahlias are probably the best-known tuberous roots.

Tubers. A tuber is simply the swollen part of an underground stem. Tuberous begonias, cyclamen—and potatoes—are all tubers.

Shop Wisely—and Early

Whether you intend to plant spring- or summer-flowering bulbs, buy them within the first week or so that they appear in the stores. Otherwise (even in the very best garden centers), they can dry out quickly and won't bloom as well the following year. Also, avoid bulbs that come in packages because

Bug-Off Bulb Bath

This special spa treatment will help your spring- or summer-blooming bulbs fend off disease germs and pesky insect pests.

> 2 tsp. of baby shampoo
> 1 tsp. of antiseptic mouthwash
> 1/4 tsp. of instant tea granules
> 2 gal. of hot water (120°F)

Mix all of the ingredients together in a bucket. Then drop in your bulbs, and let them soak for two to three hours (longer for larger bulbs). Don't peel off the papery skins! The bulbs use them as a defense against pests. Then either plant the bulbs immediately, or let them air-dry for several days before you store them—otherwise, rot could set in.

it's important to examine each one. When you do, keep these pointers in mind:

- Steer clear of any bulbs with mushy gray spots on them, as well as those that are much lighter in weight than others of the same size. These bulbs are damaged and aren't worth taking home.

- Don't worry if the bulb's papery skin is loose—that's a common and perfectly harmless condition. Likewise, if you see a few nicks, just ignore them; they won't affect the development of otherwise healthy bulbs.

A Bigger Bang for Your Buck

If your planting space is short—or if you'd simply like to get a season-long parade of color using only the time and effort it takes to dig a single hole—this tip is for you. Just gather up an assortment of spring- and summer-flowering bulbs, and proceed as follows:

Take 2

If you have a fireplace in your home and have been wondering what to do with all those ashes, try this—add them to your bulb bed before you plant. You can apply up to 15 pounds of ashes per 100 square feet. Ashes are a great source of potassium, which'll help your bulbs develop good, strong stems that don't need staking.

STEP 1. Dig a hole that's about a foot deep and as wide as you want it to be. Set in some large, summer-flowering bulbs, like lilies, crown imperials, or giant ornamental onions, and cover with 1/4 inch or so of soil.

STEP 2. Put in some slightly smaller, spring-flowering types, such as daffodils or tulips, and replace another 1/4 inch of soil (give or take).

STEP 3. Add a layer of still smaller spring bloomers, like grape hyacinths, and cover them. Finish with a layer of tiny crocuses and (of course) more soil.

STEP 4. Come spring, scatter seeds of sweet alyssum or another low-growing annual over the area.

You'll have an ever-changing show of blooms in one compact (or maybe not-so-compact) spot!

A Match Made in Heaven

On the other hand, maybe you decided you had more yard than you wanted to take care of, so you replaced much of your grass with low-maintenance groundcovers. If that's the case, then this tip's for you: Liven up that green scene by pairing your groundcovers with bulbs for a burst of spring blooms. Smaller types, like dwarf daffodils and reticulated iris, work well with low-growing covers, such as bugleweeds and deadnettle. Team full-sized daffodils with more vigorous "carpets" like periwinkles. In return for the color boost, the groundcover will perform a couple of good deeds for the bulbs—holding up the flowers when spring breezes blow and keeping soil from splashing up when April showers fall! (You can read more about all kinds of great groundcovers in Chapter 5.)

Quick Fix

When you add spring-blooming bulbs to a flower garden, ignore the common advice to put short plants in front and tall plants in back. Instead, plant your bulbs near the back of a bed or border, or in the center of an island bed. This way, you'll get to enjoy the glorious show before your larger plants start to sprout. Later on, the leaves of emerging annuals and perennials will do a good job covering up the declining bulb foliage.

Spreading Cheer—the Easy Way

Creating bulb-and-groundcover combos isn't the only low-maintenance way to put bulbs to work in your yard. Here's another trio of terrific tips for brightening your life—and lessening your workload—with bulbs:

- Grow them in containers for movable spots of color on a deck or patio. Potted bulbs also make great fillers for bare spots in spring and summer flower gardens.

- Tuck allium, gladiolus, or lily bulbs in a corner of your vegetable garden. You can leave them there for an extra touch of color, or cut them for use in summer bouquets—without ruining the dazzling display in your flower beds.

✒ Set out crocuses, dwarf daffodils, Siberian squill, and other small bulbs right in your lawn. They'll provide delightful drifts of spring color, and by the time they're through flowering, your grass will be ready for its first mowing of the season, and you can mow right over the spent foliage.

At the peak of their blooming, take pictures of your bulbs. That way, you'll know where *not* to sink your shovel when you're tending other plants in the bed.

Spring into Spring

By and large, spring-blooming bulbs are an easygoing bunch, but there are some things you need to keep in mind.

Time it right. Spring-blooming bulbs are sticklers for timing. If you put them into the ground when the soil is still warm, they won't form roots at all—though they may send up top growth in the fall. But if you wait too long, the bulbs won't have time to get well rooted before the ground freezes. So let your fingers do the testing. After a couple of frosts have hit, shove your hand into the soil. If it's cool, grab your trowel, and have at it!

Bountiful Bulb Breakfast

Give your newly planted bulbs a boost with this marvelous mix. It's packed with enough nutrients and organic matter to provide a small, but steady supply of food—thereby ensuring balanced bulb growth. This recipe makes enough for about 100 square feet of garden area.

> **10 lbs. of compost**
> **5 lbs. of bonemeal**
> **2 lbs. of bloodmeal**
> **1 lb. of Epsom salts**

Mix all of the ingredients in a wheelbarrow. Before setting out your bulbs, work this hearty meal into the soil in your planting beds. Or, if you're digging individual holes, work a handful of the mixture into the soil in each one before setting in the bulb.

Give them good drainage. Most bulbs (and all of the more common ones, such as tulips, daffodils, and hyacinths) demand well-drained soil. Before you plant, always add plenty of compost or leaf mold to the bed (see Chapter 9 for the lowdown on building super soil). If your home ground is so damp that nothing you can do will change it, grow your bulbs in containers instead.

Watch the depth. As a rule of green thumb, a bulb should be planted at a depth that's three times its size. That means, for instance, that a 1-inch crocus bulb needs a hole that's 3 inches deep, and a tulip that's about 2 inches in diameter should be tucked 6 inches into the ground. Like most rules, though, this one needs to be stretched now and then: If your soil is heavy, plant your bulbs just a little shallower than the recommended depth; in sandy soil, go slightly deeper.

Plant them right side up. Unless you find traces of last year's roots, it's not always easy to tell the top of a bulb from the bottom—especially when you're rushing to get dozens of 'em into the ground and you're runnin' out of daylight! Here's your clue: Generally, the bottom of the bulb is flatter than the top. If you just can't decide which end is up, plant the bulb on its side. A bulb will struggle to its feet from a sideways position, but it'll rarely flip itself over from a headstand.

Hands off the foliage! This year's foliage is the food supply for next year's growth. It's okay to cut the flowers, but whatever you do, don't touch the leaves until they've turned yellow and started to wither.

IT'S REALLY DEPRESSING!

Dahlia flowers come in all shapes, sizes, and colors, but once you've dug up the tubers, they all look alike. Here's a simple way to solve the identity crisis: Get a box of tongue depressors at the drugstore. Then using a waterproof, smear-proof marker, write the name of the dahlia on one side, and the color and height on the other. Drill a small hole in the top of the stick, run a string through the hole, and tie it to the tuber before you store it away for the winter. Come spring planting time, you won't have to play the "Guess the Flower Color" game!

Some Like It Soggy

While it is true that the vast majority of bulbs need good drainage, there are some exceptions. This trio thrives in moist soil.

Camassias (*Camassia*). Spikes of star-shaped flowers bloom in late spring, in shades of blue and white. Stems range from 14 to 36 inches tall, depending on the variety. These bulbs thrive even in heavy clay soil, but they do need full sun. Zones 5–8.

Checkered lily (*Fritillaria meleagris*). The flowers look like upside-down tulips on 12- to 15-inch stems, and they really *are* checkered, in either white or green against a base color from light purple to almost black. They bloom in midspring; and like shade and soil that's evenly moist. Zones 4–8.

Snowdrops (*Galanthus*). Bell-shaped white flowers bloom in very early spring on 4- to 10-inch stems. They prefer moist, shady sites but will tolerate sun. Zones 3–8.

H E L P !

Q Last fall, I planted dozens of 'Pink Impression' tulips in my garden in Savannah, Georgia. The catalog description said the stems would grow to be 28 to 30 inches tall, but mine are barely above the ground. (The flowers are gorgeous, though!) What went wrong?

A *Your climate, that's what! When tulips don't get a good jolt of cold weather, they produce short, stubby stems. In an area where winters are short and mild, you need to give the bulbs a taste of artificial winter. So keep them in the vegetable bin of your refrigerator for about 10 weeks, then plant them in late fall.*

By the way, hyacinths are prone to the same no-chill, no-thrill condition, but they can make do with a slightly shorter cooling-off period than tulips. Give the H-guys six to eight weeks in the fridge before you tuck them into bed.

FABULOUS FOOD AND DRINK

Anything that adds as much happiness to life as a flower garden does deserves a little extra-special care. But that doesn't mean you have to labor long and hard in the service of your plants. Here are my best secrets for delivering top-notch TLC in ways that will keep your load light—and your garden lush and lovely.

Wet flowers and foliage are prime breeding grounds for fungus spores, so aim your hose or watering can at the soil, *not* at your plants. And water as early in the day as you can, so that if your plants do get wet, they'll dry out before nightfall.

Water of Life

Sprinkling your garden every morning with a handheld hose may be relaxing for you, but it doesn't do much good for your flowers. The water you supply that way rarely soaks into the soil below the top inch, so your plants will form most of their roots close to the surface. This leaves them dependent on a daily water fix, and if you miss a day, they'll wilt at the merest hint of dry weather.

To encourage deep rooting—and cut down on watering time—the trick is to water thoroughly, then not water again for a week or so. To make sure you've really delivered the goods, stick a finger down into the soil after you think you've watered enough. The ground should be wet several inches down. If not, continue watering, then check again.

Listen Up!

When it comes to delivering this essential elixir to all the plants in your yard, one of the most important guidelines is to water only when your plants need it. When your flowers are thirsty, they'll speak up in one, or all, of these ways:

- Leaves droop slightly during the heat of the day, but recover in the evening once the sun goes down.

- Leaves are duller or grayer than normal.

❧ The foliage of fleshy-leaved plants shrivels slightly or feels soft to the touch.

One word of warning: When you see these symptoms, don't automatically reach for the hose. Instead, be patient long enough to check the soil—pull the mulch aside if you have to—and make sure the ground isn't actually waterlogged. Plants that have *too much* moisture can show the very same symptoms as those that don't have enough.

Some Advice That Bears Repeating

I've said it before, and I'll say it again throughout this book: There are two surest, simplest ways to keep your plants well watered and ease your labor load at the same time. First, serve up frequent, heaping helpings of organic matter— especially compost. Besides adding essential nutrients to the soil, it increases its water-holding capacity by one-third or more. (For the full scoop on making and using "black gold," see Chapter 9.)

Take 2

Believe it or not, you probably have all the equipment you need for a permanent, in-ground irrigation system right in your kitchen. What is it? Coffee cans! Just save every one you empty (and scavenge more from friends and neighbors). Dig can-size holes every few feet throughout your flower beds. Then sink a can (with both ends removed) into each hole, and fill it up with gravel. Each time you water, fill the cans to the brim. The moisture will seep into the soil, where the plants need it most.

Quick Fix

By midsummer, your annuals and perennials can start to look a little frazzled. Foliar feeding—spraying liquid fertilizer right on their leaves—gives them an instant pick-me-up. Simply fill a hose-end sprayer with diluted fish emulsion or compost tea, and spray away! (Mix the fish emulsion with water according to the package directions; for my easy compost tea recipe, see page 140.)

Second, give each of your flower beds a thick blanket of mulch. A 2- to 3-inch-deep layer of this magical material shields the ground from sun and wind, so any water that's already in the soil stays there, instead of evaporating into thin air.

Power Watering

Almost everybody enjoys a can of soda pop now and then, but for your plants, pop is more than just a refreshing treat—it's super chow. It's not the sugar or the yummy flavor that does the trick. It's the carbon dioxide, which plants need to turn the sun's energy into food. To serve up this power lunch, first surround your plants with a 3-inch layer of mulch like bark chips, gravel, or pine needles. Then twice a week during the growing season, pour a can of soda right through the mulch. The chunky covering will keep the gas under wraps long enough for the plants' roots to drink it up.

COMPOST TEA

This variation of my Classic Compost Tea (see page 315) will energize your flowers like crazy. Toss a shovelful of compost into a 5-gallon bucket. Add two heaping handfuls of salt-free alfalfa pellets (available at animal feed stores), then fill the bucket with water. Let it sit for at least two or three days, stirring once or twice a day. Dilute it with water until the tea is light brown before using it. When the bucket is empty and you're through watering your plants, spread the remaining solids on your flower beds for an extra nutrient boost.

uick Fix

If you use an overhead sprinkler to provide your plants with life-giving moisture, here's an easy way to find out whether you're serving enough liquid: Just set a few cat food or tuna fish cans, open end up, in the beds you're watering. Run the sprinkler for an hour, then check the depth of the H_2O in the cans. As a general rule, most flowers need roughly 1 inch of water per week during the growing season, whether it's delivered by you or Mother Nature.

Flower-Friendly Feeding

Follow these super-simple feeding tips and your flowers will be happy and healthy all season long.

Annuals. These one-year wonders don't stay around long, but when they need food, they need it *fast*! Sprinkle a few pinches of dry, organic fertilizer (5-10-5 is best) around each one—or give the whole bed a light dusting—at planting time. Then follow up by giving them A Floral Feast (below) every two weeks throughout the growing season.

Bulbs. These long-lasting gems appreciate a slow but steady supply of food. After considerable practice, I've found that this is the best formula: Mix 2 pounds of bonemeal with 2 pounds of wood ashes and 1 pound of Epsom salts, and sprinkle this mixture on top of beds where bulbs are growing as the shoots emerge from the ground.

A Floral Feast

For glorious color spring, summer, and fall, serve this tasty treat to all the flowers in your garden—annuals, perennials, *and* summer-blooming bulbs.

> 1 can of beer
> 2 tbsp. of ammonia
> 2 tbsp. of dishwashing liquid
> 2 tbsp. of fish emulsion
> 2 tbsp. of hydrogen peroxide
> 2 tbsp. of whiskey
> 1 tbsp. of clear corn syrup
> 1 tbsp. of unflavored gelatin
> 4 tsp. of instant tea granules
> 2 gal. of warm water

Mix all of the ingredients in a large bucket or watering can. Then water all your flowering plants with this mixture every two weeks in the morning for a spectacular display of beautiful blooms.

Perennials. Like bulbs, perennials enjoy a long-lasting meal. So in early spring, sprinkle a handful of dry, organic fertilizer (5-10-5) on the soil around the base of each plant, or spread a thin layer over the whole perennial bed. (Either pull any mulch aside and replace it after you apply the food, or feed before you mulch.)

Ask the Experts

If your plants start showing any of the signs described in "Diagnosing Diet Deficiencies" (at right), give them a good dose of an all-purpose organic fertilizer that also contains trace minerals. If that doesn't perk them up, call your local Cooperative Extension Service and ask for help. The specialists there may have you drop by with a few leaves, and chances are they'll also recommend a thorough soil analysis.

Leaves That Tell a Different Story

If your plants' leaves have brown, curled edges that look like they've been singed by a flame, the problem is not a nutrient deficiency. Those symptoms indicate that you've applied too much fertilizer, failed to mix it thoroughly with the soil, or used a product that contains too much concentrated nitrogen. As a result, at least some of the plants' roots have been destroyed. (The problem is most common with synthetic fertilizers, but fresh manure is also a frequent culprit.) Fortunately,

Take 2

When you change the water in your fish tank, or toss an over-the-hill floral arrangement into the compost bin, don't send the used H_2O down the drain. Serve it to a plant instead. That liquid is chock-full of health-giving nutrients. So is the water that you've used to cook eggs, vegetables, or pasta, or to rinse out glasses, bottles, or cans that held any of these bracing beverages:

• Beer
• Coffee
• Juice
• Soda pop
• Tea
• Whiskey
• Wine

DIAGNOSING DIET DEFICIENCIES

Discolored leaves on your plants often indicate that something's lacking in their diet. Here's how to recognize the symptoms. **Note:** This chart will help you troubleshoot problems with flowers as well as all of the other plants in your yard and garden.

NUTRIENT	SYMPTOMS OF A DEFICIENCY
Calcium	Leaf tissue turns dark from the base outward and dies because the feeder roots have died.
Iron	Leaves turn yellow between the veins; veins stay green or faintly yellow.
Magnesium	Leaf centers turn yellow or reddish. Dead spots appear between the veins.
Manganese	Leaves at the top of the plant turn yellow in the center, between the veins, but there's no sign of red.
Nitrogen	Leaves are small and yellow, sometimes turning red or purple. Severe stunting or dwarfing soon follows.
Phosphorus	Leaves are small and may fall early; edges may be scorched, purplish, or blue-green. Plant growth is generally reduced and weak, and flower and fruit production plummets.
Potassium	Leaf tips and edges are yellow and scorched-looking, with brownish purple spotting underneath. Most common in sandy soils.
Sulfur	Leaf veins are lighter in color than the tissue in between them.

if you've reached the scene in time, there is still hope for a reprieve. Here's your three-step first-aid process:

STEP 1. Dig up the victim, and thoroughly hose off any surviving roots.

STEP 2. Flush the hole thoroughly with clear water and add a half-and-half mixture of fresh topsoil and compost.

STEP 3. Follow up with a long, slow drink of water.

Too Much of a Good Thing

First, the good news: It's unlikely that you'll ever serve your garden plants too much of a secondary nutrient like calcium, iron, or magnesium. That leaves you with only The Big Three (nitrogen, phosphorus, and potassium) to worry about. Now the bad news: When an overdose does occur, there is no quick fix. Your only option is to hold back on any amendments that contain the offending element for at least two to three years, and supply added amounts of the other two. This will eventually bring the soil back into balance. A nutrient excess is trickier to identify than a deficiency, but if

Grandma's GROW-HOW

Plants' appetite levels vary, but to play it safe, always remember the words Grandma Putt lived by: "Moderation in all things." Even with organic fertilizers, more is not better. In fact, excess fertilizer can cause all kinds of problems, ranging from delayed maturity to malformed flowers and vegetables (see "Too Much of a Good Thing" above). Be especially careful to avoid an overdose of nitrogen. It will make your plants produce overly lush foliage, which will attract sap-sucking insects like aphids and scale.

you spot any of these symptoms in any of your plants, you should get a soil test immediately:

❧ Delayed plant maturity and foliage that's too leafy, too dark, or overly lush, with reduced flowering and/or poor vegetable or fruit production. This indicates too much nitrogen.

❧ Plants that show a number of deficiencies like those in "Diagnosing Diet Deficiencies" on page 143 indicate an overdose of phosphorus.

❧ Stunted plant growth and/or poorly colored, coarse-looking, or malformed flowers, fruits, or vegetables all indicate a diet that's much too high in potassium.

PRIME POSY PREDICAMENTS

As we've seen in this chapter, growing fabulous flowers is faster and easier than a lot of folks make it out to be. Of course, you may need to troubleshoot a problem or two every now and then, but if you follow the tips, tricks, and pointers in this section, that'll be a piece of cake, too!

The first key to preventing trouble in your flower garden is to keep an eagle eye out for anything that looks odd or out of place. That way, you can spot small problems before they turn into big ones.

Trespassers on Parade

In nature's grand scheme of things, all plants are created equal. But that doesn't mean you need to stand by while an unruly mob of weeds robs nourishment from your flowers! I've found that winning the battle against trespassing plants takes almost no time at all, as long as you follow these two guidelines:

❧ Keep a thick layer of mulch on all your flower beds. It's your best defense against weeds sprouting up from below—and the best way to prevent windblown weed seeds from sprouting in the soil. As a bonus, mulch also helps hold in moisture during dry spells.

❧ Anytime you're in your garden, look for weed seedlings. When you spot one, pull it up immediately—*before* it has time to set seed or send out rampaging roots.

Get Out!

This good-riddance method is the fastest way I know of to get rid of weeds in your flower beds without harming your plants. (It works like a charm in herb and vegetable gardens, too.) Here's the simple four-step process:

STEP 1. Cut each weed right down to ground level.

STEP 2. Slice the bottom off a 1-quart plastic bottle that has a screw-on top. (You'll need a bottle for each troublesome weed.) Then set the bottle over the weed, and push it into the ground about 2 inches.

STEP 3. Mix up a batch of my Weed Wipeout Tonic (at right), stick your sprayer head into the top of the bottle, and pull the trigger. Drench that weed until the potion is running off in streams. Then screw the top on the bottle. (This ensures that the tonic won't be diluted if it rains or when you water your plants.)

STEP 4. Leave the bottle in place for a couple of weeks, then inspect your handiwork. Chances are, your weed woes will be history. But if any extra-tough guys are still showing signs of life, give them another dose of the tonic. Before long, they'll go belly-up, too!

You can eliminate a lot of weed worries simply by planting what my Grandma Putt called "good-guy weeds." They're flowers that reseed like crazy, but are easy to control if they get out of hand. Sow them anyplace you have weed problems, and then just let 'em go. It sure beats waging a constant war on weeds—and their pretty little flowers look a darn sight better than thistles or plantain! These are all powerful weed fighters:

- Asters
- Columbine
- Coreopsis
- Forget-me-nots
- Johnny-jump-ups
- Poppies
- Sweet alyssum
- Violets

A Plague on the Land

Plant diseases can strike even the best-tended garden. Fortunately, it's easy to stop many of them in their tracks. The secret is the same as it is for controlling weeds: Inspect your plants every day (or as close to it as you can), and if you find any of the following symptoms, take action right away. Don't dawdle—even a short delay could spell the difference between a minor challenge for you and a fatal disaster for your plants.

Spots on leaves. Pick off all the marked leaves and toss them in the trash—not in your compost bin!

Mottled green-and-yellow leaves that are crinkled or curled up. These are all signs that nasty viruses are at work. There is no cure, so pull up infected plants and throw them away immediately.

Plant viruses are spread by sap-sucking insects like aphids, thrips, and flea beetles. There is no cure, but some everyday kitchen trash can help prevent an outbreak: Every time you empty a carton of milk, cream, or buttermilk, fill the container with water, shake it, and pour the contents onto one of your plants.

Weed Wipeout Tonic

When you've got weeds that won't take "no" for an answer, knock 'em out for good with this potent potion.

> 1 tbsp. of dishwashing liquid
> 1 tbsp. of gin*
> 1 tbsp. of white vinegar
> 1 qt. of hot water

Mix all of the ingredients together, and pour the solution into a handheld sprayer bottle. Then drench the weeds to the point of runoff, taking care not to get any of the tonic on nearby plants.

* If you don't have any gin on hand, use vodka instead.

Yellowed leaves, stunted plants, and/or wilting. These may be disease symptoms, or they could signify the presence of pests, cultural problems, or nutrient deficiencies. If a dose of a good all-purpose organic fertilizer doesn't solve the problem, call your local Cooperative Extension Service and ask for help.

Uninvited Diners

When you find hungry insects munching on your beautiful flowers, it can be mighty tempting to simply reach for a lethal spray and let 'em have it. Well, don't do it! (Remember, if you want "good" bugs to help wage your pest-control war, you need to have some "bad" bugs on hand for them to eat!) But, of course, that doesn't mean you have to surrender your garden to the multilegged invaders. As we saw with weeds and diseases, the key to stopping trouble early lies in a sharp eye—and the patience to conduct regular inspections. Here's the routine to follow:

- Brush your hand over each plant to see if any whiteflies, flea beetles, or leafhoppers jump or fly away.

- Look at the leaves. Large, ragged holes usually indicate slugs, beetles, or caterpillars. Be sure to check the undersides of leaves, where many of these little rascals like to hide.

- Inspect the stems and buds carefully because these are favorite feeding places for sucking insects like aphids and spider mites.

Grandma's GROW-HOW

Grandma Putt's flower garden looked like one of the big silk-and-velvet crazy quilts she sewed. Her beds were full of so many different kinds of flowers in so many colors, it just about took your breath away. That crazy-quilt mix kept pesky pests away, too. That's because most bad-guy bugs have definite food preferences. When they look down on a big patch of their favorite vittles, they'll drop in and chow down. But when they see a whole lot of different plants—some that they wouldn't touch even if they were starving—they generally take their appetites elsewhere.

H E L P !

Q My plants are all healthy and pest-free, but somehow they just don't seem as, well, energetic and chipper as I think they ought to be. Do you know any way I could perk them up?

A I sure do! Just mix ½ cup of apple juice per 5 gallons of water in a bucket. Next, fill a handheld sprayer bottle with the solution, and spray it on your green pals. Then get ready to watch 'em grow stronger, healthier, and much more productive! **Note:** This trick works wonders for herbs, fruits, and vegetables, too.

Keep in mind that just about all of the insects that bother flowers also plague vegetable plants. In fact, they cause a lot more trouble in vegetable gardens than they do in flower gardens! So in Chapter 6, you'll find scads of super-simple tactics for battling bad bugs.

Holey Cow!

What do you do when Rover insists on digging holes in a newly seeded area, or smack-dab in the middle of your flower beds? Draw the line! Fishing line, that is. Here's a simple two-step process that will keep the pooch out and the soil (and plants) in place:

STEP 1. Push stakes into the soil, all around the edges of the place you want to protect. Then put more stakes in a row down the middle of the area. They should sit about 7 inches above the ground.

STEP 2. Tie nylon fishing line to one of the stakes, about an inch from the top. Then, start weaving the line from stake to stake, across the mini-plot and back again. When you're finished, you'll have a big zigzag pattern. Be sure to keep the openings big enough so you can step into them easily to plant or weed.

Once the pup gets tangled up in the net a time or two, he won't prance through again! Just remember that once the plants come up, you won't be able to see the line—so when you're working in the bed, be careful you don't get trapped!

Not Here, Pal!

Can't keep Fido and Fluffy out of your big pots and planters? You've got two excellent options at your disposal:

- Soak cotton balls in orange or lemon extract or oil, and tuck them into the soil just deep enough to keep them from blowing away. Most dogs and cats hate the scent of citrus fruits. One of these homemade repellents will work for a small pot; for larger containers, use two or three cotton balls.

- Some dogs and cats aren't bothered at all by citrusy aromas (or even flavors). If that's the case at your house—or if you grow highly toxic plants like angels' trumpet (*Brugmansia*)—don't take any chances. Rub chili oil onto any leaves that are within your pet's reach. You can use either a cotton ball or a soft cloth for this job, but be sure to wear rubber gloves to avoid burning your skin.

HELP!

Q I'm so frustrated! I spent all day yesterday planting tulip bulbs. Then this morning I found them on the ground, right beside their holes, but looking untouched by tooth or claw. What could have gotten to them?

A *Sounds like a clear case of chipmunk mischief! These guys are so curious that often they dig up bulbs just to get a good sniff. Try this trick that (kooky as it sounds) has worked like a charm for me: Pop the bulbs back into their holes. Then lay a sheet over the planting bed, and set a few rocks on top to weigh it down. Leave it in place for three or four days, then take it off. By then, your scent will have faded, and I'll bet you dollars to daffodils that Chip or Dale won't bother those bulbs again!*

This Is *Not* a Restaurant!

The average backyard is full of critters that want to sink their chops into your bulbs. I've got all kinds of tricks for showing these guys the door, but these tactics work the best for protecting newly planted bulbs.

Chipmunks
- Sprinkle dried bloodmeal into the holes at planting time.

Gophers
- Before you plant your bulbs, line the bottom and sides of the hole (or planting bed) with ½-inch mesh wire. To keep the wire from restricting root growth, set it about 3 inches below your deepest-planted bulbs.

- Include bluebells (*Hyacinthoides*, formerly called *Scilla*) in your bulb garden—gophers won't go near the pretty little things!

Mice
- Circle the bed with a fence made of fine-mesh wire that extends 3 to 4 inches aboveground and 6 to 8 inches below.

- Don't mulch until after you know the ground has frozen solid.

Squirrels
- After you've planted your bulbs, lay a piece of screen wire, or an old window screen, over the bed, and cover it with about ¼ inch of soil. Once the ground has settled, remove the screen.

- Plant lots of daffodils—it's the one bulb that squirrels won't touch!

Voles
- Sprinkle Bon Ami® powder cleanser into the holes before you plant.

Take 2

Are rascally rabbits and other critters snacking on your flower and bulb shoots as fast as they appear? Simply cut the bottoms off some plastic milk jugs, and slip one bottomless jug over each group of shoots. Push the bottom inch or so of each jug into the soil to secure it. Leave the barriers in place for a few weeks, then slip them off again, and save 'em for next year.

Oh, Deer, Oh, Deer

One classic deer-chasing tip is to tuck deodorant soap, smelly old socks, pouches of baby powder, or other aromatic stuff among your targeted plants. It works, too, unless the deer are on the brink of starvation. But I don't think you want those odors in your flower garden—I know I wouldn't want them in mine! Believe it or not, there are some very attractive plants that will send deer scooting off to friendlier pastures, at least much of the time. Castor-oil plant is a guaranteed deer chaser. But it's also highly poisonous to humans and other animals, so you need to use it with caution. Safe options include catnip, chives, garlic, lavender, onions, and spearmint.

The one odiferous deer deterrent I do recommend for a flower garden is the urine of a major predator like a cougar, wolf, or coyote. You probably don't want to invite any of those critters onto your turf to guard your geraniums, but you can make the deer think you have. Search online for "predator urine." Order a bottle, and sprinkle it around the perimeter of your yard according to the directions on the package. You won't even notice the odor, but the Bambi Brigade sure will!

In most areas, deer will leave these winners alone:

Annuals
- Ageratum (*Ageratum houstonianum*)
- Garden verbena (*Verbena x hybrida*)
- Snapdragon (*Antirrhinum majus*)

Perennials
- Common bleeding heart (*Dicentra spectabilis*)
- Delphiniums (*Delphinium*)
- Irises (*Iris*)
- Peonies (*Paeonia*)

Bulbs
- Common snowdrop (*Galanthus nivalis*)
- Crocuses (*Crocus*)
- Crown imperial (*Fritillaria imperialis*)
- Daffodils (*Narcissus*)

Quick Fix

No matter what kind of predator urine you use to deter deer, you'll have to change your "brand" periodically. Deer are creatures of habit, and they quickly get used to just about anything in their day-to-day world that doesn't gobble them up—including a cougar that leaves its scent on the ground, but never seems to appear.

CHAPTER
4

RADIANT ROSES
The Queen of Flowers in a Flash

**The way some folks carry on, you'd think that a rosebush
is nothing but a disaster waiting to happen. Well, friends,
I'm here to tell you that it just ain't so! In fact, some kinds
of roses are among the fastest-growing, easiest-going
shrubs you could ever hope to find, and the bag of
tricks in this chapter will make caring for them a snap.
So go ahead—promise yourself a rose garden!**

**The key to success
with roses lies in
finding types that
suit your growing
conditions and
require only as
much care as you
have the time and
patience to provide.
Or, to put it another
way, these so-
called prima donnas
are no different
from any other
plant in your yard!**

A WONDERLAND OF ROSES

People have been cultivating roses for more than
10,000 years. In the process, they've developed a
mind-boggling multitude of colors, fragrances,
flower forms, plant sizes, growth habits, and degrees
of hardiness. And that's good news for impatient
gardeners for one reason: No matter what kind of
growing conditions you have, or what job you want
roses to perform in your yard, there's one—or more—
that will fill the bill with a minimum of time and
effort on your part. Let's take a brief look at the roster.

A Rose for Every Purpose

Serious rose growers divide their beloved beauties
into five basic categories. Once you know the

differences, you can choose the type that requires only as much care and attention as you want to give it—and not find yourself saddled with plants that will be nothing but time-consuming nuisances.

Hybrid teas and grandifloras. These are the best known of all roses. They both bloom from spring through frost, producing long stems with long, pointed buds that open into large, high-centered blossoms. The difference between them is that hybrid teas generally have only one blossom at the end of each stem, while grandifloras produce their blooms both individually and in small clusters. Unfortunately, the plants themselves are almost skimpy-looking, with both flowers and foliage tending to cluster toward the top. They look best when planted in groups of at least three, with shorter plants at their "feet" to hide the bare, lower stems.

Landscape roses. This is a sort of catchall classification consisting of roses that are used in the same way you'd use other flowering shrubs: as groundcovers, hedges, or background plants in mixed borders. Floribundas, polyanthas, rugosas, musk roses, and English roses all fall into this category. Unlike hybrid teas and grandifloras, these plants look good even when they're not blooming. What's more, many of them are the answer to an impatient gardener's prayers—cold-hardy, disease-resistant, and as close to trouble-free as a living thing can get.

Old garden roses. These are species and pioneer hybrid roses that date back to 1867 and earlier. They vary considerably in hardiness, length of bloom

HOPEFUL NEWS FOR HYBRID TEA LOVERS

Hybrid tea roses have earned a reputation as the spoiled brats of the plant world—and most of them do everything they can to live up to it! Of all roses, they're the most prone to pests, diseases, cold-weather damage, and other cultural problems. But plant breeders are constantly working to produce hardier varieties. New ones come out almost every year, so if you have your heart set on a hybrid tea, just make sure you do your homework. To find the best choices for your yard, consult gardening magazines and specialty catalogs, the Internet, your local gardening club, and (of course) your local Cooperative Extension Service.

time, and growth habit (meaning that they can also fall into the landscape or climbing categories). But they all have one thing in common: the powerful fragrance that no modern hybrid can match.

Climbing roses. This type produces canes that range anywhere from 6 to 30 feet long. They can't support themselves, as true vines do, but when properly trained and tied, they function in exactly the same way.

Miniature roses. These are "scale models" of hybrid teas, landscape roses, and climbers. The bush types tend to stay dainty and compact, but many of the climbers and groundcovers produce canes 8 feet or more in length. This makes them ideal in a small yard, where you want the look of a rose without the bulk of the big types. The one downside of minis is that most have little or no fragrance.

Quick Fix

When shopping for a climbing rose, choose one that will match the size of its support structure when the plant reaches maturity. If the canes aren't long enough, you won't get the coverage you want; if they're too long, you'll find yourself with a *lot* of pruning to do.

HELP!

Q I'd love to try my hand at growing roses, but I sure don't want to spend my summer weekends spraying, pinching, and pruning. Can you recommend a fuss-free rose for me?

A I sure can! Rugosa rose, a.k.a. beach rose, hedgehog rose, or sea tomato, is a truly trouble-free shrub. It hates being sprayed and never needs pruning. Just give it full sun and well-drained soil, and stand back—it'll give you a bounty of fragrant, white, clear pink, or purplish pink flowers from late spring into fall, followed by large, plump, tomato-red hips. The glossy, disease-resistant foliage is green in summer and yellow in fall. In short, this rose is everything an impatient gardener could ask for!

Standards of Elegance

A standard, or "tree," rose is not a specific category like those we discussed earlier. It's simply one that's been altered to grow on a single, tree-like stem. The process involves grafting the bottom of a stem of one kind of rose onto a rootstock, then grafting the canes of another kind (the showy part) onto the top of the stem. Hybrid teas, floribundas, and polyanthas—both full-size and miniature—are all popular candidates for this special procedure. My favorites, though, are the "weeping" standards made from rambling, climbing, or groundcover roses. Many garden centers sell these elegant creations, but as you might expect, you'll find the greatest variety at nurseries and in catalogs that specialize in roses.

Well Rooted

The vast majority of rosebushes available at your local garden center are also really two plants in one: the canes of a showy variety grafted onto the roots of a hardier type. If you live in a cold climate, look for roses that have been grown from cuttings (called *own-root* roses). Why? Because if severe winter weather kills the top of a grafted rose, any shoots that appear in the spring will come from the roots—and what the new plant will look like is anybody's guess. But if an own-root bush dies back, the new growth will be the very same rose you started with!

READY, SET, PLANT!

Even though roses are flowering shrubs, you can't treat them quite like other shrubs at planting time. They demand a little specialized treatment to get them started on the right root so they'll thrive in your yard with the least amount of attention from you. The process isn't difficult, but it is important to do it right. Read on for everything you need to know.

Grandma Putt used to plant parsley in all her rose beds because she said it made the roses' fragrance more intense. Don't ask me why, but it sure worked—and it still works in my garden today!

Their Place in the Sun

Believe it or not, you can solve 90 percent of your rose-growing problems before you even put the bushes in the ground just by giving them the best possible growing conditions. If you home in on exactly the right location, your roses will take off at a gallop! Here are three points to consider when selecting a site:

🌿 Give them as much sunlight as possible. That means at least six hours a day, and ideally eight or more throughout the growing season. Although some roses can survive in less light, most of them won't bloom well, and they'll be more prone to diseases.

🌿 An open, airy site goes a long way toward keeping diseases from getting a foothold. A south- or east-facing piece of ground, with some sort of shelter or windbreak to the northwest side, is a rose's idea of heaven on earth.

🌿 Roses need fertile, well-drained soil with a pH that's between 5.5 and 6.5. Amend yours as necessary, according to the guidelines in Chapter 9. But what if the only sunny, airy site in your yard is hopelessly hard or soggy—or maybe so sweet or sour that no amount of tinkering will fix it? Just build raised beds, and fill them with a half-and-half mixture of quality topsoil and compost.

Take 2

When you've planned a garden wedding or other outdoor gathering, and you're concerned that your roses won't reach their peak of bloom in time for the big event, this trick just *might* save the day: Spread aluminum foil on the ground between the bushes. (This is an excellent way to recycle gently used foil.) The extra light reflecting off the foil should hasten their blooming by a full two weeks. Of course, you'll want to apply a more attractive mulch before the guests arrive!

Go Bare

When it comes time to buy roses, you can choose between bare-root and container-grown plants. My advice is to go with the bare-root versions because they seem to settle in more quickly than their potted counterparts. Just one word of caution: Don't buy your bare-root babies at the local garden center. Instead, order them from a top-notch mail-order nursery to ensure your plants a better start in life. When you order plants through the mail, they'll be delivered in a nice roomy carton with their whole natural root system intact and gently swathed in sphagnum moss (or a similar wrapping). And they'll show their gratitude by quickly springing to life in your garden!

Plan Ahead

Having sung the praises of bare-root roses, I must confess that they *do* have one drawback: They need to be planted while they're dormant, in either late fall or very early spring, when the weather can be mighty chilly. (On the other hand, you can plant container-grown roses any time the ground isn't frozen; see "Planting a Container-Grown Rose" on page 161.) The simple solution to this dilemma is to plan ahead. In early fall, dig the holes and get the soil ready according to the directions in "Planting a Bare-Root Rose" (at right). When your roses finally arrive, it takes just minutes to get them settled in the ground. Then after your future bloomers are all snug in their beds, you can rush indoors for a cup of warm cocoa!

Bare-Root-Rose Booster Bath

To get your bare-root roses off to a strong, healthy start, give them a preplanting bath in this energizing elixir.

> 1 tbsp. of baby shampoo
> 1 tbsp. of corn syrup
> 1 tbsp. of 5-8-5 or 5-10-5 garden fertilizer
> 1 gal. of warm water

Mix all of the ingredients in a bucket, and soak the roots in the solution overnight. Then after you've planted your bare-root babies, sprinkle the mixture around your established rosebushes—they'll love you for it!

Planting a Bare-Root Rose

Whether you're planting a hybrid tea rose or one of its less finicky cousins, there's just one note: If your new rose is a climber, make sure your trellis or arbor is in place *before* you put the plant in the ground. If you plant first and install the support structure later, you could wind up damaging a lot of roots—and getting plenty of scratches from thorny canes in the process. The road to success begins with this five-step process:

Dig the planting hole.

STEP 1. Dig a hole that's at least 16 inches wide and 16 inches deep.

STEP 2. Mix about one-third of the excavated soil with plenty of composted (*not* fresh!) manure. A 3-inch layer, or half of a 40-pound bag, will do the trick.

STEP 3. Shovel half of this mixture into the hole, and mound it into a cone.

STEP 4. Set the plant in place with its roots arranged around the cone, and gently cover the roots with more of your amended soil. Continue filling the hole with alternate shovelfuls of soil and the manure-soil mixture from your wheelbarrow.

Mix the soil with composted manure.

STEP 5. Finish by sprinkling a tablespoon of Epsom salts over the soil surface—it's a powerful source of magnesium, which roses crave. Then water slowly and deeply, following my shrub-watering guidelines in Chapter 2. Follow up with a drink of my Rose Start-Up Tonic (see page 161), and top that off with a 2- to 3-inch layer of organic mulch.

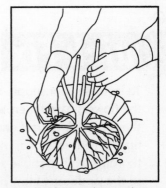

Set the plant in place, with its roots arranged around the cone.

The Question of Depth

The ideal planting depth for roses varies, depending on where you live and the way the plant has been propagated.

Own-root roses. If your winter temperatures stay above 10°F, set the plant so that the crown (the point where the roots and stem join) is even with or just a little below the soil surface. In cold-winter areas, setting the crown about an inch below the surface will provide extra protection from severe weather.

Grafted roses. In mild-winter regions, plant your roses with the graft union (the knobby-looking area just above the roots) at or slightly above the soil surface. In colder climates, the deeper you bury the union, the better chance your plant will have of surviving frigid weather—but the fewer canes it is likely to produce. So you can position the graft just above ground level, and protect it against the cold—while praying for a mild winter! Or you can opt for security over lushness and set the union anywhere from 1 to 4 inches below ground level.

AN A-PEELING MEAL

Whenever you plant a rose, do what I do: Toss a couple of banana peels into the hole before you fill it up with soil. But don't stop there—every time you eat a banana, bury the skin about an inch deep beside one of your rosebushes. These power-packed "wrappers" are full of nutrients that roses need for good health, including potassium, phosphorus, magnesium, calcium, sulfur, sodium, and silica.

uick Fix

To increase your supply of roses, snip off 6- to 8-inch-long stem tips after all the flowers have fallen, and remove all of the leaves except for one or two at the top. Stick the cut end into a raw potato, then plant the cutting (potato first) in your rose bed, with half of the stem's length below the ground. Water thoroughly, then shove a glass jar over the cutting, a little way into the soil, so the jar doesn't blow over. Come spring, when you remove the jar, you should see a brand-new baby rosebush!

Planting a Container-Grown Rose

The procedure for planting a rose that's been grown in a pot is almost the same as it is for a bare-root bush. Here's the routine:

STEP 1. Before planting, water the rose thoroughly, but leave it in its pot until the last possible minute to keep the roots moist.

STEP 2. Dig a hole that's about twice as wide and twice as deep as the root-ball, and prepare the soil according to Steps 2 and 3 in "Planting a Bare-Root Rose (see page 159)." In this case, though, flatten the soil cone slightly so that the root-ball can sit on top of it.

STEP 3. Take the rose out of its container. (If it doesn't want to budge, run a knife around the inside edge.) Using your fingers, loosen the soil on the root-ball, and gently untangle any coiled roots.

STEP 4. Set the plant on top of the cone, adding or removing soil as necessary to reach the right planting depth (see "The Question of Depth" at left). Spread the loosened roots down over the sides of the cone as much as possible.

STEP 5. Finish up just as you would with a bare-root rose.

Rose Start-Up Tonic

Here's the perfect meal to get both bare-root and container-grown roses off to a good, healthy start in life.

> 1 tbsp. of dishwashing liquid
> 1 tbsp. of hydrogen peroxide
> 1 tsp. of vitamin B1 plant starter
> 1 tsp. of whiskey
> 1/2 gal. of warm water

Mix all of the ingredients in a watering can. Then pour the solution all around the root zone of each newly planted (or transplanted) rosebush.

TENDER LOVIN' ROSE CARE

Well, now that you've seen how simple it is to choose, plant, and even propagate roses, let's take a look at the routine TLC they require. Don't worry—this is not the big, time-consuming headache that some folks make it out to be. In fact, it's downright easy—and a lot of fun, besides!

To give your roses a potent dose of magnesium and potassium, simply bury avocado skins in their beds near the base of each bush.

Please Pass the Chow

Roses are renowned for their hearty appetite, but it's easily satisfied with this simple two-part plan:

- ☙ In mid- to late spring, mix 4 parts bonemeal, 1 part Epsom salts, and 1 part 5-10-5 dry, organic fertilizer in a bucket or tub. Then give each bush 1 heaping tablespoon of the mixture, or work in 4 pounds per 100 square feet of rose bed. Store any leftovers in a tightly sealed container for later use.

- ☙ Every three weeks or so after that, give each plant 1 pint of an elixir made from 1 cup of beer, 2 teaspoons of instant tea granules, and 1 teaspoon each of dishwashing liquid, fish fertilizer, hydrogen peroxide, and organic rose food mixed in 2 gallons of warm water.

The crucial thing to remember is to stop fertilizing roses about eight weeks before you expect the first frost in your area. (Because that date can vary, my rule of green thumb is to close the "restaurant" by July 15 in the North and August 15 in the South.) Feeding after that time will encourage the plants to produce tender, new growth, which will be prone to winter damage. You *should*, however, apply a mixture of 1 cup of bonemeal and 1/2 cup of Epsom salts around the base of each bush before the ground freezes and you mulch your roses for the winter. This snack won't promote new shoot growth, but it will give the roots a big boost before their long winter's nap. Then tuck your roses in tight with a hearty layer of mulch so they'll be snug as a bug in a rug until spring.

Water Well—and Carefully

Like most garden plants, roses need about 1 inch of water each week while they're actively growing. Your mission is to monitor the output from Mother Nature's "sprinklers" so you can make up for any deficiency. As we discussed back in Chapter 2, the best tool for delivering moisture to a shrub (or any other plant) is a soaker hose. That's especially true for roses, which tend to attract fungal diseases like a picnic attracts ants.

As further protection against diseases—and to conserve moisture in the soil—keep your roses mulched with at least 2 inches of organic material, such as pine needles, shredded bark, or compost.

HOW SWEET IT IS!

Impatient gardeners can't wait to see their roses in full bloom. If that sounds like you, then try this sweet trick: To make cut rosebuds unfurl lickety-split, simply stir a spoonful of sugar into their water. They'll open up right before your very eyes!

It's in the Pipeline

A climbing rose—especially one of the old-timers—looks great growing up the trunk of a tree and into the branches. There's only one problem: The tree's roots tend to drain off most of the moisture, and the rose's roots dry up. To make sure the rose gets its thirst quenched, sink a 2-foot length of 2-inch-diameter pipe into the ground near the bush. Rain will fall into the pipe and travel straight to the rose's roots. During dry spells, shove your hose nozzle into the pipe, and let the water trickle in slowly for 15 minutes or so.

Quick Fix

The classic rose-pruning advice is to always trim just above a bud and to slope the cut at a 45-degree angle away from the bud. But guess what? After years of practice, I've found that simply whacking whole plants back by half with hedge trimmers works just as well. Granted, the plants don't look so glamorous at first, but once they leaf out, you'll hardly notice the difference.

Rose Pruning Demystified

When you first start growing roses, learning to prune them in exactly the right way can be downright intimidating. But don't fret—with these simple guidelines and just a little practice, you'll soon be doing the job like a pro:

- First, follow my "3-D" rule: Trim out any dead, diseased, or damaged stems, cutting back to healthy, white-centered wood.

- When you spot crossing or rubbing canes, remove the smaller of the two. The reason: Repeated rubbing can cause disease-drawing wounds in the wood.

- Prune weak or spindly branches. They won't bloom well, so there's no point in keeping them on the bush. (On a large rose, such as a hybrid tea, "spindly" means any shoot that's narrower and shorter than a pencil.)

- On established roses, remove up to one-third of the oldest canes each year. This will encourage vigorous, free-flowering new growth to form.

- If you have hybrid teas, floribundas, or shrub roses that bloom right through the growing season, your clipping job doesn't stop with just an annual pruning. You also need to snip off faded flowers—or cut lots of fresh ones for indoor bouquets. The more you cut, the more flowers your plants will produce. In fact, they'll reward you with gorgeous blooms well into fall!

Grandma's **GROW-HOW**

No matter how careful I was, I always ended up getting pricked and scratched as I tended to my roses. That is, until I remembered this trick from Grandma Putt: Use clothespins! Even if you never dry your laundry on a line anymore, don't get rid of your old clip-type clothespins. Stash a few with your garden tools, and whenever you go out to cut roses for bouquets, use one handy clothespin to hold each thorny stem as you snip it off. That way, you'll get no unexpected jabs.

When you're finished pruning, coat each cut surface with a dab of white glue. It'll keep pests and diseases from moving into the cane.

The Bedtime Ritual

Just like small children, roses appreciate a little extra attention before they go to sleep. First, to get them in the mood for their long winter's nap, stop removing spent flowers in late summer or early fall, three to five weeks before the first expected frost in your area. Also, stop fertilizing in midsummer (see "Please Pass the Chow" on page 162), but keep on watering so your plants don't go to bed thirsty.

If you live where winter temperatures dip below 0°F (Zone 6 and north), it's a good idea to protect hybrid teas, grandifloras, floribundas, and most English roses. Once the ground has frozen, pile shredded bark, soil, or

SCAT, CATS!

If roving cats are making mischief in your yard, roses can be mighty handy to have around. How so? When you prune the plants, spread the thorny canes on freshly tilled soil to keep Fluffy from using it as a litter box. Or lay them on the ground under birdbaths, feeders, and nesting boxes to protect your fine-feathered friends. (This trick will also keep raccoons out of your vegetable patch—or your garbage can.)

HELP!

Q I'm confused as all get-out about when to prune my roses. Spring, summer, fall—what's the best time?

A It all depends on the kind of roses you've got. Prune continual bloomers, like hybrid teas, in late winter or early spring—just as some of the buds on the largest canes are beginning to swell, but before the plants start sending out new shoots and leaves. For roses that bloom only once in late spring to early summer (like many shrub and old roses), do your pruning after all the flowers have faded. Otherwise, you'll lose this year's blossoms.

compost over the base of the stems in an 8- to 12-inch-tall mound. Remove the mulch in early spring, so new shoots can easily emerge.

Climbing roses respond well to additional winter protection, especially in Zone 6 and north. How much protection depends on the climate:

- In extremely cold regions and for marginal varieties, remove the plants from their supports and bend them down to the ground (very carefully so as not to break the stems!). Cover the plants with 6 inches of soil, wait until the ground has frozen, and then add enough straw mulch to cover the mound to a depth of about 3 inches.

- In less frigid regions and for hardier climbing types, pack straw around the canes while they are still attached to the trellis or support. Then wrap burlap around the straw, and hold it securely in place with twine.

ROSES ARE *NOT* BORN TO TROUBLE

Like any other plants, roses can attract their share of miseries. But most of those problems are easy to solve—and even easier to prevent. Here are my best secrets for doing both.

Anytime your roses are looking a little run-down, rake away the mulch, then sprinkle 2 or 3 tablespoons of Epsom salts around each bush. Lightly scratch the salts into the soil, and put the mulch back. You should notice a big difference in just a few weeks.

Here's to Good Health!

Roses are notorious for being fungus magnets, but that doesn't necessarily have to be the case. Just follow this simple problem-prevention plan:

- Start with disease-resistant plants, and give them the kind of healthy surroundings we talked about earlier: a site with well-drained soil, full sun, and good air circulation.

- Install soaker hoses in the beds so the plants' leaves will remain dry whenever you water.

❧ Regularly inspect your bushes, and remove any diseased leaves the minute you spot them; that way, you'll stop trouble before it gets out of hand. If the fungi have gotten a head start on you, clip off all the affected growth, and spray the plant from top to bottom with my Fungus-Fighter Tonic (see page 223).

❧ At the end of the growing season, give your rose beds a good, thorough cleanup. Cut back the canes, rake up all dropped leaves and other plant debris, and dispose of it. This will deprive the fungi of a cozy winter hideaway. (If you're certain the debris is free of pests and disease germs, toss it into the compost bin; otherwise, send it off with the trash.)

If you practice this routine faithfully, you stand a pretty good chance of keeping your roses entirely fungus-free. And even if a disease does strike, the plants should be strong enough to fend off major damage.

In Good Company

A lot of folks rely on companion planting to keep their vegetable crops growing strong (see Chapter 6). Choosing the right neighbors is a super-fast way to work wonders for your roses, too. In particular, pairing them with any member of the onion family can help protect your plants from three of a rose's most dreaded adversaries: black spot, mildew, and aphids. You have plenty of attractive options, like common chives, which have pretty pink

Quick Fix

Nothing can ruin the look of a rose faster than a fungal disease called powdery mildew. It looks just like it sounds: dusty, grayish white spots that start on the leaves and spread to the whole plant. To keep this nasty stuff at bay, just spray all of your roses once a week, beginning in early spring, with a 50-50 mixture of milk and water. Spray early in the day so that the foliage can dry before nightfall, and make sure you cover the entire plant from top to bottom, including the undersides of all the leaves.

flowers that are a beautiful addition to any garden. And many low-growing ornamental onions also make fine rose companions. Two of my favorites are the yellow-flowered lily leek and the rose-purple to pink-flowered nodding onion. Check online or at your local nursery for even more options.

Public Rose Enemy Number One

A number of insects target roses (see "Uninvited Guests" on page 170), but by far the most bothersome of the bunch are Japanese beetles. Unchecked, they can turn leaves, buds, and flowers to shreds almost overnight. Here are three simple ways to end their dining pleasure.

The shakedown. Japanese beetles hate to eat alone, so hundreds of them will zero in on one plant and ignore the bush right next to it. That makes them prime candidates for mass drowning. Simply fill a wide bowl with water, and add a few drops of dishwashing liquid to break the surface tension. Hold the bowl under a beetle-infested branch and shake it gently; the pests will tumble into the soapy water and that'll be all she wrote! Just one note: You need to perform this trick in the morning or evening. At those times of day, when you knock the beetles from their perches, they tend to drop straight down; if you disturb them at midday, they generally fly off to make mischief elsewhere.

The cocktail party. If you'd rather not stand around shaking buggy branches, set a pan of soapy water on the ground about 25 feet from plants you want to protect. In the center of the pan, stand a can or jar with an inch

JUMPIN' GERANIUMS!

Geranium maculatum is a delicate-looking plant with pretty little pink flowers—you'd sure never take it for a killer! But just place it where you've got Japanese beetle problems, and stand back. As if by magic, the beetles are drawn to it, and when they eat the leaves, they die! Other kinds of geraniums deliver a less potent punch: Their leaf juices don't kill the pests, but they do knock them out for eight hours or so—thereby giving you time to scoop them up and drown them in a bucket of soapy water.

or so of grape juice in it. (Japanese beetles go gaga for grape juice!) Then cover the top of the can with a piece of window screening. The beetles will make a beeline for the juice, fall into the water, and drown.

The hit squad. You don't have to fight the beetle wars alone: There are some powerful allies in both the plant and animal kingdoms that are ready to do battle. Garlic, rue, tansy, catnip, and larkspur all release chemicals that send Japanese beetles packin'. A lot of birds gobble up the pests by the bushelful, and two different kinds of tachinid flies kill 'em off in other ways. You can find the flies for sale in garden-supply catalogs, and for the lowdown on enticing winged warriors to your turf, see Chapter 10.

To end your Japanese beetle woes once and for all, get some milky spore disease (*Bacillus popilliae*) from a garden center or catalog, and apply it to your turf according to the package directions. It stays in the soil for years, killing grubs as they hatch.

Grandma Putt's Simple Soap Spray

This old-time remedy kills off just about any soft-bodied insect you can name—which is why you'll find it recommended as a time-saving weapon of choice, particularly for roses. And you couldn't ask for a simpler recipe!

½ bar of Fels-Naptha® or Octagon® soap, shredded*
2 gal. of water

Add the soap to the water and heat, stirring, until the soap dissolves completely. Let the solution cool, then pour it into a handheld sprayer bottle, and let 'er rip. Test it on a few leaves first, though, because some plants are ultra-sensitive to soap. And be sure to rinse the residue off the foliage after the bugs have bitten the dust because lingering soap film can damage leaves.

* You'll find Fels-Naptha and Octagon soap in either the bath soap or laundry section of your local supermarket.

UNINVITED GUESTS

It's no secret that roses are top menu choices for many hungry insects. The good news is that these visitors rarely cause fatal damage if you catch them in time. Examine your plants every day, or at least every few days, and spring into action at the first sign of trouble. Here's what to look for and how to respond.

DAMAGE	UNINVITED DINER	WHAT TO DO
Curled, sticky, and/or distorted leaves	Aphids	• Remove them with a strong spray of water from your hose. • For severe infestations, apply Grandma Putt's Simple Soap Spray (see page 169).
A hole in the end of a pruned stem	Cane borers	• Cut off and destroy (don't compost) infested canes. • Apply white glue to the pruning cuts.
Flower buds and young shoots that turn black and die	Rose midges	• Remove and destroy any and all affected plant parts. • Spray with Grandma Putt's Simple Soap Spray.
Brown, spotted petals; deformed buds that never open; young leaves distorted and yellow-flecked	Thrips	• Blast them off with your hose. • Remove and destroy infested leaves and flowers. • Spray with Grandma Putt's Simple Soap Spray. • Encourage (or buy) predatory mites.
Oval, round, or scalloped holes in leaves	Leaf-cutter bees	• Remove the damaged leaves if they bother you. Otherwise, do nothing—these tiny, nonstinging bees are important pollinators of many garden plants.

CHAPTER
5

VERSATILE VINES AND GROUNDCOVERS
Hardworking Landscaping Helpers

I can't think of any other plants that perform such heroic
feats around the old homestead while asking so little
in return. In other words, they're just what the doctor
ordered to cure any gardener's impatience! In this chapter,
you'll find some of my best tried-and-true tips for
putting vines and groundcovers (including ornamental
grasses) to work in your yard—and helping them live
up to their fullest problem-solving potential.

VINES TURN EYESORES INTO ASSETS

Think about it: What other plants can turn a
chain-link fence into a hedge, a blank wall into
a haven for hummingbirds, or a wide-open arbor
into a cozy hideaway? Of course, they can't do the
job all by themselves. But if you choose the right
vine for the task at hand, and one that's happy in
your growing conditions, then all you need to do
is give it some basic TLC. It'll solve some of your
most perplexing yard-care dilemmas—fast!

**If you want to plant a
privacy screen and you
have a tiny yard, even the
slimmest shrubs will hog
a lot of valuable space.
So do yourself a favor:
Install a fence or sturdy
trellis, and cloak it with
vines of your choice.**

Double Your Pleasure

How would you like to keep your spring-blooming shrubs in flower all summer long? Or perhaps turn evergreen shrubs into fountains of color? Then plant annual vines around them. With just a little guidance from you, the stems will wind their way up through the shrubs—no trellis required! Morning glories, hyacinth beans, and scarlet runner beans all offer months of colorful flowers, and they're a snap to start from seed. For the simple directions, see "Sow, Sow, Sow Your Seeds" on page 109.

Just one word of caution: Don't put your climbers too close to the shrub's base, or they'll be shaded out of existence before they get started. Instead, plant the seeds just outside the farthest reaches of the shrub's stems. That way, the seedlings will get all the sun and rain they need to thrive. Once the stems start to climb, point them in the right direction, and then stand back and marvel at the double feature!

These are some of my favorite vines for growing at ground level:

- **Climbing hydrangea (*Hydrangea petiolaris*)**

- **English ivy (*Hedera helix*)**

- **Five-leaved akebia (*Akebia quinata*)**

- **Honeysuckles (*Lonicera*)**

- **Mountain clematis (*Clematis montana*)**

- **Sweet autumn clematis (*C. terniflora*)**

- **Virginia creeper (*Parthenocissus quinquefolia*)**

Going Down!

If you've got a steep slope that's difficult, time-consuming—or even downright dangerous—to mow, then the right vine can ease your load in a hurry. Many vines will happily cascade down a hillside, smothering grass and weeds in the process. Just plant them at the top of the slope, point them downward, and let 'em go. (To provide the ideal top-of-the-hill starter bed, cook up a Super Soil Sandwich following the directions in Chapter 9.)

When planting hillside vines, remove the leaves halfway up the stem of each plant so it can direct its energy to root formation. Bury the root-ball and bare stem in an angled trench. Then each year in late spring, pinch the growing tips to encourage side shoots to form, and use wire pins to direct those new shoots toward open spots you want to fill in. Cut back any wayward stems several times a year—or mow regularly around the edges of the planting to keep it in check.

Support Your Local Vines

All vines climb in one of three ways. Recognizing these different methods can help you choose the right support structure for your vine—or the right climber for the structure you want it to adorn.

Clinging vines. Rootlets, or "holdfasts," attach the stems firmly to any surface they encounter. English ivy and Virginia creeper are two prime examples. These vines make perfect cloaks for tree trunks, stone walls, or solid fences. Simply plant them at the base of the structure you want them to cover, and they'll scramble upward. (Just keep them away from aluminum or vinyl siding, or wood walls that may need painting periodically.)

Tendril vines. Little shoots that grow out from the stems hold these climbers to their supports. Grapes and sweet peas fall into this category. Clematis climb in a similar way, but they wrap their whole leafstalk around any structure that's thin enough. Strings, netting, branches, and small trellis slats will work fine for the lighter tendril types, but grapes demand a stout, strong arbor made of wood and heavy wire. If the plant already has long shoots, arrange them on the support in the direction you want them to go. Fasten them loosely with twine or coated twist ties until the tendrils begin to grip (it shouldn't take more than a day or so).

Twining vines. As the name implies, these types twist their stems around their supports. Annual

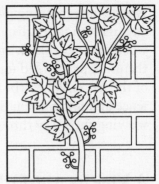

Clinging vines use "holdfasts" to attach themselves to surfaces.

Tendril vines send out little shoots that wrap themselves around thin supports.

Twining vines twist their stems around their supports.

173

twiners like morning glories and black-eyed Susan vine grow happily on any lightweight trellis, chain-link fence, or even string. On the other hand, woody twiners like wisteria need the sturdiest arbor or trellis you can give them. Plant the seed (or, in the case of wisteria, the transplant) at the base of the fence. When the first long stems appear, gently guide them up the fence and fasten them lightly with twine or twist ties. Once the vines start weaving their way through the grid, they'll need no more help from you.

A Vine by Any Other Name

Technically speaking, procumbent (a.k.a. scrambling) vines are not vines at all, but simply plants that have ultra-long, weak stems. This category, which includes climbing snapdragon, bougainvillea, and some varieties of honeysuckle and jasmine—as well as indeterminate tomatoes and climbing roses—lacks any support mechanism. That means you need to attach the stems to a support structure. If you're using an open work system like a chain-link or rail fence, lacy iron gate, or window frame, use twine or twist ties to fasten the growing stems to various uprights and cross pieces. In the case of a flat surface like a door or a solid-board fence, insert screws or nails, and tie the stems to them.

HELP!

Q This summer, I tried to grow moonflower vines through my shrubs, but they started blooming so late in the season, I barely got a half-dozen flowers before the first frost hit and killed the vines. Do you know any trick that will make them bloom earlier?

A *If you want blooms earlier in the season, you need to give your moonflowers a jump start in spring. Sow the seeds indoors in peat pots, two or three weeks before your last frost date, and move 'em outside to the garden in early summer. They'll get growing in a jiffy, and before you know it, they'll be blooming to beat the band!*

Deck the Walls

Vines look fantastic when they're growing on
a brick or stone wall or a solid-board fence.
But unless you take a few precautions, they
can wind up doing more harm than good.
To protect your walls and your plants, train
the vines on a lattice trellis that's stationed
about 6 inches away from the wall or fence.
Besides keeping the surface clean and dry,
this maneuver will let air circulate behind
the vine—and that'll go a long way toward
stopping dastardly diseases in their tracks!

Four Steps to Vonderful Vines

Midspring is the perfect time for planting
perennial vines, and the process couldn't be
simpler. First, overspray your planting site
with my Flower Garden Soil Booster (see
page 110). Then proceed as follows:

STEP 1. Dig a hole that's 12 to 18 inches
across and about 1 foot deep.

STEP 2. Set the plant in the hole so the
crown (the point where the roots and
stems meet) is about even with the soil
surface—or 1 inch below ground level
for clematis.

STEP 3. Fill in around the roots with soil, then water well.

STEP 4. Spread a 2-inch-thick layer of organic mulch over the soil, keeping
it an inch or so away from the stems.

Be sure to put your support structure in place *before* you plant your vines. If
you set a trellis into the ground when the vine is already growing, you could

---

SUPPORT 'EM IN STYLE

The best trellises don't
simply support vining
plants; they also add
visual pizzazz to a
garden. If you'd like an
out-of-the-ordinary
touch for your yard,
you just might find
the perfect decorative
relic at a garage sale,
or right in your own
attic. Consider these
unusual possibilities:

• Iron garden gates

• Iron window bars

• Multipaned window
frames (minus the
glass, of course!)

• Old doors

• Old wooden ladders

• Orphaned brass or
iron headboards or
footboards

• Shutters

end up cutting the roots, or even trampling the plant. And it's guaranteed that you'll have to step on and compact the soil. **Note:** If you're planting bare-root vines, follow the instructions in "Planting a Bare-Root Rose" (see page 159).

Prudent Pruning

Most perennial vines grow just fine without fancy pruning, but it's important to remove dead, diseased, and damaged stems the minute you see them, any time of year—which deprives pests and disease organisms of easy access to the plant. Aside from that, a quick trim every few years will keep your vines looking their best. The golden rule is to prune *after* the flowers have faded. The exact time will vary depending on your climate, but generally, you want to clip spring-flowering vines, like Carolina jessamine, Dutchman's pipe, and five-leaved akebia, in early summer. Summer-flowering vines, like climbing hydrangea, honeysuckles, and passionflowers, should be trimmed back in the fall.

Take 2

Instead of growing lightweight annual vines on plastic mesh or nylon cord, use biodegradable twine made of cotton or hemp. That way, at the end of the season, you can just pull down the plants and the "trellis" and toss the whole bundle into your compost bin, or bury it in the ground. Over time, it will break down, enriching your soil—and saving you the hassle of separating the organic matter from the synthetic stuff.

The Queen of the Climbers

For sheer impact, clematis can't be beat. The large-flowered hybrids come in just about every color, except for pure yellow, and in many multicolors. They have flat, single, semi-double, or double blooms up to 8 inches across. As befits royalty, though, these beauties are a little particular about their home ground. Old-timers put it this way: "Clematis like to have their head in the sun and their feet in the shade." So plant your queens where the stems and flowers will get full sun, but the roots will be shaded by other plants—or simply keep the soil covered with a thick layer of mulch.

A lot of folks tell me they steer clear of clematis simply because they're confused about when to prune them. Actually, once you know which type you've got, the process is a snap. The key lies in the timing.

Early-blooming clematis. These bloom in early spring to early summer. They don't really need annual pruning, but if the vines are starting to look messy, trim them right after they flower. Examples include alpine clematis and anemone clematis.

Early, large-flowered hybrids. These bloom from late spring into early summer and may rebloom in late summer. Give them an early-spring shape-up by cutting out any dead or damaged parts and trimming off the vine tips, just above any pair of plump, healthy buds. Examples include 'Barbara Jackman', 'General Sikorski', 'Niobe', and 'The President'.

uick Fix

There are plenty of good ways to fasten vines (and floppy plants) to their support structures. But when you do the job with strips of old panty hose, you get a special bonus: The nylon will attract static electricity, which will give your plants an added boost of grow power.

The Royal Diet

For such an elegant-looking plant, clematis has a very down-to-earth appetite. Just feed yours a helping of this home-cooked meal first thing in the spring, and they'll reward you with flowers fit for a king (or queen).

> **5 gal. of composted horse or cow manure***
> **½ cup of bonemeal**
> **½ cup of lime**

Shortly after the last frost, combine all of the ingredients in a wheelbarrow, and spread the mixture over the root zone of your clematis. Then bid her bon voyage, and watch her grow to town!

* Don't use fresh manure; it will burn the roots of your clematis and any other nearby plants.

Late-flowering clematis. These bloom from summer to early fall. Cut them back each year in early spring to 8 to 12 inches above the ground, just above a pair of healthy buds. Examples include 'Ernest Markham', 'Jackmanii', 'Polish Spirit', and sweet autumn clematis.

Wonderful Wisteria

For my money, there is no more beautiful sight on earth than a wisteria vine pouring out a fountain of purple or white flowers in late spring. Some folks think keeping these woody wonder vines shipshape is a major pain in the grass. But all it takes is a little snipping three times a year, which is a small price to pay for such a knockout show! Here's the annual to-do list.

Early summer. As soon as the flowers fade, trim back each side shoot to about 1 foot. If there are so many side shoots that you can hardly see what you're doing, just cut out some of them altogether, right back to the main stem. And don't worry—you can take out well over half of them and not hurt the plant.

Mid- to late summer. As the side shoots grow out again, they can get long and scraggly looking. So get out your clippers and trim 'em all again to about a foot beyond the early-summer cut.

Late winter or early spring. Tidy up your vines by pruning the side shoots back to 1 foot (about where you made the early-summer cut the previous year).

> ## BEWARE OF BERRY-BEARERS
>
> Watching birds gobbling up English ivy berries is loads of fun, but there's just one problem: After eating the berries, the birds excrete the seeds. Before you know it, seedlings are popping up all over the place and growing like wildfire. So unless you want your whole yard (or neighborhood) filled with English ivy, trim it back twice a year or so, before it can flower and produce berries. For a large planting, use hedge shears or a lawn mower with the mowing deck set on high. For a small patch, hand clippers will work just fine. And be sure to wear gloves and long sleeves because contact with English ivy can irritate your skin.

GROUNDCOVERS MAKE PERFECT PROBLEM SOLVERS

To paraphrase Mr. Shakespeare, a perennial by any other name would look as lovely—and work just as hard. I say this simply because many people use the word *groundcover* as though it were a separate botanical classification. Well, it's not. Groundcovers are simply tough-as-nails perennials that lose no time in (as the name implies) covering ground. And that trait can solve some of your most challenging landscape problems. Plus, many plants that can function as groundcovers are beautiful enough to grace any flower garden. Here's how to use these hard workers in your yard.

If you have a piece of ground where grass won't grow, but you lack the time and patience for a soil-improvement project, plant any of these winners. They all thrive in poor soil:

- **Coltsfoots (*Petasites*)**

- **Common periwinkle (*Vinca minor*)**

- **Ivies (*Hedera*)**

- **Pachysandras (*Pachysandra*)**

Have They Got a Deal for You!

If you find that your patience for lawn-care chores grows shorter with each passing year, do yourself a favor: Replace some—or even all—of your turfgrass with groundcovers, and let them do more while you do less. Here's the rundown.

Less trimming. Replace the turf under trees with shade-tolerant spreaders and put an end to tedious trimming around your tree trunks.

The basic feeding, weeding, watering, and pest-control drill is the same for groundcovers (and vines) as it is for any other annuals and perennials. So deliver routine TLC according to the simple guidelines in Chapter 3.

Less mowing. Grass needs mowing, but most other groundcovers don't. Blanket slopes and other hard-to-mow places with plants that you can let grow without needing a weekly "haircut."

Less weeding. A struggling lawn leaves plenty of room for weeds to move in—and leaves you to referee the resulting battle for root space. Give up on unhappy grass and let a more suitable groundcover crowd weeds right out of the picture.

Less raking. Sturdy groundcovers under trees will "absorb" a lot of leaves—they'll simply sift down to ground level where they'll feed the groundcover. The bonus: No raking required!

Speed Them to Success

Give groundcovers what they need to succeed, and they'll take off like Seabiscuit out of the starting gate. Follow these pointers to make sure your plants get off to a strong start and grow quickly to fill in bare areas:

- Do the math. Most groundcovers should be planted 6 to 10 inches apart. Measure the space you want to fill, and calculate how many plants you'll need per square foot. Don't skimp on plants, unless you're willing to wait longer for complete coverage.

- Say no to straight rows. A diamond planting pattern will fill the space more efficiently.

- Don't skip breakfast. Send plants off to the races with a hearty helping of my Groundcover Starter Chow (at right).

A MONEY-SAVING SHOPPING TIP

Filling a sizable space with groundcovers can get pricey if you set out in the spring to buy enough plants to fill the area. So instead, do your shopping when temperatures are rising and plant prices are falling. Look for bargains in mid- to late summer, when garden centers are eager to reduce their stock, and plants in pots are crowded and in need of division. You'll often find that you can afford twice as many containers and then get two or three plants from each pot.

🍃 Set up the sprinkler. Even drought-tolerant plants need watering when they're getting started. Make sure new plantings get about an inch of water each week, whether from rain or your faucet.

🍃 Manage with mulch. Some spreaders may take up to three years to fill in their new homes. In the meantime, cover bare ground between 'em with weed-blocking, soil-protecting mulch.

🍃 Yank weeds while they're young. Pull 'em out before they start spreading.

A Balanced Approach

The very trait that makes a plant a good groundcover—the ability to spread quickly with little or no help from you—can also make it a menace. Here's a trio of tips for ensuring that your living carpet will remain just that, and not a monster bent on conquering the whole neighborhood.

Take 2

If you're like me, you have a steady supply of leftover coffee grounds. Don't throw them out; instead, sprinkle this black gold on the soil around your vines and groundcovers. Try it and I guarantee that you'll end up with the biggest, bloomingest plants on the block!

Groundcover Starter Chow

When you plant groundcovers in well-prepared soil, they'll take off like lightning. And they'll cover ground even faster when you give them a healthy serving of my starter chow at planting time.

> **3 parts bonemeal**
> **1 part Epsom salts**
> **1 part gypsum**

Mix all of the ingredients in a bucket. Place ½ cup of the mixture in each planting hole, and spread another ½ cup on the soil surface to encourage rapid groundcover expansion.

Think "location, location, location." When using groundcovers in a flower bed or confined area, choose less vigorous types like barrenworts. In larger, open areas, go with more aggressive spreaders like Japanese pachysandra or wood anemone.

Encourage competition. One of the best ways to keep groundcovers in check is simply to plant two different kinds next to each other, and let 'em duke it out. It seems to keep them both under control.

Give them second-class accommodations. I don't mean you should neglect them, just don't provide your groundcovers with their ideal growing conditions. A case in point: Sweet woodruff will tolerate any kind of soil, and any light from dense shade to full sun, but it performs best in a moist site that gets morning sun. If you put it there, it'll take over your whole yard before you know it. On the other hand, if you plant it in dry shade, it will still thrive, but it won't stray very far.

How to Spot a Monster

If you're new to the groundcover game, it's not always easy to tell how well behaved a plant will be once it's planted in your yard. And the last thing you need is an aggressive green grower getting out of control. These clues

When planting groundcovers, it can be tricky to get the spacing just right—but it's a snap if you use this simple trick. Just find a piece of welded-wire garden fencing with 3-inch-square openings. Mark the corners of the planting area with stakes and string, then lay the fencing flat on the soil at one corner of the plot. The grid will tell you exactly where to plant, whether you're going with a diamond pattern or traditional straight rows. For 6-inch spacing, set a plant in the center of every other "hole" in the grid. For 9-inch spacing, place a plant in the center of every third "hole," and so on. When you finish a section, carefully lift the fencing and move it to the next portion of the planting area. The result is perfect spacing every time!

TOPS FOR TRICKY SPOTS

If your yard has areas where tending to turfgrass is a lot of trouble, then maybe it's time to replace that high-maintenance stuff with groundcovers (including a few vines) that will perform like champs. Here's the cream of the crop.

SOGGY SPOTS

- Dwarf Chinese astilbe (*Astilbe chinensis* var. *pumila*)
- Golden creeping Jenny (*Lysimachia nummularia* 'Aurea')
- Japanese primrose (*Primula japonica*)
- Lady's mantle (*Alchemilla mollis*)
- Rushes (*Juncus*)

DRY, PARCHED SPOTS

- Beach wormwood (*Artemisia stelleriana*)
- Lamb's ears (*Stachys byzantina*)
- Lavender cotton (*Santolina chamaecyparissus*)
- Prickly pear (*Opuntia compressa*)

UNDER TREES

- Ajuga (*Ajuga reptans*)
- Common periwinkle (*Vinca minor*)
- Hostas (*Hosta*)
- Lilyturf (*Liriope spicata*)

SUNNY SLOPES

- Creeping juniper (*Juniperus horizontalis*)
- Goldmoss stonecrop (*Sedum acre*)
- Moss phlox (*Phlox subulata*)
- Mother of thyme (*Thymus serpyllum*)
- Tawny daylily (*Hemerocallis fulva*)

SHADY SLOPES

- Ajuga (*Ajuga reptans*)
- Common periwinkle (*Vinca minor*)
- English ivy (*Hedera helix*)
- Japanese pachysandra (*Pachysandra terminalis*)
- Wintercreeper (*Euonymus fortunei*)

will help you sniff out potential super-spreaders before they get a foot, er, root in the door:

➤ Be wary of plants that have a reputation for growing "almost anywhere." That's a sure sign that they're capable of growing *everywhere*, too.

➤ Look 'em in the roots. The creeping crawlers most likely to scramble out of control are plants that spread by rhizomes and stolons. **Note:** Rhizomes and stolons are horizontal stems that grow parallel to the soil surface, forming new plants at nodes along the way. The difference between the two is that rhizomes grow under the soil, while stolons grow over the soil surface.

➤ Say a polite "No thanks" to friends and neighbors who have "plenty to share" of a particular groundcover—that's often code for a plant that's growing out of control in their yard.

Keep in mind that the list of plants that are considered to be invasive varies widely across North America. All sorts of growing conditions—such as high and low temperatures, rainfall and humidity, as well as soil texture and pH—help determine whether a plant is a rampant rambler or a well-behaved soil saver. So check with your state Department of Natural Resources or your local Cooperative Extension Service to find out which plants are considered big no-no's where you live.

Productive Pinning

Here's a smart trick that'll save you time *and* money when you're planting a groundcover that spreads fast like bugleweed or deadnettle. Buy just half the recommended number of plants

Grandma's
GROW-HOW

To keep people and pets from wearing a path through your groundcovers, do what Grandma Putt did: When you plant new ones, leave spaces for the well-worn trails your family and visitors already use. If a path appears after planting, go with the flow, and lay some stepping stones there to prevent folks from trampling your plants and compacting your soil in the process.

you need, and then trick the plants into growing even faster than usual by stimulating lots of extra root growth. The secret is to use wire pins to tack down the growing tips of the stems every 6 inches or so. Bringing the tips into close contact with the soil triggers them to send out roots at their nodes (the places where a leaf joins the stem). Those new roots pump in extra water and nutrients, and that speeds up the production of still more new shoots. The more pins you pop in, the better your results will be!

This technique is also the fastest, easiest way to anchor a vine or a climbing rose that you're using as a groundcover (see "Going Down!" on page 172).

Grow More Groundcovers

If you don't have the budget to buy a lot of groundcover plants all at once, then start small and grow your own inventory. It's easy to do with a technique called layering, which encourages plants to form roots along their stems to make new "baby" plants. This technique works

It's easy to make plant pins for your groundcovers. Just use wire cutters to snip wire clothes hangers into pieces about 6 inches long, and bend each section into a "U" shape. Then press them down into the soil against the growing plant tips.

HELP!

Q I'm tired of spending time fussing with my lawn—especially fighting a never-ending war with grubs. I plan to replace the grass with low-maintenance groundcovers, which I understand are more grub-resistant. But do you know a quick, easy way I can get rid of the grubs that are already there?

A *I sure do! Just cultivate the soil thoroughly, and you'll bring all the grubs to the surface, where birds will polish 'em off pronto. If you do your digging in spring or early fall, tilling 3 to 4 inches deep is good enough. Once the weather turns cool, though, the grubs head deeper; then you'll need to till the soil anywhere from 4 to 8 inches deep.*

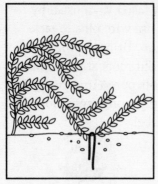

Anchor the stem in place with a pin made from a wire clothes hanger (see page 185).

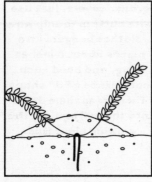

Mound soil over the stem.

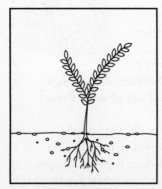

When roots have formed, move the baby plant to its permanent location.

well for any groundcover that has spreading stems—even woody types like bearberry and cotoneaster. With a little layering, you can turn 25 plants into 100 in a single growing season! Here's all there is to it:

STEP 1. Gather your gear. You'll need a small sharp knife, rooting hormone, wire pins, hand pruners, and a trowel.

STEP 2. Choose a spreading stem on one of your groundcovers, and use the knife to gently scrape away the outer bark. Dust the scraped area with rooting hormone.

STEP 3. Hold the scraped area down so that it touches the soil surface, and anchor it in place with a wire pin.

STEP 4. Mound 1 to 2 inches of soil over the stem. Repeat this procedure with as many stems as you can.

STEP 5. Check the mounded soil frequently, and water to keep it moist, but not saturated.

STEP 6. After a few weeks, tug on the layered stems. If you feel some resistance, that means that roots have formed. Use the hand pruners to cut the stem between the mother plant and the baby plant.

STEP 7. With the trowel, carefully lift the rooted plantlet out of the soil, and then replant it in the area you want to cover.

A Yearly Ritual

Although groundcovers demand little in the way of TLC, they put on their best show when you perform one annual ceremony: Cut the whole patch back by about a third of its height. Depending on the size of the area (and your patience level), you can do the job with hedge shears, hand pruners, or a string trimmer. As for timing, clip summer- or fall-flowering groundcovers in the spring, and trim spring bloomers right after they finish flowering.

New Life for Old Groundcovers

Sometimes an aging groundcover starts to thin out, and bare ground shows through among its leaves. If it's planted near or under trees, chances are that the trees have grown larger and are casting too much shade. In that case, don't fight Mother Nature. Instead, interplant a shade-loving groundcover, and let it gradually take over. If shade's not the problem, then most likely your soil is suffering from malnutrition. In either case, my Terrific Topdressing (below) will recharge those sickly-looking plants fast!

Terrific Topdressing

Bring new life to old groundcovers by serving them healthy portions of this fabulous formula.

> **20 parts Milorganite®***
> **10 parts earthworm castings***
> **5 parts ground-up fresh apples**
> **$1/2$ bushel of peat moss**
> **1 can of beer**
> **4 tsp. of instant tea granules**
> **2 gal. of water**

Combine the Milorganite, earthworm castings, apples, and peat moss in a wheelbarrow, and scatter the mixture generously over any ailing groundcover. Then mix the beer and instant tea granules in the water, and immediately pour the solution over the Milorganite mixture. Your hardworking groundcover will be back in business in no time at all! (By the way, an annual springtime application will keep all of your groundcovers growing great guns.)

* Available at garden centers, in catalogs, and on the Internet.

ORNAMENTAL GRASSES SAVE TIME AND TROUBLE

Just like the eager-beaver perennials we call groundcovers, ornamental grasses (and their close cousins, rushes and sedges) can replace parts of your lawn or add razzle-dazzle to your flower beds with a fraction of the time and effort required by turfgrass and most flowering plants. In fact, just about the only attention these low-care wonders need is a quick cutting once a year. What more could an impatient gardener ask for?

Any of these ornamental grasses will say "Y'all come!" to scads of songbirds:

- Blue-eyed grass (*Sisyrinchium graminoides*)

- Fountain grass (*Pennisetum setaceum*)

- Little bluestem (*Schizachyrium scoparium*)

- Maiden grass (*Miscanthus sinensis* 'Gracillimus')

- Switch grass (*Panicum virgatum*)

- Zebra grass (*Miscanthus sinensis* 'Zebrinus')

Make the Most of Ornamentals

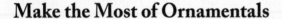

Replacing a little—or a lot—of tired, time-consuming turf with ornamental grasses can turn a ho-hum yard into a real showstopper. Follow these terrific tips to put maximum pizzazz into your landscape.

Grow 'em in groups. Avoid the tufted look of one grass plant here and another over there—that makes more work, not less! Ornamental grasses are at their best in swaths of three or five (or more), so you can really appreciate their color and texture through the seasons.

Use 'em as a backdrop. Tuck perennials and flowering shrubs in and around them. These grasses are stars in their own right, but they're also great background plantings for bright flowers.

Dress up difficult sites. These plants can be picture-pretty, but that doesn't mean they're too dainty to tackle tough conditions. See "Ornamental Grasses on the Job" (page 192) for a guide to which species to use where the growing gets tough.

Let the wind blow. Plant ornamental grasses in a spot where you can see—and hear—the wind rustling through their blades. You just might like their natural "music" better than your neighbor's wind chimes!

Skip fall cleanup. Some ornamental grasses have seed heads that birds will dine on during the winter months; others just look pretty when they're glazed with ice or dusted with snow.

Warm or Cool?

Like their turf-type cousins, ornamental grasses can be split into cool-season and warm-season groups. That tells you when they do their best growing—and when they'll do less for your landscape during their dormant periods. Here's the scoop:

Take 2

The time to cut ornamental grasses is early spring, just as new growth is starting to appear. And as payment for performing that simple chore, you get a nice crop of "hay" that you can chop up and use for mulch or add to your compost bin.

↝ Cool customers, such as blue fescue, are often evergreen or semi-evergreen, and they grow year-round in mild-winter climates. They tend

Quick Fix

When a heat wave hits, some parts of your lawn can be baked by the sun's blazing rays. Most vulnerable are strips of grass adjacent to paved areas, such as driveways, patios, and sidewalks; areas next to fences or walls; and spots just outside of glass doors or big, ground-level windows. To protect the turf, plant buffer zones of dry-heat lovers between the grass and the heat reflectors. In front of walls or fences, go with rugged ornamental grasses. Extra-tough groundcovers work well below windows and along paved surfaces. Just remember that the plants will need more water than they would if they were growing in a cooler setting.

to get growing early in the spring and usually flower before summer arrives. They may go dormant in the hot part of summer, then perk up and start growing again when the cool weather returns in the fall.

🌱 Warm-weather winners, such as Japanese silver grass, start growing a little later in the spring, bloom in summer, and enter dormancy in the fall—often with a change in foliage color that mimics the changing leaves of deciduous trees.

Give 'Em the Grow-Ahead

If you launch your non-lawn grasses with some good old TLC, they'll repay you with many years of (almost) carefree good looks. Here's your easy five-step action plan:

STEP 1. Prepare the soil, loosening it to about 6 inches deep and working in an ample inch or so of compost. Clear out any weeds that might compete with the grasses while they're just getting going.

STEP 2. Space the plants according to height. For example, give a grass that'll grow 2 feet tall similar side leeway. If coverage is a concern, you can tighten up the spacing a little, but don't pack 'em too close or you'll wind up having to dig and divide to relieve overcrowding.

If your ornamental grasses die out in the center, dig them up and divide them according to the guidelines in Chapter 3 (see "Divide to Multiply" on page 130). Replant only the vigorous outer portions of each clump.

What if your plants are too big to dig up? Not to worry! You have two simple options: Either use a spade to cut out pie-shaped wedges, lift them out one at a time, and replant the healthiest ones. Then fill in the remaining holes with soil. Or take the easy route, and use a post-hole digger to clean out the center of the clump. Set a small plant of the same type of grass in the hole, fill it with fresh soil, and you're good to go.

STEP 3. Set plants in the ground at the same depth as they grew in their pots or in the nursery. Aim to put the crown—where the blades and roots meet—right at the soil surface. Add a handful of my Ornamental Grass Breakfast (below) to the soil in each planting hole.

STEP 4. Water the young plants thoroughly, and tuck them in with an inch or two of mulch, which will help keep moisture in and weeds out.

STEP 5. It's important to water your ornamental grasses regularly during the first growing season, but that's all the pampering the grasses will need, at least initially. You'll want to hold off on any further feedings, because they can make your grass plants prime targets for pests and diseases.

THE KINDEST CUT OF ALL

Most warm-season grasses look great all winter long, but come springtime, they need a pretty harsh haircut to get ready for another growing season. Handheld pruning shears are fine for smaller plants, but you'll need heavy artillery to tackle the big guys, like *Miscanthus*. So go at 'em with long-handled loppers or—faster yet—a string trimmer that has a saw blade attached.

Ornamental Grass Breakfast

To give ornamental grasses a super start, plant them in early spring in well-prepared holes along with a good helping of this hearty recipe. It's just what they need to really get up and grow!

> **2 lbs. of crushed dry dog food**
> **2 lbs. of dry oatmeal**
> **1 handful of human hair**

Mix all of the ingredients together in a bucket. Toss a handful of the mixture into each planting hole and work it into the soil. Set in the plants, backfill with soil, then scatter any leftover chow on top of the soil.

ORNAMENTAL GRASSES ON THE JOB

Trade in some of your turf and eliminate some of the tricky spots in your yard with these hardworking, good-looking ornamental grasses. You'll find these and many other easy-care winners at nurseries that specialize in ornamental grasses, as well as in many garden centers, in catalogs, and online.

LOW-CARE SUPERSTAR	HOW IT GROWS	WHERE IT GROWS BEST
Indian grass (*Sorghastrum nutans*)	Clump-forming with light green-to-blue foliage that turns orange in fall; long, feathery, reddish flower clusters in late summer; grows to 3 ft. tall with 6-ft. flower stalks	Sun, dry soil, warm season, Zones 4–9
Japanese silver grass (*Miscanthus sinensis*)	Clump-forming with silvery leaves that turn shades of red and yellow in fall; silver-to-purple flower plumes from midsummer into fall; grows to 3–5 ft. tall with flower stalks of 6–10 ft.	Sun, moist soil, warm season, Zones 5–9
Quaking grass (*Briza media*)	Clump-forming with delicate flowers that shake in the breeze throughout the growing season; grows to 1–2 ft. tall with flower stalks of 2–3 ft.	Shade or sun, moist soil, cool season, Zones 4–10
Tufted hair grass (*Deschampsia cespitosa*)	Airy flower clusters age from green to gold to bronze above narrow, dark green leaves; grows to 2 ft. tall with flowers to 3 ft. tall	Shade, moist soil, cool season, Zones 4–9
Variegated hakone grass (*Hakonechloa macra* 'Aureola')	Spreading with green-striped yellow leaves that resemble bamboo; grows 1¹/₂ to 2 ft. tall	Shade, moist soil, warm season, Zones 6–9

CHAPTER
6

MOUTHWATERING VEGGIES

A Hasty, Tasty Harvest

Why would an impatient gardener even think about growing food crops? I'll tell you why: When you grow your own vegetables, you're rewarded with a lot more than just a steady supply of food. You can get the kind of sweet, rich, old-time flavor and texture that comes only fresh from the garden—from varieties that commercial farmers don't grow. So harvest the tips, tricks, and tonics in this chapter, and get growing!

When you're choosing a site for your garden, get out early in the morning and look for the spot that feels the toastiest: A place that warms up early in the day will also warm up early in the spring, thereby giving you a jump on the growing season.

DOING THE GROUNDWORK

I know I've said this many times before, but it bears repeating: The first step on the road to success—and lower maintenance—in any garden is careful planning. That's particularly true in a vegetable garden because vegetables in general are a lot more finicky about their location and growing conditions than other kinds of plants are. But don't let that hold you back! The tips in this section will put you well on your way to a heavenly harvest in a hurry. Chances are, as you're pondering your future plot, you'll also rekindle some mighty happy memories. (Remember all those warm summer mornings you spent in Grandma's garden?)

Basic Decisions

A vegetable garden can be as small as a window box, as big as your whole backyard, or any size in between. So before we talk about planting and growing vegetables, peruse the list below, and check off all of the statements that apply to you. Your answers will help you decide not only what you want to grow, but also how big to make your plot, how to lay it out, and how much time you'll need to spend on it. And remember: There are no right or wrong answers—this is *your* garden!

From my garden, I want:

❧ Vegetables with old-time, fresh-picked flavor

❧ Varieties that I keep reading about in magazines and seeing on television, but can't find at my local supermarket

❧ Produce that's been grown without pesticides or synthetic fertilizers

❧ Food that I know hasn't been genetically engineered

❧ A lower food bill

❧ A big harvest for preserving and sharing

❧ Just enough food for my family and me to eat fresh

❧ An attractive addition to my yard

No matter how many of the above statements you checked off, keep three pointers in mind to help minimize your workload and maximize the pleasure you get from your garden.

Keep it small. If you're new to growing vegetables, follow Grandma Putt's golden rule for happy gardening: Decide on a size that you can handle cheerfully and comfortably, then reduce it by a third.

PLEASE PASS THE SUNSCREEN

If Ol' Sol doesn't shine on your yard all day long, don't fret! Not all veggies are die-hard sun worshippers. Most greens, including lettuce, spinach, collards, and kale, can tolerate some shade—especially during the hottest part of the day. So can Swiss chard and peas.

THE FAMILY FEAST

How big your garden needs to be depends (of course) on how many people you want to feed. Here's my rule of thumb for figuring out a plot that will keep you in fresh vegetables all summer long with a plentiful supply to put by for the winter—or share with friends and neighbors.

IF YOU'RE FEEDING (PERSONS)	MAKE YOUR GARDEN (FT.)
3 or 4	10 x 10
4 to 6	15 x 15
6 or more	30 x 30

Keep it close to your house. Or as close as your yard's layout will allow. That way, you'll be better able to spot tiny weeds before they grow into big ones. You'll notice insect pests while there's still time to pick them off by hand or send them fleeing with a blast from the garden hose. Plus, you'll know just when your new vegetables are ready for picking, and you won't miss a minute of their sweet, fresh flavor!

Keep it as close as possible to a hose hookup. Otherwise, you'll spend a lot of time toting a watering can back and forth because vegetables are a thirsty bunch. Most of them require at least an inch of water every week, and some need more than that. (Eggplant, for instance, demands a whopping 4 inches of water each and every week!)

Minds of Their Own

Throughout this book, I've assured you that for every kind of growing conditions in your yard, you can find plants that will thrive there. Well, vegetables are different in that regard because they're mighty picky about where they set down their roots. Analyzing your yard to find exactly the right site *will* take a little time and patience, but it's your key to a bountiful harvest. These are the general conditions most vegetables need for top performance:

- Six to eight hours of direct sun a day—more if possible

- Gentle air circulation (no gusty winds)

- Well-drained, loamy soil that's rich in nutrients

Other factors are also crucial to food-gardening success, but in this case, individual vegetables have distinct preferences.

The length of your growing season. It begins with the last frost in spring and ends with the first frost in fall. This number determines whether the vegetables you want to grow will have time to ripen in your garden. Some, like lettuce and radishes, mature in a few weeks. But others, like corn and peppers, can take 100 days or more.

How hot it gets. For instance, potatoes and carrots prefer cool temperatures, while peppers and tomatoes want all the heat they can get for as long as

HEAD FOR A HILL

The ideal site for a vegetable garden is a gentle, easy slope with no buildings, trees, or big shrubs nearby to block light or airflow. In the North, a south-facing incline is best. It'll warm up quickly in the spring and take its time welcoming Jack Frost in the fall. In the South, look for a slope that faces north; it won't get quite so hot during the dog days of summer.

uick Fix

Although most vegetables have general preferences for a certain kind of weather, chances are you can still grow whatever you're hankering for. Just adjust planting times to suit your climate, and choose varieties that are bred to thrive in your particular growing conditions. Plant breeders are constantly turning out new, weather-resistant varieties, so to find the latest and greatest, study seed catalogs and websites (especially the site maintained by your state university's horticulture school).

they can get it. (See the American Horticultural Society's website at www.ahs.org. There, you can either download the AHS Plant Heat Zone Map or order a printed version.)

Humidity. Although many plants can handle the heat just fine, the combination of heat and humidity will quickly do most of them in. This is especially true in the Deep South, where even the most die-hard sun lovers benefit from afternoon shade.

Day length. A few vegetables, including onions and spinach, are sensitive to the number of daylight hours they get. If it's not just right, they won't produce well.

DESIGN FOR SUCCESS

Now that you know what you want from your garden, and you've found the best spot for your plants to put down roots, it's time to design their home on your range. These tips will help you plan a plot that appeals to you visually and makes it easy for you to care for your vegetables from planting through harvest time.

In a vegetable garden, size, shape, and plant placement are not just aesthetic matters. Your choices can spell the difference between a garden that's as easy as pie to care for and one that will give you nothing but headaches.

Consider the Future

Although planting beds can be any shape you want, as you're pondering your plan, keep these two considerations in mind:

- If you'll have to mow around your garden, the simpler its shape is, the easier the job will be.

- You must be able to reach every plant without stepping on and compacting the soil in the process. You can either make each bed narrow enough so you can reach into the center easily, or break up larger beds with pathways every now and then.

Rise Up!

Besides saving space in your garden, growing crops in raised beds is the best way to ensure both good drainage *and* better moisture retention. But those aren't the only reasons to use these elevated marvels. Just consider the following advantages.

A broader plant palette. An enclosed, raised bed is just a big, bottomless container, so you can fill it with soil that suits the requirements of any—and every—kind of plant.

Earlier planting. Soil in raised beds warms up earlier in the spring because more of it is exposed to sunlight. That means you can get heat lovers off and running sooner.

Easier maintenance. You don't have to reach so far to pull weeds and harvest crops. In fact, because you can make them as high as you want, you can garden comfortably even if you use a wheelchair or have trouble bending over.

Good looks. Since the walls can be made of just about any material that will hold soil, raised beds can make an attractive addition to your yard.

Problem prevention. The walls hold the soil (and plants) inside, even in heavy rain, and they help deter weeds and many pests.

Grandma's GROW-HOW

Grandma Putt always told me that patience is a virtue. And when it comes to gardening with raised beds, she was right. An impatient gardener will ask, "Why spend the time to build raised beds?" Well, besides the reasons I've given above, raised beds will actually save you time and money—you won't have to spend a small fortune improving your yard's problem soil. Plus, your crops will produce better in raised beds because they're growing in loose, fertile topsoil that never gets walked on. And you can grow twice as many crops in the same space because you don't need to build garden paths. As impatient as I am, I know that a little time and effort spent creating raised beds pays off in a big bountiful harvest later on.

The Building Process

You can make raised beds out of wooden beams, salvaged lumber, rocks, bricks, cement blocks, and even sheets of recycled metal. If possible, start in late summer or early fall, and proceed as follows:

STEP 1. Mark off the site. I like to use stakes and string in a lawn. On a hard surface like brick or asphalt, I use chalk. (Don't forget to keep each bed narrow enough so that you can reach in to tend your plants easily!)

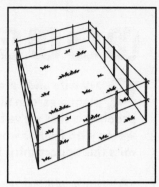

Mark off the site for your raised bed.

STEP 2. Build your planting bed to whatever height you want.

STEP 3. Fill the bed using my Super Soil Sandwich recipe in Chapter 9. Then go about your business and let the whole thing "cook" through the winter. Or, if it's already spring and you need to get your crops planted quickly, just make the top layer 4 to 6 inches of good-quality topsoil, or a half-and-half mixture of compost and topsoil. Soak it thoroughly with my Super Soil Sandwich Dressing (page 312), wait two weeks, and then plant to your heart's content.

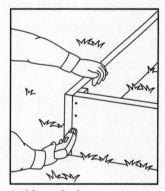

Build your bed.

A Word About Walls

While it *is* true that you can build a raised bed from almost any material under the sun, there are a couple of points to keep in mind if you want to avoid trouble:

❧ If you live in a hot climate, build your beds from light-colored material that reflects the

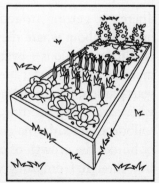

Vegetables thrive in easy-care raised beds.

HELP!

Q My wife and I are enthusiastic cooks, and we want to plant a garden filled with flavorful vegetables. The problem is that we've been invited to spend a couple of weeks with friends who have a house on Cape Cod, and we don't want to miss this opportunity. Do we have to give up our dream garden?

A *Not at all! Just pay special attention to the "days to maturity" sections in your seed catalogs, and choose varieties that won't need to be picked while you're gone. And, of course, ask someone to handle the watering chores in your absence. Then you can take off without a care in the world—or at least about your vegetables!*

sun's rays, like stone, or wood painted with white water-based paint. If the sides are dark, the intense heat they absorb could cook your plants' roots. At best, it will give them a thirst that just won't quit.

🌱 Avoid pressure-treated lumber and old railroad ties. They both contain toxic chemicals that can leach into the soil and into your vegetables.

WHAT GOES WHERE

There's no getting around it: Vegetables have strong opinions about where they'll bed down and with which companions—even if it is for only a few months. So no matter how eager you are to start your garden, the guidelines about what should go where are worth heeding, because all plants send out soilborne and airborne chemicals that can either help or hinder the growth of other nearby plants. Don't fret, though: Compiling your garden's annual "guest list" is a snap. These hints will put you on the road to a nice congenial gathering.

You can arrange plants in your vegetable garden in any way that appeals to you—in single rows or intermingled—and in any shape that fits your garden size and doesn't hinder harvesting.

Why Family Matters

Most of the plants in a particular family have pretty much the same nutritional needs. They also tend to attract the same pests and diseases. And both of those factors figure into an important part of garden planning called crop rotation (see "The Wheel of Life" on page 202).

If you're a beginning gardener, a knowledge of vegetable families is also a highly useful planning tool. That's because if you don't have a clue about what to plant with what, you just need to remember this rule of green thumb: When in doubt, plant vegetables near other members of the same family. They may not help each other—but they won't cause any harm either. Here's the roster:

Beet or goosefoot (*Chenopodiaceae*): Beets, chard, spinach

Cabbage or mustard (*Cruciferae* or *Brassica*): Broccoli, Brussels sprouts, cabbage, cauliflower, collards, horseradish, kale, kohlrabi, mustard, radishes, rutabagas, turnips

Carrot (*Umbelliferae*): Carrots, celery, parsley, parsnips

Cucumber or gourd (*Cucurbitaceae*): Cucumbers, gourds, melons, pumpkins, squash

Grass (*Gramineae*): Corn

Mallow (*Malvaceae*): Okra

Grandma's GROW-HOW

Grandma Putt taught me that for just about every gardening rule, there's at least one exception. And in the case of vegetable family life, that exception is the tomato or nightshade clan. Tomatoes and their pepper and eggplant cousins will behave like angels when living next door to each other. But like feuding siblings, tomatoes and potatoes just don't care for each other's company. Also, since potatoes need a lower pH than the rest of the family, they're seldom grown with any of their relatives.

Morning glory or bindweed
(*Convolvulaceae*): Sweet potatoes

Onion or lily (*Liliaceae*): Asparagus, chives, garlic, leeks, onions, scallions, shallots

Pea or legume (*Leguminosae*): Beans, peanuts, peas

Sunflower (*Compositae*): Artichokes, endive, lettuce, sunflowers

Tomato or nightshade (*Solanaceae*): Eggplant, peppers, potatoes, tomatoes

The Wheel of Life

Crop rotation may sound like a complicated procedure, but it's really not. It simply means growing plants in different parts of your garden each year. Rotation pays off in two ways.

Nutrition. Although all plants need the same basic kinds of nutrients, they need them in different quantities and different combinations, and they take them from different levels of the soil. When the same kind of plant grows in the same spot year after year—no matter how much fertilizer you provide—eventually the supply runs out. But if you let the plant change places with one that favors a different set of nutrients, the soil will replenish itself.

Pests and diseases. Insect pests and disease-causing organisms also have favorite foods. They feast on their victims during the summer, then spend

IT'S A QUESTION OF HEIGHT

Determining where to plant tall crops like corn and sunflowers, and ones that grow on high supports like tomatoes and some beans, depends on the climate. In most parts of the country, it's usually best to put them on the far west side of your garden so they can shield the more tender plants, like lettuce, from the west wind and the hot afternoon sun. But if you live way up North, where heat can be hard to come by even in summer, you'll probably want to keep those high, vertical shapes on the north side of your garden. That way, they won't cast cold shadows on their shorter neighbors.

the winter in the same spot, fast asleep in the soil. If they wake up in the spring to find that their first choice of food has been replaced by something they don't care to eat, they starve and die out.

Givers and Takers

One key variable to keep in mind as you rotate your crops is their appetite levels. Plants fall into three types: big eaters, lighter eaters, and what I call givers. The givers actually return nutrients to the soil if you plow them under

EAT UP!

One of the keys to fast and easy vegetable success is to rotate crops according to their appetite levels. Here's the rundown in a nutshell.

BIG EATERS	LIGHT TO MODERATE EATERS
• Broccoli	• Beans*
• Brussels sprouts	• Beets
• Cabbage	• Carrots
• Cauliflower	• Kale
• Celery	• Leeks
• Corn	• Onions
• Cucumbers	• Peanuts*
• Eggplant	• Peas*
• Lettuce	• Peppers
• Melons	• Radishes
• Okra	• Spinach
• Potatoes	• Sweet potatoes
• Squash	• Swiss chard
• Tomatoes	• Turnips

Although these legume crops will add nitrogen to the soil if you plow them under in the fall, they do *need a little nourishment during the growing season.*

at the end of the growing season. Beans, peanuts, and peas fall into the givers category; so do "cover crops," like clover and buckwheat.

The three things to remember are to replace a big eater with a lighter eater or a giver; replace a deep-rooted plant with one that has shallow roots; and never put a plant where a member of its own family grew the year before.

IN THE BEGINNING

Vegetables are like any other plants: The better start you give them, the better they'll perform, and the less time you'll have to spend fussing with them. In this section, I'll share some secrets that will put you on the fast road to a big, healthy harvest.

Plants or Seeds?

In the spring, at any garden center, you'll see table after table covered with vegetable seedlings. So—especially if you're impatient to get growing—doesn't it make sense just to buy plants, take them home, and tuck them into your garden? Well, sometimes yes, and sometimes no. Here's how to make the call.

To get a bigger veggie harvest, just plant bigger seeds. In any given batch, the larger seeds germinate faster and produce stronger seedlings than the smaller ones do—and that grow power translates into a bigger yield. The reason is simple: Larger seeds contain more food to boost the baby plants along.

Buy started plants when:

- The vegetables you want to grow need an early start indoors, and you don't have the time, the space, or the inclination to do the job yourself.

- You want to be certain of getting vegetable varieties that will grow well in your climate.

- You want instant results for a container garden or an ornamental planting.

- You're happy with whatever varieties the garden center has for sale.

Start from seed when:

🌱 You want to grow varieties you can't find at the garden center.

🌱 The vegetables you want to grow are not sold as transplants. Root crops, as well as cucumbers, squash, melons, corn, and beans, fall into this category.

When you're at the garden center, look for young, sturdy, stocky plants without blossoms. A plant that's leggy, lanky, or already blooming is too old and stressed out to perform well in your yard. Gently remove each plant from its container, and make sure no roots are growing around the outside of the soil clump. It indicates that the plant has been in its pot too long. And if you see any signs of pests or diseases—including a whitish powder or chemical odor on the leaves—take your business elsewhere. That's a sign that either the grower or the store has problems that you don't want in your yard!

Before you head off to your local garden center, call and ask when they plan to put a new shipment or their own homegrown stock out for sale. On that day, try to get there shortly after the place opens. That way, you'll have the best selection of plants, and they'll still be fresh and rarin' to grow in your yard. This last point is crucial if you shop in a supermarket or big-box store, where after-delivery TLC can be spotty at best.

Life in the Great Indoors

Most vegetables are a snap to start from seed indoors. First, find the ideal starting date on the seed packet (generally, it's from three to six weeks before the last expected frost in your area). Then follow this simple four-step procedure:

STEP 1. Fill clean, shallow containers with sterilized, commercial seed-starting mix, and dampen (but don't soak) it. Then plant your seeds according to the depth and spacing instructions on the packet.

Cover the flats with clear plastic to retain moisture.

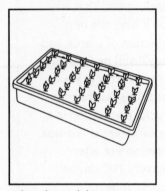

When the seeds have germi-nated, move the containers to a spot that gets 12 hours of light a day.

As soon as the first two real leaves appear, move each seedling to an individual pot.

STEP 2. Wrap the containers loosely in clear, plastic bags (or cover them with plastic wrap) to hold in moisture, and put them in a warm spot—the top of your refrigerator is perfect. Check your future crops every day, and mist the soil with water if it feels dry.

STEP 3. When you see the first signs of life (usually a thin stem, followed by a pair of small, plump cotyledons, a.k.a. seed leaves), take off the covers, and move the flats to a spot where the seedlings will get at least 12 hours of light a day, whether from the sun, grow lights, or a combination of both. Then spray the seedlings with chamomile tea spray (see Grandma's Grow-How at right).

STEP 4. As soon as the first two real leaves appear, move each seedling to an individual pot filled with pasteurized commercial potting mix. Don't touch the fragile stems; instead, use a spoon to lift out the little root-ball and set it into its new home. Then just look after the tiny tykes as you would any other houseplants until it's time to move them outdoors.

Reluctant Travelers

Most vegetables do okay on the journey from seed flats to garden soil. But some others want to sink their first little roots into a good home and settle in for the long haul. If your growing season is too short for these homebodies to start life in your garden, sow the seeds in pots that can go right into the ground at transplanting time. Use pots that are 2 to 2 1/2 inches wide, and sow several seeds in each pot. When the youngsters have two sets of true leaves, snip out all but the strongest seedling. Veggie crops like beans, carrots, corn, cucumbers, melons, okra, parsnips, peas, radishes, rutabaga, and squash (including gourds and pumpkins) are all cranky travelers.

To get your seeds off to a disease-free start, indoors or out, lightly sprinkle Jell-O® powder on the soil with a saltshaker. As your young plants grow, feed them more Jell-O; the gelatin helps the plants hold water, and the sugar feeds the microorganisms in the soil.

Home on the Move

You can buy pots made from biodegradable materials like pressed peat moss or paper fiber. They work fine, but I prefer to make my own supply. In addition to costing less than commercial versions, they break down much faster in the garden, thereby allowing the seedlings' roots to stretch out sooner and get off to a quicker, stronger start. I have two favorite types of starter homes.

Sod pots. These are best for big seeds like squashes and cucumbers. First, dig up a piece of turf that's about 3 inches deep, and cut it into 2-inch-square chunks. (Just make sure the grass hasn't been treated with any herbicide, which will kill your seeds.) Turn the sod pieces upside down, set

Grandma's GROW-HOW

Damping-off is a foul fungus that can spread like wildfire through a tray of seedlings, wiping them out overnight. To keep it from getting a toehold, do what Grandma Putt always did: Put four chamomile tea bags in a small bucket or heat-proof pitcher, pour 1 quart of boiling water over them, and steep them for at least an hour (the stronger, the better). Remove the tea bags, and mix in ¼ teaspoon of baby shampoo. Pour the solution—which, by now, should be at room temperature—into a handheld sprayer bottle, and gently mist-spray your seedlings as soon as the first green shoots appear. Just one dose is enough.

them into a flat that has drainage holes in the bottom, and tuck two or three seeds into each piece.

Newspaper pots. These work best for small- to medium-size seeds. You will need a mold (a soft-drink can is perfect) and a supply of newspaper. Just cut a strip of newspaper about 12 inches long and 6 inches wide. Wrap the paper around the can lengthwise, with about 4 inches covering the side of the can and 2 inches hanging over the bottom. Fold that extra piece onto the bottom of the can, and press it tight with your fingers. Take away the can, and presto—you've got yourself a pot! Build as many as you need, fill them with seed-starting mix, and put them into flats with holes in the bottom for drainage. Make sure you pack 'em in tight so they don't unravel, and sow your seeds.

Kindergarten, Seedling Style

Whether your young transplants have been coddled in your home or in a greenhouse, they'll need a little preparation before they're ready for life outdoors. The traditional hardening off process entails setting the pots or flats in a shady, protected area for a short period each day, gradually increasing their outdoor time over the course of a week. That's easy enough if you're around to ferry the seedlings in and out, but if your day job can't accommodate that schedule, try this ultra-simple hands-off approach:

STEP 1. Find a protected spot under a leafy shrub, where the seedlings will be shaded all day, and water the ground thoroughly.

STEP 2. Set your potted seedlings on the damp soil, and water them well.

Take 2

Potato eyes are more likely to sprout if you start them indoors, and paper egg cartons make perfect starter pots. Just cut your seed potatoes into pieces (make sure each one has at least one eye), and tuck a chunk into each section of the carton. Fill them with sterilized potting soil, and keep it moist. When green shoots start to appear, cut the sections of the carton apart, and plant them directly in your garden.

Quick Fix

Just before you're ready to set your seedlings in the garden, water them with a solution of 2 ounces of salt or baking soda per gallon of water. This elixir will temporarily stop growth and increase the plants' strength so they can face anything Mother Nature throws their way (well, *almost* anything).

Then spray the shrub's foliage above them until it's dripping. This will keep the young plants from drying out and dying during the day.

STEP 3. Repeat this process over the course of a week, moving the youngsters into a little more sun each day.

A Bumper Crop—It's a Blanket Deal!

When you're fixin' to grow heat-loving crops like squash, tomatoes, peppers, or corn, black plastic mulch (available at most garden centers) can lead the way to a faster, happier harvest. Here's all you need to do: First, get your planting beds ready in the fall, and cover them with a thick layer of leaves or straw. This will keep the ground as warm as possible through the winter. Come spring, take off the organic stuff and replace it with black plastic mulch to heat up the soil in preparation for planting. (For the exact timing, check the soil-temperature guidelines on your seed packets or transplant labels.)

The next step depends on where you live. If your summers get steamy, take the plastic mulch off your beds *before* you plant your seeds or set in your transplants. Otherwise, later in the season, the soil will heat up too

A BLOOMIN' GOOD TIME

When you start warm-weather crops like tomatoes and peppers indoors, it's important not to transplant them too early. There's no need to guess at the right time. Just do what Grandma Putt did and get the job done when the peonies and black locust trees bloom.

much. Once the plants are on their way, spread an organic mulch around them to keep the soil cool and weeds out.

In regions where the soil needs all of the warming help it can get, leave the plastic on the ground. Just cut slits in it where you want to sow your seeds or insert your transplants. Then anchor the sheet securely in place at planting time. If it shifts even a tad, it'll cover the seedlings and smother them.

Bring on the Clouds

Try to do your planting on a drizzly, overcast day. The transplants will settle in more quickly when the sun's not out to bake them, and you won't have to worry so much about keeping the whole crowd moist as they wait their turn. But if you're in a period of nonstop sunshine, don't fret: Just gather up baskets, cardboard boxes, or even straw hats, and set them over the young ones as you work. If you use boxes, prop up one side of each carton on a stone or brick to let some air in. Let your plants keep their caps on for a day or so, then take them off, and let the sun shine in!

HELP!

Q When I visited a friend in Santa Fe last year, he gave me seeds from his favorite hot peppers. The plants grew fine in my garden here in Portland, Oregon, but the peppers took forever to mature! And they weren't nearly as hot as the ones I tasted at my friend's house. What went wrong?

A *Nothing. While it is true that some kinds of peppers are naturally hotter than others, weather plays a crucial role. First, a pepper that's grown in hot, dry territory like New Mexico will always be hotter than the same variety grown in the Northwest, where the soil is richer and the weather is cooler and damper. Second, the cooler the weather, the longer it takes a pepper to mature. A pepper that takes 70 days in Santa Fe might take up to 100 days in Portland.*

Timely Tomato Planting

For most vegetables, the transplanting process is simple. You just dig a hole and set in the plant at the same depth it was growing in its pot. But tomatoes demand special treatment. First, don't rush to get your tomatoes into the ground—wait until the soil temperature is at least 55°F and you're fairly certain the air won't get any chillier than 45°F at night. (But keep row covers handy, just in case!) I always give my tomatoes a good support system, so I set them 15 inches apart down the middle of a 30-inch-wide bed. If you don't plan to grow yours on stakes or trellises, leave 2 feet between determinate (a.k.a. bush) types and 3 feet between indeterminate (a.k.a. vining) ones. As for planting, you have a choice of two techniques.

When the blossoms on your plants turn into green tomatoes, stretch aluminum foil on the ground between the plants, and anchor it along the edges with stones or bricks. The reflected light can increase your yield, especially in cloudy weather, and speed up the ripening of the fruit by a full two weeks!

The hole method. This is the system to use if you live in a warm climate. Simply dig a hole about the size of a basketball. In the bottom, put a layer of compost or well-rotted manure mixed with a handful of bonemeal and

Tomato-Booster Tonic

For the tastiest tomatoes in town, treat your plants to this terrific tonic.

> 2 tbsp. of Epsom salts
> 1 tsp. of baby shampoo
> 1 gal. of water

Mix all of the ingredients in a bucket or watering can, and thoroughly soak the soil around each tomato plant as it flowers. The result: More growth, which equals more flavor!

1 teaspoon of Epsom salts. Then set the plant in so that only about the top 4 inches stick up above the soil. (Clip off the lower leaves with scissors first.)

The trench method. This technique works especially well in cool regions or when you're trying to get a jump on the season because the roots grow up close to the surface where the soil is warmer. Make a 6-inch-deep trench the whole length of your planting bed. Spread a thin layer of compost along the bottom, then trim off the leaves from all but the top 4 inches of the stem. Lay each plant in the trench horizontally, with the 4-inch leafy part curved up out of the ground. Pack soil around it so it stays in place, then cover up the rest of the stem.

Whichever planting style you choose, take a tip from Mary Poppins and me, and add a spoonful of sugar to each hole or each plant's section of the trench. Your tomatoes will be so sweet and juicy, you'll want to eat them for dessert!

Later on in the season, when flowers begin to appear on the plants, serve up a healthy drink of my Tomato-Booster Tonic (see page 211).

VEGGIE GARDEN TLC— FAST AND SIMPLE

Even if you've chosen the perfect site for your garden and selected vegetables that were bred to perform likes champs in your climate, your plants will still need a certain amount of care. These tricks will help you deliver it—and you'll have plenty of time and energy left over to enjoy your own season in the sun!

Don't use any nitrogen-rich fertilizer (organic or otherwise) late in the growing season: It will stimulate leafy growth and make your plants easy targets for a killing frost.

Five Steps to Fabulous Feasting

Here's what you need to know about feeding your garden all season long. If you follow this routine, your garden will bless you with a tremendous harvest in the fall:

STEP 1. To get your vegetable garden ready for the big growing season, you should begin your preparations two weeks before you intend to plant your crops. First, you need to apply some of my Vegetable Power Powder (below) to the soil and work it in well.

STEP 2. Then immediately mix 1 can of beer, 1 teaspoon of tea granules, and 1 cup each of antiseptic mouthwash, mild dishwashing liquid, and regular cola (not diet) in a bucket. Fill your 20 gallon hose-end sprayer with the solution, and apply it to the soil to the point of runoff.

STEP 3. Before you plant your seeds, soak them overnight in my Seed-Starter Tonic (see page 16). It can actually speed up germination time by 75 percent!

STEP 4. About 10 days after planting and every three weeks for the rest of the growing season, feed your plants with my All-Season Green-Up Tonic (see page 26).

STEP 5. Every other week or so, serve your vegetable garden a nice big drink of my Compost Tea (see page 315).

Vegetable Power Powder

This simple formula will help get your garden off to the best possible start in life. (The recipe makes enough to cover 100 square feet of garden area.)

> 15 lbs. of dry, organic fertilizer (either 4-12-4 or 5-10-5)
> 5 lbs. of gypsum
> 2 lbs. of diatomaceous earth
> 1 lb. of sugar

Mix all of the ingredients together, and put them into a handheld broadcast spreader. Set the spreader on medium, apply the mixture over the top of your vegetable garden, and work it into the soil.

Drink Up, Gang!

Most vegetables need at least an inch of water a week. That's about 62 gallons for every 100 square feet of garden area—and that's a lot of H$_2$O! No matter where you live, it's likely that you'll have to provide a lot of the moisture yourself, so keep this handful of pointers in mind as you serve up drinks.

Use a soaker hose. It's the most efficient way to deliver water all the way down to your plants' roots.

Keep your soil well stocked with organic matter. This is the best way to improve the soil's structure and increase its ability to hold water. Good soil structure also encourages large, healthy root systems, and that's a plant's best defense against drought.

Mulch heavily. You'll conserve water, keep down weeds, and discourage pests all at the same time.

Plant drought-tolerant varieties. Garden centers and catalogs offer more and more every year. In particular, many heirloom vegetables tend to need much less water than modern hybrids do.

Don't overdo it. Too much water will cause more damage than too little. It will drown your plants' roots and wash away essential nutrients. To find out how much moisture your particular vegetables need, check seed catalogs or a comprehensive vegetable-gardening book.

Grandma's GROW-HOW

If water is in short supply where you live, remember Grandma Putt's rule of thumb: The more parts of a plant you eat, the more water-thrifty it is. Beets, onions, turnips, lettuce, and other greens top the list because the whole plant is edible. Corn ranks at the very bottom because a single cornstalk will use 54 gallons of water during the growing season to produce just one or two ears of corn.

Bring on the Thunder!

Have you ever noticed how your lawn and garden seem to suddenly green up after a storm? That's because the electricity in the air joins oxygen with nitrogen to make nitric oxide (the chemical compound that delivers nitrogen to your plants). But you don't have to just sit around praying for storm clouds to appear—you can create the same atmosphere yourself, as farmers and gardeners have been doing for centuries. They call it electroculture, and it can actually improve the health of your plants and increase the size of your harvest. Try it yourself, using these three techniques:

◄ Grow cucumbers, indeterminate tomatoes, and other vine crops on metal trellises or fences.

◄ Use only metal poles for staking.

◄ Tie up your plants with strips cut from nylon garments, like slips or old panty hose. (If you don't know how that could attract electricity, just ask any woman about "static cling"!)

Quick Fix

To make the most of a thunderstorm's grow power, use copper pipe for staking and grow your vining plants on copper arches. Just get some flexible copper tubing, cut it into the lengths you need, and bend them into shape. Or build a simple trellis using copper pipe, standard connectors, and plumber's cement instead of wood and nails. (Look for plans on the Internet or in a garden-project book.) It's best to buy your gear at a plumbing-supply store, where it'll cost a fraction of what you'd pay at a hardware or building-products store.

Oh, yes, there is one more thing to remember. Once you've made your garden an electrical magnet, make sure you get out of it the minute you hear thunder!

The Big Cover-Up

Even if you think you've got your growing season all figured out, trust me; you don't. Because, just when you least expect it—at the beginning *or* the end of the growing season—Mother Nature can turn down the thermostat and send the north winds blowing. And, if you're not Johnny-on-the-spot, all your hard work can go right down the drain. The simplest way to protect your harvest is to buy floating row covers and toss them over your plants at the first sign of frost. Besides keeping out chilly breezes, they fend off pests. But there are plenty of other ways to do both those things, and for much less money.

Old nylon net curtains. Use them exactly as you would commercial row covers. Then, when they've accomplished their mission, run them through the washing machine, and store them away until you need them again.

Plastic milk cartons with the bottoms cut off. Put one over each tender plant, and push it a couple of inches into the ground so it doesn't blow away in the wind.

Panty hose. Just cut off a leg and slip it over a baby plant, enclosing it in the foot end. Then tie the bottom tight.

Newspaper. Make a tent and set it over your plants. Fold out the bottom edges and weight them down with rocks so the sheet doesn't blow away.

My Weed-Management Policy

Every gardener ends up going to war against weeds. In fact, no matter how vigilant you are, weeds are bound to appear in even the best-tended gardens. Regardless of what kind of planting space you're working

Take 2

Believe it or not, having a stash of brown paper grocery bags on hand can save you a lot of time and effort in the garden. How so? Because you can use them to plant your crops and protect them in one easy step. Just dig your planting hole, then set a bag inside so that 10 inches of bag sticks up above the soil surface. Fill it with soil, roll down the top of the bag, and plant your seedling. At the first sign of frost, roll up the bag collar and fasten it closed with a spring-loaded clothespin. When all danger of frost has passed, cut off as much of the bag as you can, leaving the rest to break down and add organic matter to the soil.

with, by following these simple guidelines you'll help keep weeds from getting the upper hand.

Seed heavily. Weeds pop up in any bare soil they find. When you're direct-sowing vegetables (or flowers, fruits, or herbs), cover the space with the plants you want in your garden. Later, you can thin the seedlings so they're the right distance apart.

Don't rush to get warmth-craving plants into the ground. When heat lovers have to struggle to grow in cold soil, weeds can do them in fast.

Use transplants. Young plants take off the minute you set them into the ground. That means they can start shading out weeds right from the get-go. Plus, when something green does pop up, you'll know it's a weed, and you can pull it without worrying that you're removing your future food.

Mulch early and mulch often. A thick layer of organic mulch will stop weeds from popping up among your plants. It will also keep fungi in the soil from splashing up on stems and foliage.

Nettle Tea

You may think of stinging nettles as just annoying, and sometimes painful, weeds. But in fact, they can be powerful garden allies. For one thing, they pack a load of nitrogen that's as potent as manure, but without any risk of burning roots. For another, they give off chemicals that repel plant-munching insects, but are perfectly harmless to all living creatures. So what are you waiting for? Brew a bucket of this powerful tea, and put it to work in your vegetable garden—and all over your yard!

> 1 lb. of stinging nettle leaves
> 1 gal. of hot water

Put the nettle leaves in a bucket, pour in the water, and let the mixture steep for at least a week. Strain out the leaves, and water your plants with the brew. (I use an old-fashioned watering can for this job.) Then toss the soggy, but still-nutritious leaves into the compost bin, or bury them in the garden.

Your Summertime Agenda

For a vegetable gardener, the livin' gets a whole lot easier in the summertime. It's not like the spring, when you're rushing to get everything into the ground, or later in the fall, when you're scrambling to harvest all your crops before frost lays them flat. In fact, it's easy to just lie back in your hammock and gaze up at God's blue sky. Well, don't get too comfortable! Life may move at a slower pace in the summer, but there are still chores to be done—and you need to be persistent about doing them. So play it safe: Keep this list taped to the fridge, just so you don't overlook anything when you get an attack of the midsummer lazies:

☙ Make sure your garden is getting plenty of water.

☙ Check for sagging stems and tie them up before they break.

☙ Keep an eye out for any signs of pests or diseases.

☙ Pick vegetables as soon as they're ripe (see "Is It Ready Yet?" below).

☙ Serve up frequent drinks of my Compost Tea (page 315).

☙ Inspect the mulch now and then, and add more if needed.

Is It Ready Yet?

Different varieties of vegetables are on different ripening schedules. But it's not all that difficult to figure out when it's time to

Take 2

Don't haul your dirty veggies back to the kitchen to clean them (and then have to clean the kitchen). Instead, wash 'em off right in the garden and keep your kitchen spic-and-span. Just rustle up any old container that has holes in it, fill it with veggies, aim your hose, and fire away. Here's a handful of good choices:

• Colanders

• Dish drainers

• Plastic baskets

• Plastic mesh produce bags, hung from tree branches or laundry lines

• Salad spinners

harvest. If you're not certain whether something is ready to pick or not, be on the lookout for these clues.

Color. Fleshy-fruited veggies like tomatoes, peppers, winter squash, and pumpkins turn color as they ripen. Read your seed packet or catalog description carefully so you know what color to look for (it's not always what you might expect!).

Gloss. Healthy, growing veggies are shiny and glossy. If their skin is dull, you've waited too long. Watermelon is the exception to this rule: When it's ripe, its skin is dull. (For more on watermelon and other fruits commonly grown in vegetable gardens, see Chapter 7.)

Size. Lots of vegetable crops, including peppers, potatoes, cucumbers, zucchini, and leafy greens, are ready to eat whenever they look like they are. If you don't think you can trust your eyes, then just take a bite. Your taste buds don't lie.

COME AND GET IT!

The time for harvesting different crops varies because some vegetables take longer to ripen than others. By following this checking schedule, you should catch everything at its peak of flavor—before it heads downhill.

CHECK EVERY DAY	CHECK EVERY OTHER DAY	CHECK EVERY THIRD DAY	CHECK ONCE A WEEK*
• Broccoli • Lettuce	• Beans • Corn • Cucumbers • Okra • Strawberries • Summer squash	• Beets • Carrots • Eggplant • Onions • Peas • Peppers • Tomatoes	• Gourds • Melons • Pumpkins • Winter squash

* In hot climates, or if the weather's hotter than normal for your area, check these every day.

Hints for a Happy Harvest

When it's time to bring in your bounty, there are several guidelines you need to keep in mind. First, try to pick your vegetables in the morning, when their sugar content is highest. But if the plants are wet, give them time to dry off. If you harvest (or do any other garden work) when plants are wet, you're likely to spread diseases. Take your time and work carefully, because bruised or scratched vegetables spoil quickly, and damaged plants are sitting ducks for pests and diseases. It never pays to be impatient at harvest time. Use your fingers to pick thin-stemmed vegetables like peas and beans, and ones that slip easily from the vine like tomatoes. And use a sharp knife or clippers to cut tough- or brittle-stemmed crops. Veggies like cabbage, peppers, broccoli, eggplant, and squash can be damaged badly if you try to pull or tear them from their stems.

Eating Happily Ever After

Whether you plan to eat your veggies fresh from the garden at their peak of flavor, or sock them away for the long winter ahead, they'll last longer if you follow these tips:

◆ Leave an inch or two of stem on pumpkins, peppers, and squash.

Big commercial growers generally harvest their crops all at once and send 'em off to market. But home gardeners get to bring in the bounty all summer long—and you owe it to yourself to keep a close eye on your plants and pick whatever you find that's ripe, for a couple of reasons. One is flavor. Most vegetables taste their best when they're young and tender. The other is that you'll get a bigger yield. That's because the way a plant looks at it, once it produces its offspring (in this case, seed-bearing vegetables), its job is done. So if you leave overripe veggies on the vine, the plant will simply close up shop. But if you keep harvesting, the plant will keep producing.

❦ Remove the tops from root crops.

❦ Rush anything you pick to the fridge or another cool place.

❦ Wash only what you plan to use right away.

The Bedtime Ritual

Good garden care doesn't end with the last harvest. Your plot needs some TLC so it will be ready to produce another bumper crop next year. This four-step routine will put you on the high road to success:

Till legume crops into the soil.

STEP 1. Till any legume crops under, so they'll add their nitrogen to the soil. Clear off all other plants (except for asparagus, rhubarb, or other perennials!), and toss them in your compost bin.

STEP 2. For every 100 square feet of garden area, work in a mixture of 25 pounds of gypsum, 10 pounds of organic fertilizer (either 4-12-4 or 5-10-5), and 5 pounds of bonemeal.

Work gypsum, fertilizer, and bonemeal into the soil.

STEP 3. Spread a thick layer of newspaper over the garden, add a layer of leaves over that, and top it all off with straw. After a lot of trial and error, I've found that this is the worms' very favorite bedtime blanket. It keeps them warm and busy all winter long, so come spring, your planting beds will be rarin' to grow.

STEP 4. Overspray the mulch with my Super Soil Sandwich Dressing (see page 312).

Spread newspaper, topped with leaves and straw.

SICK BAY—AWAY!

Don't worry! I didn't include this section to frighten you. In the first place, plant diseases most often plague big, single-crop commercial growers. Second, if you follow the planning and planting guidelines throughout this book, you can prevent a good 90 percent of your problems. And when unhappy circumstances do put your crops at risk, the tips in this section will help you rise to the challenge—fast.

The key to fending off vegetable ailments is the same as it is for the other plants in your yard: Find disease-resistant varieties that will thrive in your climate and give them the TLC they need to grow strong and healthy.

The Most Unwanted List

There are hundreds of different plant diseases in the world, but only a tiny fraction of them could ever appear in your yard. Here are the three you are most likely to see in your vegetable garden.

Bacterial wilt. Tomatoes are the most frequent victims. In early stages, soft brown lesions appear on stems and grow until the plant is girdled. Then the stems develop brown streaks and, finally, they dissolve into brown jelly. There is no cure, but you *can* head off trouble by:

~ Using row covers to protect plants from cucumber beetles. Just remove the covers when the plants bloom so insects can pollinate the blossoms.

~ Rotating crops on a four- to five-year cycle.

Fusarium wilt. This is caused by a fungus that blocks plants' vascular tissue, so stems and leaves wilt and droop. When you water them, they perk up, but they're soon droopy and wilted again. In cool, damp weather, fluffy pale pink or white fungi may grow from the blocked spots. Fusarium can live in the soil for up to 20 years, and unfortunately, no fungicide can kill it. To control the disease:

~ Dig up afflicted plants and put them in the trash. Then remove as much soil as you can from the former root zone, and dispose of it, too.

🐦 Solarize your soil before you plant anything else in that spot (see "Let the Sun Fight Your Battles" on page 351).

🐦 Control striped cucumber beetles, which spread the disease.

Tomato mosaic virus. Tomato family crops as well as beans, beets, cucumbers, melons, and potatoes are common victims. Leaves turn yellow to pale green and may be mottled, deformed, and smaller than normal. Plants are stunted with a greatly reduced yield. The virus can live in the soil for up to five years. Your mission is to:

🐦 Remove and destroy infected plants immediately, and avoid touching other plants because the virus is spread by contact.

🐦 Change your clothes and disinfect your hands and tools before you return to the garden.

🐦 Plant only resistant varieties.

🐦 Don't let anyone smoke in or near your garden, or enter your garden with even an unlit cigarette.

Fungus-Fighter Tonic

This potion is a godsend for fending off fungal diseases of all kinds on both edible and ornamental plants. And it's so safe you could even mix it into cookie dough!

> ½ cup of molasses
> ½ cup of powdered milk
> 1 tsp. of baking soda
> 1 gal. of warm water

Mix the molasses, powdered milk, and baking soda into a paste. Place the mixture into an old panty hose toe or a cheesecloth pouch, and let it steep in the warm water for several hours. Strain, then pour the remaining liquid into a handheld sprayer bottle, and mist your fungus-prone plants every week during the growing season.

Villainless Crimes

These two common garden ailments look and act like diseases, but they're actually cultural problems.

Blossom-end rot. It attacks squash, tomatoes, peppers, and watermelon. A dark, watery spot starts at the blossom end of a fruit and grows slowly until it's covered the whole thing. Small fruits usually drop off quickly. Larger ones often stay on the plant. The cause? Too little calcium in the soil, or long periods of wet weather followed by a dry spell. Your prevention plan:

🍂 Before your growing season starts, test your soil. If it needs calcium and the pH is also low, add limestone. If the pH is not low, add gypsum.

🍂 Mulch to maintain even moisture.

🍂 Go very easy on all fertilizers.

Cracking. This appears on tomatoes, celery, and rhubarb. In tomatoes, it's caused by a sudden change in soil moisture, and it makes them crack lengthwise. In celery and rhubarb, the problem is a deficiency of the trace element boron, which causes the leaf stems to split. To head off trouble:

🍂 Mulch tomatoes to maintain even moisture, water during dry spells, and pick fruit as soon as it's ripe.

🍂 Test your soil before the growing season starts, adding boron if necessary.

HOW SWEET IT IS!

Here are three super-simple secrets for growing the sweetest, juiciest tomatoes in town:

• Don't use any high-nitrogen fertilizer on your tomato plants. Too much nitrogen encourages leaf growth at the expense of flowers and fruits.

• Avoid cultivating around tomatoes. You want to disturb the roots as little as possible. Instead, use a 2-inch layer of mulch to keep out weeds and help retain water.

• If you notice the leaves curling on your tomato plants, it means they aren't getting enough water. Be sure to give them a thorough soaking at least once a week, and more often in hot, dry weather.

GARDEN-VARIETY GATE CRASHERS

The way some folks talk, you'd think that planting a vegetable garden is like opening a five-star restaurant for every pest in the county. Well, friends, it just ain't so! It *is* true that there are some hungry bugs, birds, and four-legged critters that'd like to sink their chops into your harvest. But fending them off is a lot easier than you might think. Here are a few specialized tricks for dealing with some of the uninvited guests you're most likely to see in your vegetable garden.

You'll find more of my trouble-avoidance tips and tricks to help win the war on pests and diseases in Chapter 10.

Tomato Hornworms

Just a few of these giant caterpillars can defoliate a tomato plant in a flash, then polish off the fruit. They target every member of their namesake family, as well as peas, okra, squash, grapes, dill, and many flowers. Here's what to do:

- Kill young hornworms with Btk (*Bacillus thuringiensis* var. *kurstaki*). For best results, wait until the caterpillars are just big enough to chew a hole through a leaf. At that stage, they'll be able to ingest a lethal dose of the bacteria, but won't have had time to cause much damage to your plants.

- After the harvest, cultivate your soil thoroughly down to 5 inches or so. You'll destroy many of the hornworm pupae and bring even more up to the surface, where they'll be eaten by birds or killed by cold weather.

If you're new to gardening, or to your area, ask your neighbors what insects and other critters they've had trouble with and how they've handled it. This can save you a lot of time and trouble because a "pest" that causes major damage in one region may be completely harmless in another.

❧ If hornworms plagued your garden in the past, spray your plants with Btk when you transplant them, and repeat the application every two weeks until blossoms appear.

Cucumber Beetles

These villains dine on the entire cucurbit clan, including melons, squash, gourds, pumpkins, and their namesake crop, plus early beans (both lima and snap), corn, peas, potatoes, radishes, and tomatoes. The larvae feed on roots and fallen fruit. Adults chew ragged holes in foliage, flowers, stems, and fruits—injecting fusarium wilt and cucumber mosaic virus in the process. Here's how to act fast before the disease germs spread:

❧ When adults appear in spring, handpick and drown them in soapy water.

❧ Polish them off with a dose of my Peppermint Soap Spray (below).

❧ Deter them by planting masses of marigolds, which also repel squash bugs, tomato hornworms, and whiteflies.

❧ If the beetles have already delivered the deadly diseases to your yard, solarize the soil to kill any lingering larvae before you plant anything else in that space (see "Let the Sun Fight Your Battles" page 351).

Peppermint Soap Spray

This brew is a nightmare come true for hard-bodied insects like beetles. The secret weapon is peppermint. It cuts right through a bug's waxy shell so the soap can get in and work its fatal magic.

> **2 tbsp. of dishwashing liquid***
> **1 gal. of warm water**
> **2 tsp. of peppermint oil**

Mix the soap and water together, then stir in the peppermint oil. Pour the solution into a handheld sprayer bottle, take aim, and fire.

* Do not use detergent or any product that contains antibacterial ingredients.

Squash Bugs

These insects primarily target squash (both summer and winter types, including pumpkins), but they also go after cucumbers, melons, and gourds. They are true bugs with sucking mouth parts that drain the juices out of leaves, often killing whole plants in the process. You may first notice pale green or yellow specks on the leaves that soon enlarge into brown patches. Other parts of the plant may suddenly wilt and turn brittle. Eventually, the vines turn black and die. Your best battle tactics are:

Before you launch your attack on squash bugs, look around and make sure that they're really the guilty party. Their sucking produces damage that looks very similar to the symptoms of fusarium and verticillium wilts, two deadly diseases that are spread by cucumber beetles and squash vine borers.

- As soon as your plants bloom, start inspecting leaves for egg cases. Clip off any that you find, drop them into a bucket of soapy water, and toss the whole mess into your compost bin.

- Put a piece of thin board or heavy cardboard under each of your cucurbit plants, and check back frequently. You'll find hordes of squash bugs under the board. Then you can simply smash them with a hoe or your foot.

- Go out early in the morning, when the bugs are drowsy, and sweep 'em up with a wet/dry vacuum cleaner. (Put an inch or two of soapy water in the reservoir first.) If you don't have a wet/dry model, use a handheld version, and dump the bugs into a bucket of soapy water when you're done.

Quick Fix

To guard against both cucumber beetles and squash bugs, grow your crops in tires. Just set the tires on top of your prepared planting bed, and tuck two or three seeds into each one. Later, thin the seedlings to one per tire—choosing the strongest one, of course. No one quite knows why, but something in the rubber does a remarkable job of repelling both types of insects.

Bug Off, Bunnies!

Mother Nature blessed rabbits with the cutest good looks this side of a teddy bear store. Unfortunately, she also equipped them with razor-sharp teeth and an appetite for any plant under the sun. On the bright side, rabbits are just about the most timid critters on the planet, and that gives you some simple ways to bid them a fast farewell. This trio is the cream of the crop.

Give 'em the hair of the dog . . . and the human. Lay circles of it around your plants, and hang bags of it from fences, trellises, and branches. Hairdressers and dog groomers are usually happy to supply as much as you want.

Shine light in their eyes. Fill 1-gallon glass bottles with water and set them in and among your plants. Sunlight bouncing off the glass startles rabbits (and other animals, too).

Make 'em smell danger. Round up all the old (preferably stinky) shoes you can find and scatter them around your garden. Set out a new supply every few days so that the odor is always fresh.

Rampaging Raccoons

These masked marvels are some of the cleverest, most conniving—and most gluttonous—critters on God's green earth. Raccoons will eat just about anything they can get their paws on, but here are several simple ways to keep them out of your vegetable patch:

❧ Gather up all the electric fans you can find, and set them in place around your garden. (Be sure to use outdoor-grade extension cords.) Then, just

Quick Fix

Here's something that should be music to the ears of any impatient gardener: One of the easiest ways to make your garden less tempting to rabbits may just be to slack off a little in your weeding chores. How so? Well, a recent scientific study on the food preferences of bunnies revealed that these were their favorites, paws down:

- Crabgrass
- Daisy fleabane
- Dandelions
- Knotweed
- Lespedeza (the one shrub in this weedy roster)
- Ragweed

I've dug down deep into my almost endless files, searched all of the nooks and crannies, and come up with my best 124 gardening secrets that'll get you growing like gangbusters quick as a wink. From lawns and flowers to your favorite potted plants, there's a little something for everyone. Check out:

So get ready 'cause here goes nothing—and I really mean it: You can have the prettiest yard and garden in town by using a whole lot of nothing like old newspapers, torn window screens, and empty milk jugs to name just a few.

For more of my terrific tips, tricks, and tonics, check out my website: **www.jerrybaker.com.** It's packed with plenty of handy how-to information to keep everything in your home, yard, and garden in tip-top shape!

Lush and Lovely Lawns

1 Easy Seeding

To evenly distribute grass seed, punch several holes in the bottom of a bucket, and fill the bucket with seeds. Then, walk back and forth across your lawn, gently shaking the seeds out of the bucket.

2 Screen Saver

Place your old window screens over areas of your lawn that you've just reseeded. The seed will stick, <u>and</u> be protected from hungry birds. You can even spray paint the screen green before placing it if you want it to blend into its surroundings.

DRAT!!!

3 Give It Some Grub

Treat your lawn to a great late-summer snack. Just mix all of the leftover lawn, garden, and flower food you have taking up space in your garden shed, and apply it with your hand-held spreader set on the medium setting.

4 Compost Cuisine

Compost is great for your lawn! So sprinkle a light layer over the grass in both spring and fall for super results.

5 A Spot of Tea

To repair a small bare spot in your lawn, place a moist teabag on the spot, and sow grass seed on top of it. The bag will provide much-needed moisture and nutrients.

6 Read the Meter

Place a clean, empty can on your lawn at the farthest sprinkling point. Then stop watering when your handy, dandy "meter" is 2 to 3 inches full.

7 Hose Holster

Keep your garden hose from knotting, tangling, and twisting by loosely coiling it around the bottom of an old garbage can or other large container.

8 Mole Patrol

To reclaim your lawn from pesky moles, sprinkle used kitty litter in and along their mole runs. The aroma will drive the little rascals right out of your yard!

Terrific Trees, Shrubs and Evergreens

9 Pipe Down!

Use hollow, plastic pipes as plant supports. When it's time to water, you can pour H_2O right down the pipe and straight to the roots.

10 Stand Up Straight

To keep a tree you're planting straight, tie the trunk to a long 2 X 4 that's sitting at ground level. Backfill the hole and pack down the soil, then remove the board, and your tree will be standing straight as an arrow.

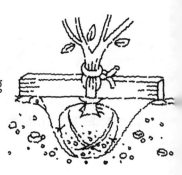

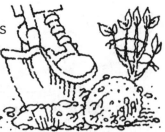

11 Movin' Right Along...

Transplant your evergreens in either late fall or early spring for the best results. And make sure you take a good size ball of earth around their roots to get them off to a good start in their new home.

12 Relocate Your Shrubs

Before moving bushes to new locations in your yard, loosely tie the branches together. You'll have an easier time digging up the roots and wind up with few—if any—broken branches.

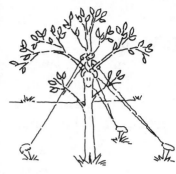

13 Keep It Loose

All newly planted trees need to be staked to prevent them from being blown down or tipped over by heavy snow. But don't stake them too tightly in place—they need to bend naturally in the wind.

14 See Ya, Suckers!

Nip suckers from plants as soon as you see them. If you don't, they'll run wild and eventually crowd out the portion of the plant you want to grow healthy and tall.

15 Not Welcome Mat

Scatter cut-up thorny rose and/or berry stems in the mulch around your trees to discourage would-be snackers like mice and other tree trashin' thugs.

16 Stone Hedge

Protect your trees from the rough edges of decorative stones by first wrapping a layer of landscape fabric around the base of their trunks. Cover the fabric with 2 inches of dried, brown grass clippings, then place the stones on top of the clippings.

Terrific Trees, Shrubs and Evergreens

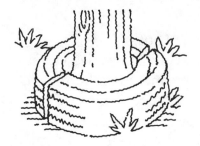

17 **It's a Wrap!**
Protect tree trunks from lawn mower damage by cutting an old tire in half, and then placing each half around the trunk.

18 **Safety First**
When you're bringing in the heavy equipment to work on the landscaping in your yard, protect your trees from construction gear by surrounding the trunks with planks held on with bungee cords.

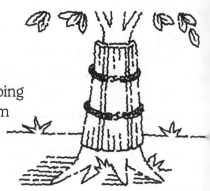

19 **Bug Off!**
To keep bugs from troubling your trees, spray a 10-inch wide strip of burlap on one side with sticky insect trap coating (like Tangle-Trap®). Secure it to the tree with a panty hose leg around its middle, allowing the top half of the burlap to drape over the bottom half. Bugs will get trapped between the two sticky surfaces.

20 **Leaf Eater**
Fill a metal garbage can halfway with fallen leaves that you've raked up. Then lower a string trimmer into the can, power it up, and chop the leaves to make mulch.

21 First Aid for Trees

To help your ailing trees in winter-time, wrap them with 4-inch strips of burlap from the ground up to the first branch. The burlap acts as insulation, keeping the tree cool and moist until the temps warm up again.

22 Tater Crate

Keep fresh cuttings moist for a brief time while you transport them from one area of your yard to another by poking small holes in a raw potato, and gently inserting the cuttings right into the holes.

23 Nuts to Weeds

Believe it or not, peanuts are a weed's worst enemy. So surround trees and shrubs with a 4-inch layer of peanut shells for the weed-killin'est mulch around.

24 Winterize Your Shrubs

You can protect small shrubs from wicked winter weather with a tomato cage. Just line it with sheets of newspaper and fill the empty space with fallen leaves.

Bloomin' Beauties

25 The Rule of Four

Always transplant seedlings on a cloudy or overcast day, and never, ever make the move until the precious babies have at least four leaves. The second set—"true leaves"—are needed to help withstand transplant shock.

26 Gesundheit!

Make sure you give your annuals a good soaking when you water them—but not a cold! Aim at their toes, not their nose. And don't sprinkle their clothes.

27 Bumbershoots

Save your old, broken umbrellas because the ribs make excellent, long-lasting supports for flowers. Paint them green, and they will hardly be visible among your blooming beauties.

28 Clean 'Em Out

Remove dead flowers from annual and perennial bedding plants as soon as you can, otherwise they could spread infection and disease to their healthy counterparts.

29 Peony Perfection

If you want your peonies to produce the plumpest blooms on the block, then pick off the side buds when they are very small, leaving only the main end bud on each stalk.

30 Hanger Hang-Ons

Out-of-shape wire hangers make great garden stakes. Simply straighten out the bends at the corners— but leave the hook intact to link onto sturdy plants.

31 Six-Pack Support

Use plastic six-pack pop can holders to support wayward vines. Attach one side to a permanent object like a fence post, and loop the vines through the holes. The holder will support the vines, but give and stretch as the plants grow.

32 Bloomin' Barrel

Drive a stake into the center of a barrel, and stretch string from the stake to the edges. Plant vines around the edges and train them to grow up the strings.

Bloomin' Beauties

33 Rollin', Rollin', Rollin'!

Make a movable bed of flowers out of an old toy wagon. Drill a few drainage holes in the bottom, add a thin layer of gravel, top with soil, and plant. When it's time to mow, simply roll the posies out of the way!

34 Put a Bonnet on It

To save your sunflower seeds, cover the flowers with netting tied underneath. That way, the seeds won't fall off and birds won't get to snack on 'em.

35 Petunia Protection

Cover your precious petunias with cardboard boxes before a hard rain. That way, you'll keep the colorful blooms from being flattened in a storm.

36 ID Tag

After lifting tender bulbs for the winter, brush away the loose dirt, then use a felt tip marker to write the plant name and color directly on the bulb. You'll save yourself a whole lot of guesswork come spring.

37 Defrost Your Flowers
If your plants get hit unexpectedly by a heavy frost overnight, water them lightly the next morning. This'll thaw them out quickly, and you'll save many of them.

38 Fresh Flower Dryin'
To preserve fresh-cut flowers, hang them upside down in a dark, well-ventilated place (like your garden shed) until they've dried. Hanging them upside down will help keep the colors bright and beautiful.

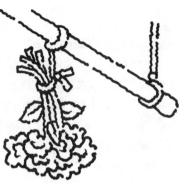

39 Ouchless Roses
Use a pair of nail clippers to trim the thorns from fresh-cut roses before arranging them in a vase.

40 Cut Rose Alert!
Place roses in water immediately after cutting them. Then, once  you're inside, cut the stems again on a slant while holding them under running water. This keeps air from getting into the stems, and helps the roses last longer.

Vibrant Veggies

41 Worth Its Salt

Use an old salt shaker to sow small seeds in the rows of your vegetable garden. It will distribute the tiny little fellas more evenly and keep them from getting lost in the shuffle.

42 Do the Can-Can!

After planting your veggies, bury cans (with both ends removed) between the plants, then fill the cans with rocks. When it's time to water your vegetable garden, pour directly into the cans so the water is delivered straight to the roots.

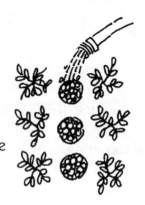

43 Tape It Up

Save broken stems on tender, young seedlings by making small splints out of toothpicks, then scotch-taping them into place.

44 Precipitation Protection

Defend young plants from the elements by covering them with caps made of panty hose. Tie the tops together, slip one over each plant, and pull the bottoms closed.

45 Spud Sower

A hand-held bulb planter is perfect for planting potatoes. Make holes 8 inches deep every 12 inches or so, plant the piece of potato in it, and then backfill with soil from the hole.

46 Egg 'Em On

Eggshells make great seed-starting pots. Poke a hole in the bottom, fill 'em with soil, and plant your seeds. When transplanting, simply crack the shells slightly, and then bury the plants, eggshell and all.

47 Thug Thwarter

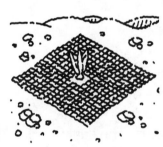

To protect your tender seedlings from bugs, slugs, and other thugs, cut out 7-inch squares of old window screens, and make an opening in the center of each to place your plants through. The static electricity generated will keep the bad guys at bay.

48 Draw the Line

Use your finger to draw a ring in the soil around new plants. The water collected in this mini-basin will go straight to the roots and help your plants grow.

Vibrant Veggies

49 Foil Garden Felons

Aluminum foil reflects light—which some insects can't stand! So lay it down as a mulch around your squash, cukes, and corn to keep the local bug population in check.

50 Mosey Along, Moles

You know that deep bass fiddle sound you can make by blowing across the top of a soda pop bottle? That sound scares moles off, pronto. So bury bottles up to their necks around the edge of your garden, and let the wind do the whooshing.

51 Pet Patrol

To keep rabbits and other small varmints out of your veggie patch, wrap bunches of dog or cat hair in old nylon stockings, and hang them in various areas. The critters will think that Fido or Fluffy is on duty.

52 Give 'Em a Pinch

If you want to grow whopper tomatoes, pinch off all of the suckers that develop between the branches. This will make the plant stronger and the fruit bigger.

53 Fork It Over

A bent up, mangled, or old kitchen fork makes a great cultivation tool, particularly in those hard-to-reach, delicate areas like your herb garden. You can also use them as wind chimes, so don't toss 'em!

54 Cultivate Your Cukes

Put Isaac Newton's theory to work in your garden. For perfect cukes, grow them on a fence or trellis—gravity will straighten them out.

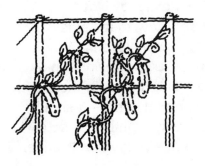

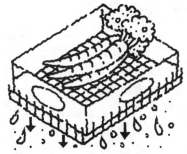

55 Silk-Free Solution

Here's a neat harvesting trick—to remove the silk from your corn, rub a damp paper towel along the ear. The silk will cling to the paper, not the corn.

56 Keep 'Em Clean

Replace the bottom of a wooden box with chicken wire for a fresh-picked vegetable cleaning station. Then you can rinse your veggies off right in the garden.

Fabulous Fruit

57 Melon Minder

To prevent melons from rotting on the ground, cut clean plastic milk jugs in half, and place one half under each growing melon.

58 Ready, or Not?

Here's how to tell whether or not your melons are ripe for the picking: Check the blossom end (opposite the stem) by pressing on it—it should give way slightly and smell kind of sweet when it's ripe.

59 Card the Cantaloupes

Protect your melons from marauding menaces by setting them on top of pieces of cardboard or thin Styrofoam. Earth-bound bugs won't get to sample the juicy goodness.

60 Holey Sock!

Don't toss your old cotton socks. Cut one hole in the bottom that's big enough to fit your fingers through, and another one for your thumb. Then pull it on over your berry-picking hand to protect your arms from thorns and branches.

61 Nutty Berries

Before your strawberries ripen, paint some walnuts red and place them around the plants. One nibble of a nut and the birds will steer clear.

62 Clip the Pits

Paper clips make good cherry pitters. Simply unbend the main curve of the wire, then use the large end as a handle and the small end to scoop out the cherry pits.

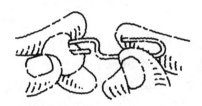

63 Panty Hose Picker

For an easy, breezy fruit picker, attach a stiff wire hoop to the end of a pole, and stretch a leg from a pair of panty hose around it. You'll be able to pick fruit from high branches without bruising it.

64 Grape Expectations

Cover ripening grape bunches with brown paper bags to keep birds away. Just make sure you cut slits in the bags before placing them on the clusters so the grapes won't be gasping for air.

Handy Garden Helpers

 Pipe Up!

Make a simple "conveyor belt" out of PVC pipes to move heavy planters from one place to another in your yard. Lay them next to each other, place the planter on top, and start rolling, moving the last pipe to the front as you go.

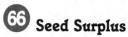 **Seed Surplus**

Store leftover seeds in their original packet, clipped shut, and filed in a recipe box along with other seed packets.

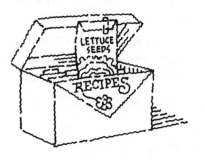

 **Get in the Green Zone**

An old football helmet makes a great plant container. Just add some soil and a little plant, and hang the whole shebang up by the face guard.

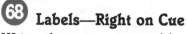 **Labels—Right on Cue**

Write plant names on old billiard balls and use them as crafty, eclectic labels in your vegetable garden.

69 Fabulous Flatware

Use an old butter knife as a sturdy stake for your fragile spring seedlings.

70 Curdy, Wordy Markers

For weatherproof plant labels, cut clean, empty cottage cheese containers into strips and use a permanent marker to write the plant names on them.

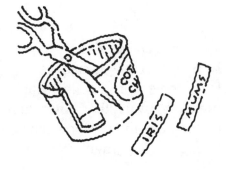

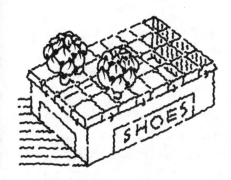

71 Think Inside the Box

To dry top-heavy plants like artichokes and alliums, make a drying rack out of chicken wire stapled to an old shoebox.

72 Solar Tiles

Flat tiles set beside your plants will soak up enough of the sun's heat during the day to keep your greens cozy during chilly nights.

Handy Garden Helpers

73 Steady Eddie

When you're working on soft or uneven ground and need to climb a stepladder, keep it steady by placing the legs in four large, empty coffee cans.

74 On Bended Knee

Don't toss away those plastic foam trays your butcher wraps meat on—wash them thoroughly, then use them as kneeling pads in your garden.

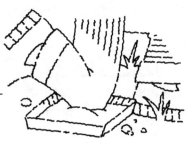

75 Terrific Traction

Ice-melting salt is deadly to plants, so next time your forecast calls for icy weather, scoop some wood ashes out of your fireplace. The ashes will keep you from slipping, but won't keep your grass from growin' come spring.

76 Flower-Shower Cap

If your hanging plant doesn't have a saucer, pull a shower cap over the bottom of the container while you water, temporarily securing it to the planter with a rubber band, if necessary.

77 Got Milk?

Cut the bottoms off empty plastic milk jugs and set the tops over your tender plants to extend your growing season even after the weather turns chilly.

78 Tie the Knot(s)

For quick and easy storage of your onions, put one bulb in the leg of old panty hose, tie a knot above it, add another onion, tie a knot, and so on, until the leg is filled, Hang the onions in a cool, dry place. Then, when you need an onion, simply cut underneath the lowest knot.

79 Can-tainer Garden

Add clean, empty soda pop cans upside-down in the bottom of large containers to keep the planters light enough to lift. You'll wind up using less potting soil, too.

80 Mighty-Fine Twine Dispenser

Set a clay pot over a ball of garden twine for a handy holder that will prevent the cord from tangling as you pull it through the hole.

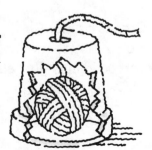

Tools of the Trade

81 Clever Compost Cooker
Recycle old tires by turning them into an instant compost bin. Stack up three or four tires and fill 'em with paper, grass, kitchen scraps, manure, and other compostable materials.

82 What a Crate Idea!
You'll get debris-free compost every time if you load it into an old milk crate and shake, shake, shake! Only the good stuff will come out and fall right where you want it in your garden.

83 Wrap It Up
Don't get rid of an old tire rim, because it makes a great place to hang your garden hose. Mount it near the spigot and wrap your hose around it. That's all there is to it—no more snarled hose!

84 Greens on the Go
An empty old milk jug makes it easy to transport seedlings. Just cut away the top of the jug, poke some drainage holes in the bottom, and set the plants inside.

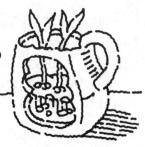

85 News You Can Use

To protect young plants from frost, cover them with a sheet of newspaper held in place with bricks or large stones.

86 Fantastic Funnel

Punch a hole in the bottom of half an eggshell, and use it as a handy, disposable funnel to fill your sprayers.

87 Clean with Cobs

Scrub your grubby garden tools clean with old, dried corncobs. When you're done, just toss the cobs on the compost pile.

88 Clean Water

If you're collecting water from your rain spout, slip an old panty hose leg over the bottom of the spout, and hold it in place with a rubber band. That way, the water in your rain barrel will be clean and clear.

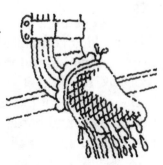

Tools of the Trade

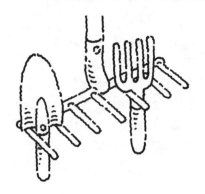

89 Rake Recycling

Instead of throwing out an old rake, use it as a tool holder. Simply hang the head upside down in a convenient place, and suspend your tools between the tines.

90 Sand Bucket Storage

Use a pail of clean, dry sand to store your small garden tools in. The sand will keep them "heads up" and rust-free when you're not using them.

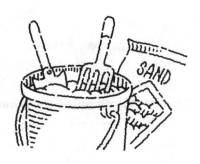

91 Yell "Oh!"

Do you have a bad habit of losing your garden tools in the grass? Here's a simple solution: Paint the handles bright yellow, and then you'll always be able to spot them.

92 Go Postal

Stop making countless trips back and forth from the garden to the shed. Get yourself a mailbox, decorate it as you wish, and place it in a convenient location in your yard. Store your gloves and garden tools in it. The "garden-box" will keep 'em all high, dry, and handy!

93 Cut 'Em Off

Thin your seedlings by snipping the weaklings off with scissors. It's much less damaging to the remaining plants than trying to yank or snap them off.

94 Handle with Care

When pruning any particularly thorny branches, hold them back out of your way with a pair of barbecue tongs for easy, "ouchless" pruning.

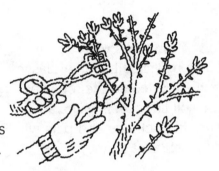

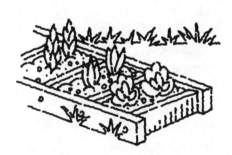

95 Among the Rungs

An old step ladder makes a great herb garden. Simply lay the ladder down on a flat area, fill the opening between the rungs with soil, and plant a different herb in each section.

96 Hang It Up

Keep your garage neat and clean by making a wall-mounted tool rack. Insert a screw eye hook in each of the handle ends, and then hang the tools on finish nails that you've pounded into exposed wall studs or crossbeams.

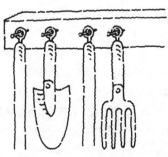

Pest Patrol

97 A Sticky Situation

Hang red plastic balls in your apple trees after you've coated them with petroleum jelly. The goopy surface will trap flies and keep apple maggots away from your fruit.

98 Pesticide Protection

Place pesticide bait in a plastic bottle, buried so the top is at the soil line. Pests will crawl in and die, but kids and pets will stay safe and sound.

99 Foiled Again!

Loosely wrap strips of aluminum foil around vegetable seedling stems to protect the tender young greens from cutworms.

100 Defend the Fruit

To protect grape clusters from bugs, birds, and other snackin' bad guys, loosely wrap the bunches in bags of cheesecloth.

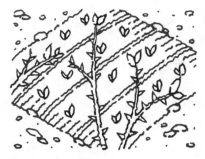

101 Seedbed Savers

Keep tender-footed critters away from freshly planted seeds by covering the beds with thorny rose bush trimmings or holly branches.

102 Mosey On, Mole!

Is your yard up to its elbows in moles—and their ankle-twisting runs? Pick up a bunch of child's pinwheels at the dollar store, and stick them in the runs every 10 feet. The vibrations will drive 'em nuts and send 'em packing!

103 Bye-Bye Fruit Fly!

Trap pesky fruit flies by pouring a little cola in the bottom of a take-out drink cup and pushing a straw partway through the lid. The flies crawl in, but they won't be able to get out.

104 Soothe a Sting

Take the zing out of a bee sting by gently rubbing the area with a freshly sliced potato. Ahhhh, that's better.

Beautiful Birds & Butterflies

105 Splish, Splash!
Hollow out the top of an old tree stump to make a shallow basin for birds. Just fill it with water, stand back, and watch the birds enjoying their bath.

106 Prickly Protection
Nesting birds go to great lengths to protect their hatchlings from cats. Give 'em a hand by planting a climbing rose at the base of the tree in which they've made their home.

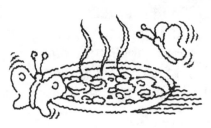

107 Peanuts! Get Your Peanuts!
Enjoy hours of wintertime bird watching fun. Simply thread peanuts, kernels and all, onto a sturdy string, and drape it across the branches of a nearby tree.

108 Bring on the Butterflies
Leave dishes filled with a mixture of stale beer or over-ripe fruit and juice in your yard. It'll attract a bevy of beautiful butterflies!

BEAUTIFUL BIRDS & BUTTERFLIES

109 Presoak Your Planters

Soak clay pots for a day in mild soapy water before planting in them. If you don't, and you start with dry pots, they'll suck all of the moisture out of your potting soil, leaving your dirt desert dry.

110 Bottle Top Tip

Protect your tender, young potted seedlings by placing the top half of a plastic pop bottle over them. Give 'em a little air by removing the twist-off cap.

111 Keep 'Em Moist

To keep a potted plant from getting thirsty, tuck a wet sponge in the potting soil right below the roots before tucking in the plant.

112 Pencil It In

Make sure your leggy plants don't get tipsy by using a wooden pencil as a stake. Just insert the pencil into the soil, next to the plant, and then tie them together with a small strip of panty hose.

Happy Houseplants

113 Freshen Up

When rooting plant clippings in water, add a lump of charcoal to the glass. It will help slow plant decay and fight bad odors. Just don't use charcoal that's been doused with lighter fluid.

114 Super Shells

Crush your empty eggshells and use 'em as the drainage layer in the bottom of your pots instead of pebbles. They'll make your planter lighter and add valuable nutrients to the soil.

115 Soil Softener

If the surface of the soil they're planted in gets hard and crusted, seedlings aren't strong enough to force their way through. So, keep the soil soft by adding 1 teaspoon of baby shampoo per quart of warm water.

116 Gentle Watering

Fasten a panty hose foot to a garden hose to make a terrific diffuser for watering delicate container plants.

117 Mist Shield

When misting house-plants, hold a piece of cardboard over the fragile flowers as a shield so that only the hardier leaves get wet.

118 Clean and Green

Dislodge dirt and dust from your prickly and fuzzy houseplants with a hairdryer set on "cool" or "low."

119 Wick Away

Water your houseplants while you're away on vacation with an old-fashioned wick system. Put one end of the wick in a gallon of water, and bury the other end in the soil next to the plant.

120 Careful Clippin'

Whenever you clip the brown tips off your houseplants, be sure to leave a bit of brown border. You'll only cause more damage if you cut through the live tissue.

Happy Houseplants

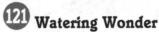

121 Watering Wonder

You'll give your houseplants a slow, steady supply of water if you place ice cubes on the soil in their pots. The melting ice will keep their thirst quenched.

122 Collar the Bad Guys

Don't throw out your dog's old flea collars—recycle them by cutting them up and placing them on the soil of your houseplants to get rid of insects.

123 Clean That Cactus

Use an old toothbrush to clean dust from prickly cacti without poking your fingers.

124 Water Right!

Borrow a turkey baster from your kitchen gadget drawer when it's time to water your houseplants. It'll hurry the H_2O right to the roots and keep the leaves perfectly dry.

before you go to bed, turn 'em all on. Repeat this trick every night for a week or so, and the raccoons will head for calmer pastures.

- Lay a 3-foot-wide strip of any sticky, slippery, or sharp material around the garden perimeter. When the raccoons' sensitive, hairless feet touch the surface, they'll clear out fast. Good choices include plastic sheeting, wire mesh, jagged stones, and smooth, round pebbles.

- Cover individual plants with wire-mesh cages that are anchored firmly to the ground. Use screening that has ½- to 1-inch openings so that insects can get in to pollinate the blossoms. And make sure the structures are big enough to hold the plant at maturity.

- To protect bigger crops like corn and vining tomatoes, prop old window screens or bushel baskets against the cornstalks or tomato supports.

> ### SURE DOESN'T SMELL LIKE FOOD!
>
> Raccoons hate the scents of bleach and ammonia. So fill old margarine containers or other small bowls with either of the aromatic fluids (don't mix them), and set them among your vulnerable plants. The greedy gluttons will go elsewhere for dinner.

Great Galloping Gophers!

Evidence of gophers is sometimes mistaken for that of moles because the two little critters share the same simple approach to life: Dig it, man! But moles eat only grubs and other insects; any damage they do to plants is a by-product of their enthusiasm for the chase (see Chapter 1). Gophers, on the other hand, are rodents that eat nothing *but* plants, and plenty of them. Fortunately, you have several excellent options for protecting your veggies.

Lay some flat fences. Line the bottom and sides of each planting hole—or the entire bed if it's small enough—with ½-inch galvanized wire mesh. Lay the screen about 2 feet underground, and make sure it covers the sides all the way up to a few inches above the soil surface. Don't leave any gaps because gophers can squeeze through even the tiniest openings.

Hot-Pepper Punch

Almost without exception, animals share one common trait: a profound disgust for anything that tastes or smells hot. All you need to do to deter any critter—from a teeny-tiny mole to a great big, beautiful deer—is spray their stomping grounds, or your vulnerable plants, with this fiery potion.

> ½ **cup of dried cayenne peppers**
> ½ **cup of jalapeño peppers**
> **1 gal. of water**

Add the peppers to the water, bring it to a boil, and let it simmer for half an hour. (Keep the pan covered, or the peppery steam will make you cry a river of tears!) Let the mixture cool, strain out the solids, pour the liquid into a handheld sprayer bottle, and spritz your plants from top to bottom. To ensure continued protection, reapply after every rain.

Splurge on spurge. Run down to the garden center and buy as much gopher spurge, a.k.a. mole plant *(Euphorbia lathyris),* as you can afford. Then plant it all around the perimeter of your garden. The roots produce an acrid, milky juice that sends gophers packing, pronto!

Sound 'em out. Like a lot of critters, gophers are very sensitive to sound vibrations. So gather up six or eight empty glass bottles and half-bury them, top ends up, in a line near the gophers' hangouts. When the wind passes over them, it'll make a scary noise that'll send the little guys scurrying in a hurry. **Note:** This trick will also help keep voles, groundhogs, and rabbits out of your vegetable garden.

Help—or Trouble—on the Wing

Most birds gobble up so many destructive insects during the growing season that they're worth their weight in hundred-dollar bills. And besides eating up the bugs that munch on your veggies, they'll polish off the ones that like to bother you and your four-footed family members. Birds that hang around for the winter also chow down on hibernating bugs and future bugs, a.k.a. eggs. On the other hand, some birds can make real nuisances of themselves, especially at spring planting time.

So how do you tell the varmints from the volunteers? It's simple: Just take a close look. If a bird has spindly legs and a short, thick, cone-shaped beak, it's a seed eater—and you want it to steer clear of your veggie patch, at least until your plants are well past the seedling stage. But if you see a bird with either a thin and pointy or short, wide, and gaping type of beak, you've found a friend.

A bird with a thin and pointy beak eats insects, and plenty of them. It'll poke that beak into all those tiny places where bugs hide, and gobble them up from the ground, too. Wrens, warblers, kingbirds, phoebes, and all kinds of flycatchers fit this bill.

On the other hand, a bird with a short, wide, and gaping beak grabs food on the fly. Swifts, swallows, nighthawks, purple martins, and whip-poor-wills all snatch pesky pests as they're streaking through the air.

HELP!

Q I had to take my bird feeder down because raccoons were coming right up on my deck, opening up the lid, and eating all the seed! The birds don't come around anymore, and I miss them so much. Can you tell me how to keep the rascals away from my feeder?

A *Here's a neat trick you can try: Hook up a motion detector to a couple of strong spotlights aimed at the feeder. The birds will be able to feed in comfort during the day, but when the raccoons come around at night, the sudden, bright light will send them scampering. This method will also keep deer and other critters out of your garden—that is, provided it's close enough to a power source.*

Bye-Bye, Birdie!

When birds are helping themselves to your seeds or vegetables, the only guaranteed way to protect your crops is to cover the plants with nets or floating row covers. Simply surrounding your garden with things that flash or whip around in the wind will also keep down some of the damage. Just remember to use a combination of objects, not just one, and change them every so often so the birds don't get used to thinking of them as part of the scenery. Any of these items will do the trick:

- Aluminum pie and cake tins

- Helium-filled Mylar™ balloons

- Pinwheels

- Small mirrors

- Strips of Mylar

- Whirligigs

- Wind socks

Quick Fix

Aluminum foil is a surefire weapon that'll guard your crops from flying insects of all kinds. But if you have a lot of plants to protect, leave the foil in the kitchen and buy some reusable, silver-colored mulch at the garden center. It'll do the same good job and last for years. Just remove the glittery stuff when the weather gets hot, or the intense sun could burn lower plant leaves.

Hooray—Foiled Again!

You may think of aluminum foil as simply a handy kitchen aid. But actually, its strength and flashy, light-reflecting texture make it one of the most potent tools you can have in your pest-control arsenal. Here's how to put it to work outside.

Make your garden cat-free. And your bird feeders, too! Fill empty 2-liter pop bottles halfway with water, and add a few drops of bleach to keep algae from growing. Then drop two or three long, thin strips of aluminum foil into each bottle, and set the containers every few feet around the area you want to protect. The constantly changing reflections from the foil and water will make cats think twice before they venture closer.

PEST-CHASING PLANTS

Just as many insects are repelled by the chemicals in certain plants, so are a lot of four-legged critters. Here are some especially beautiful plants that can work as true guardian angels in your vegetable garden (or anyplace else in your yard).

TO KEEP THESE AWAY	PLANT THESE IN YOUR VEGETABLE GARDEN
Cats	Common rue (*Ruta graveolens*)
Deer	Russian sage (*Perovskia atriplicifolia*)
Dogs	Pot marigold (*Calendula officinalis*)
Groundhogs	Nasturtium (*Tropaeolum majus*)
Mice	Perennial sweet pea (*Lathyrus latifolius*)
Moles	Mole plant (*Euphorbia lathyris*)
Rabbits	Mexican marigold, a.k.a. Mexican tarragon or Texas tarragon (*Tagetes lucida*)
Squirrels	Crown imperial (*Fritillaria imperialis*)

Erect a flashing fence. To keep birds and four-legged critters like rabbits and raccoons away from your garden, pound stakes into the soil at 3- to 4-foot intervals all around the plot, and run twine between the stakes. Then cut aluminum foil into strips about 1 inch wide and 5 inches long, and tape them every foot or so to the twine.

Foil cutworms. All vegetable and flower seedlings are vulnerable to these pests. To bar the "door," wrap foil loosely around the stem of each tender young plant. The foil should extend about 2 inches below the ground and 3 inches above. You can remove the wrapping when the stalk is about ½ inch in diameter because at that stage, it's too thick for the cutworms to damage.

Foil squash vine borers, too. Don't let the name fool you. In addition to all types of squash, these borers target tomatoes, peppers, and eggplant. Protect your harvest by wrapping a 2- to 3-inch strip of aluminum foil around the base of each plant—and keep it there right through the growing season. Check it frequently, though, and loosen the foil or apply a longer strip as necessary.

Take 2

Even after it's done protecting your plants, aluminum foil can still give you a hand in the garden—as long as it's fairly clean, of course. Just crumple foil pieces into a ball, and use it to scrape mud off your shovels and other tools. In the process, you'll also sharpen the tools' edges a bit.

Fend off slugs. These slimy villains will sink their jaws into just about any kind of plant under the sun. But the good news is that they can't get through a coat of metallic armor. To protect single-stemmed plants, wrap a 1-inch-high band of crinkled aluminum foil around the bottom of the stem. For multi-stemmed plants, make a foil ring that's long enough to encircle the whole base of the slugs' target.

Deter flying insects. When placed on the soil around plants, aluminum foil will deter aphids, moths, thrips, whiteflies, and other destructive and disease-spreading insects. How? The light reflecting off the foil confuses the bugs so much that they can't land. When you use this trick, it's important to poke holes a few inches apart in the foil so that water can get down to the plants' roots. Also, check on it periodically to see if the shiny covering is reflecting too much hot sun onto the foliage. If the plants' lower leaves appear dry or crinkled, remove the foil immediately and give your plants a nice, cool drink of water.

CHAPTER 7

FIRST-CLASS FRUIT

Sweet Treats from Trees, Bushes, and Vines

What's your favorite fruity delight? A warm slab of apple pie fresh from the oven? A basket filled to the brim with blueberry muffins front and center on the breakfast table? Or a big slice of watermelon on a hot summer day? No matter what kinds of fruit tickle your taste buds, I have good news for you: With no more time and effort than it takes to grow flowers or vegetables, you can treat yourself and your family to the kind of old-time flavor and freshness you'll never find in the supermarket produce aisles.

TASTE-TEMPTING TREE FRUITS

A lot of folks are convinced that growing a great (or even edible) crop of tree fruit is a constant battle against every kind of pest and disease under the sun. Well, friends, don't listen to them! Oh, I will admit that fruit (and nut) trees can attract their fair share of trouble. And, just like any other kinds of plants, they need a certain amount of tender loving care from you if they're going to grow strong, healthy, and productive. But the fact is, when you're fully armed with my tips, tricks, and terrific tonics, fruit trees are no harder—and

Short on space? No problem! Nearly all fruit trees come in dwarf forms that thrive in big pots. Bush and vine fruits, including strawberries, blueberries, raspberries, and even grapes, also enjoy life in containers.

no more time-consuming—to live with than their just-for-show cousins.

Find Fruits That Suit

The process for selecting fruit trees is a combination of the procedures I recommended in Chapter 2 for choosing ornamental trees and in Chapter 6 for selecting vegetables. These pointers will put you on the high road to maximum pleasure and minimum trouble with your fruiters:

◈ Seek out fruit types and varieties that thrive in your region and the growing conditions in your yard. And whenever possible, choose trees that are native to your area. Your local native plant society or a native plant nursery can steer you in the right direction.

◈ Grow the kind(s) of fruit that you and your family like best. After all, why devote time, effort, and yard space to something your crowd thinks is just okay?

HARMONY AT HOME

You say that almost everyone in your family favors a different kind of fruit, but you have room for only a single tree? Don't worry. Just plant a combination tree that has four to six different varieties of apples, pears, or plums grafted onto a single trunk. Or go with a fruit cocktail, a.k.a. fruit salad, tree that sports an assortment of peaches, plums, nectarines, and apricots. You can find these wonders of modern horticulture in many nurseries and (of course) on the Internet.

◈ Whatever type of fruit trees you decide to plant, find the most flavorful kinds possible. As with vegetables, the tastiest varieties of fruit rarely appear in supermarkets or even at farm stands. So crank up your favorite Internet search engine and type in "heirloom fruits." You'll find dozens of nurseries and catalogs that specialize in these flavor-packed superstars.

It Takes Two to Tango

And in the case of fruit trees, it also takes two to produce a good crop. That's because most kinds can't pollinate their own blossoms; they need another

H E L P !

Q My fruit trees have always produced great crops, but for the past couple of years they've been bearing poorly. They seem as healthy as can be, and they bloom to beat the band every spring. What do you think the problem might be?

A *It sounds like poor pollination—a problem I hear about a lot these days for one simple reason: Fruit trees depend largely on bees to pollinate their blossoms. But in recent years, disease, predatory mites, and pesticides have been killing off honeybees by the millions all over North America. I suggest that you rustle up a "herd" of Orchard Mason bees, which you can find at many garden centers and on the Internet. These gentle but powerful pollinators are solitary nesters (they don't form hives), and they're perfectly safe to have around even if you have small children on the scene.*

tree of a different variety to deliver the goods. Even trees that are technically self-pollinating generally produce much more fruit when they have help. (The same goes for nut trees.) So do yourself a favor, and plant two trees— but not just any two trees. A good fruit tree catalog will give you the complete rundown on which varieties make the best teammates.

If planting two trees isn't an option, here's a quick-fix alternative: Find a friend or neighbor who has a compatible variety, and ask for a few blooming sprigs. Sink the branches into a bucket of water, set them near your tree, and the birds and bees will take it from there.

Just as Easy, But . . .

I know I said that fruit trees are no more trouble to care for than the ornamental versions are, but they can be mighty finicky about their home ground. If your young 'uns are going to get up and grow the way you want them to, you need to pay close attention to these factors when you choose and plant your saplings.

Timing. Fruit trees prefer to be planted in early spring, when they're completely dormant. If you can't do the job then, or if the nursery can't guarantee delivery before the buds begin to open, wait until next year.

Location. Most fruit trees like full sun, and they demand plenty of elbow room. Catalogs list the spacing requirements for full-size, semi-dwarf, and dwarf trees. Choose whichever size you've got room for, and if there's any doubt at all, go with a smaller version. Whatever you do, keep new, young trees away from mature ones, which will outcompete them for water and nutrients.

Soil. All but a few kinds of fruit trees insist on near-perfect drainage. If the ground is the least bit soggy, they'll just sit in their holes and pout. Or rot.

All in the Family

Even though fruit trees have precise preferences about the place they call home, the planting process they prefer is same as it is for their ornamental relatives. In particular, avoid all temptation to beef up the soil with organic matter or any other amendments. If the roots wake up to find rich, cozy surroundings, they'll stay right there in their home, sweet hole, and you'll wind up with a weak tree that will attract lots of trouble. So to ensure your fruiting friends a happy start in life—and keep your caretaking time to a minimum—follow my simple six-step tree-planting process in Chapter 2 (see "The Up-to-Date Planting Process" on page 80).

The fruit tree feeding and watering routines are the same as they are for other trees, too. You'll also find those guidelines in Chapter 2.

Although most fruit trees and bushes need well-drained, loamy soil, there are some exceptions to that rule. In fact, elderberries (*Sambucus*) thrive with damp roots. And quince (*Cydonia oblonga*) and pears (*Pyrus*) grown on quince rootstocks are as happy as clams in clay soil with so-so drainage—thereby giving you a quick and easy way to enjoy homegrown fruit without undertaking a major drainage-improvement project.

Prune Before You Plant—Maybe

If your future fruiter is balled-and-burlapped or growing in a pot, no pruning is necessary. But if you've ordered a fruit tree by mail, most likely you will get a bare-root version. And unless the instructions you receive say the plant has already been pruned, you'll have to do the job yourself. But don't worry—it's a snap!

First, cut off any roots that are broken or have jagged edges. Next, "puddle in" the tree according to the directions in Chapter 2 (see "Bare-Root Preliminaries" on page 79). Then proceed in one of these two ways, depending on whether you've got a whip (a sapling with no side branches) or a branched youngster.

Whip. Cut it back by at least one-third. For instance, if the plant is 6 feet tall, take 2 feet off the top.

Branched sapling. First, prune off any branches that are weak, damaged, dead-looking, or too close to the ground. Then cut the top back by a third, and do the same with each strong, healthy limb. Make sure you cut just in front of an outward-facing bud, so the next branch will grow away from the trunk and the tree will spread as it should.

Whether you're pruning a whip or a young, branched tree, always cut on a slant just in front of a bud, using clean, sharp pruners.

Pot 'Em Up

If your yard is too shady or too wet for fruit trees, plant dwarf versions on your deck or patio instead. They'll do just fine in an 18- or 24-inch container in a

Grandma's GROW-HOW

If you're planting peach trees, take a tip from Grandma Putt, and put garlic on guard duty. It's a powerful coat of armor against peachtree borers, but only on one condition: The garlic has to be planted at the same time as the tree, in a circle all around the trunk. It works like a charm, though! **Note:** For the lowdown on controlling tree borers of all kinds, see page 93.

sunny area. Before you add soil, set each container on a wheeled dolly; this will make it easy to move the trees to a protected area when winter rolls around. Plant one tree per pot, and to start them off with a bang in their new quarters, give each one a heaping helping of my Potted Fruit Tree Growth Booster (below).

Some good choices for container growing include apples, dwarf peaches and nectarines, cherries, citrus (see "Citrus Time Up North" at right), figs, and olives. After three or so years, you'll need to root-prune your trees to keep them vigorous and prevent them from outgrowing their containers. When the time comes, follow this simple routine:

STEP 1. Lay the container on its side and roll it to loosen the root-ball. Pull the tree out of the container.

STEP 2. Using a sharp spade, slice off about one-third of the root-ball.

STEP 3. Repot the tree in fresh soil, tamping it down firmly in place.

Potted Fruit Tree Growth Booster

When you move your potted fruit trees to new containers, sift this fabulous formula into the soil as you work.

2 cups of crushed dry dog food*
2 cups of dry oatmeal
1 ½ tsp. of sugar
A pinch of human hair

Mix all of the ingredients together in a bucket, and sift ¼ to ½ cup of the mixture into each container. (I use a retired flour sifter for this job.) Then stand back and watch your little trees produce big results!

* Use a low-priced supermarket brand that contains corn gluten meal, an ingredient lacking in premium pet foods.

CITRUS TIME UP NORTH

You don't have to live in Florida or sunny California to enjoy the delicious taste of fresh citrus fruits plucked from your own homegrown trees. Even in the cold, snowy North, dwarf oranges, grapefruit, lemons, and other citrus trees will grow happily in pots on your deck or patio all summer long. Then when moved to a sunny spot indoors, many of them will continue handing you a happy, healthy harvest. Here's a small sampling of some of the best container candidates. **Note:** The mature sizes listed below are for unpruned trees, but you can easily keep them clipped to whatever height and width you desire.

CITRUS TREE	ANNUAL GROWTH RATE (FT.)	MATURE SIZE, UNPRUNED (FT.)
Key lime (*Citrus aurantifolia*) Zones 4–11 patio; 8–11 outdoors	2–3	H: 6–12 W: 6–8
Meyer lemon (*Citrus x meyeri*) Zones 4–11 patio; 8–11 outdoors	1–2	H: 5–10 W: 3–4
Navel orange (*Citrus sinensis* 'Osbeck') Zones 4–11 patio; 8–11 outdoors	3–4	H: 8–12 W: 8–12
Nules clementine (*Citrus clementina* 'de Nules') Zones 4–11 patio; 8–11 outdoors	2	H: 6–8 W: 4–6
Ruby red grapefruit (*Citrus x paradise* 'Ruby Red') Zones 4–11 patio; 8–11 outdoors	2	H: 15–20 W: 8–10

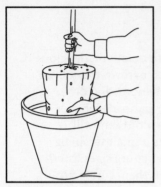

Gently set the plant into its pot.

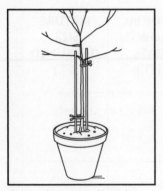

Fasten the tree to the stakes with soft cloth or broad strips of panty hose.

Firm the soil in place, then water thoroughly.

The Potting Process

In most parts of the country, spring is the best time for planting fruit trees in containers. Where winters are mild, you can do the job any time from early autumn to midwinter. (These guidelines also apply to shrubs and berry bushes.) First, choose a container that's 1 to 2 inches larger than the plant's root-ball on all sides. Next, remove any wrapping or packaging from the plant. Then proceed as follows:

STEP 1. Pour enough potting mix into the container so that the top of the root-ball lies about 1 inch below the rim of the pot. If you are planting a young tree that cannot stand on its own, insert a pole on either side of the root-ball.

STEP 2. Carefully set the plant in the pot, and gently spread the roots out if necessary.

STEP 3. If the tree needs support, secure it to the poles as described in "Tough Love for Trees" (see page 82).

STEP 4. Add more potting mix to fill the pot to within about 1 inch of the rim, holding the root-ball to keep it centered as you go.

STEP 5. Finish up by firming the soil with your hands, and watering thoroughly.

Pruning—Five for the Show

I would love to tell you that after you plant your fruit trees, you can just turn 'em loose to grow as they please, as you can with most ornamental versions. But if you do that, you'll soon wind up with unhealthy and poorly producing trees. Don't worry, though: It's a simple procedure! Just follow my general pruning guidelines in Chapter 2. As for when to do the job, it depends on what you want to accomplish. Woody fruiters need to be pruned for one of five main reasons.

To get the tree off to a good, strong start. This is done at planting time, and the advantages should be obvious!

To reduce the number of fruiting buds. Fewer buds make the plant produce fewer, but bigger, fruits. In the case of dwarf or semi-dwarf trees, it is also necessary to prevent overloading. It's best to tackle this chore in late winter, before the buds swell up.

To open up the center of the tree. Pruning in the center will ensure maximum light penetration and easier picking. Late winter is the ideal time for this procedure, too.

To force formation of fruit-bearing buds. Schedule this clip job just after the tree has blossomed.

To remove weak, damaged, and diseased wood. As in the case of ornamental trees, it's crucial to perform this first-aid procedure as soon as you spot the problem—before the disease spreads or insects penetrate the damaged tissue.

Although it's best to prune fruit trees in the winter, it's not absolutely necessary. If you'd rather not freeze your fingers, prune your trees in the summer! Contrary to "conventional wisdom," they will not "bleed" to death if you cut into them during the growing season. Wait until late summer, though, when the peak growth period has passed. And make sure you do the job at least two to five weeks before you expect the first frost. That way, the pruning cuts can heal, and any new growth will have time to harden off before Old Man Winter arrives on the scene.

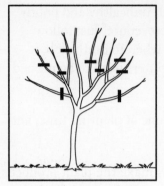

In the tree's second year, thin out vertical branches growing along the central leader.

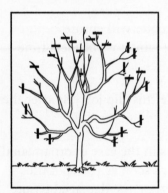

In the third year, clip only enough branches to shape the tree and keep one central leader.

From year four and beyond, continue light pruning to maintain the tree's shape.

As the Twig Is Bent . . .

So grows the tree. Only in this case, the twig is clipped. When you prune a fruit tree lightly during the first few years of its life, it will grow into the right shape, and you'll save yourself a lot of time and trouble down the road. The operative word is *lightly* because heavy pruning can delay the development of fruit-bearing spurs—and therefore your first crop. During the plant's first year, it needs no pruning at all (except for the preplanting clipping required for bare-root trees). This three-step training routine begins in year two:

STEP 1. Thin out vertical branches growing along the central leader—the main vertical branch extending upward from the trunk.

STEP 2. In year three, prune only enough to maintain a single central leader and to train the tree toward an attractive, healthy shape.

STEP 3. Starting in the fourth year, keep pruning lightly to shape the tree and (of course) remove any wood that may be damaged by weather, pests, or other mishaps.

Bend, Don't Prune!

If your fruit tree is sending up vertical branches that are churning out shoots galore but no fruit buds, you may be tempted to clip the shoots off. Well, don't do it! Instead, bend those branches down. In the spring, tie a weight (like a mesh bag filled with stones) to each branch that wants to stand at attention. Watch the positioning, though: You want to fasten the weight where it will make each branch as horizontal as possible.

Apple Tree Revival Time

If you've recently moved and inherited trees that are producing only a few small apples, it means those fruiters have not been well cared for. Well, don't fret! It's a snap to put them back into full swing. Here's the simple routine:

- Remove all of the dead and broken limbs, making clean cuts back to a side branch or the main trunk.

- Use a digging bar to poke holes in a circle around the drip line (the tips of the farthest branches) of each tree, approximately 3 feet apart and 8 inches deep.

- Put low-nitrogen fertilizer (15 pounds per tree) into the holes.

- If you see any cankers (openings in the trunk's bark that ooze sap), stuff a cotton sock with willow leaves and soak the pouch overnight in 3 gallons of water. Then pour the tea into a handheld sprayer bottle and apply it to the wounds.

In no time flat, your trees will be churning out bushels of delicious apples!

IT'S NOT RETIREMENT TIME YET!

Got an old apple tree that just doesn't want to work anymore? Put life back into that old-timer with this simple trick: In the spring, when younger trees have just put out their blossoms, take a sharp knife and carefully strip a ring of bark about $\frac{1}{2}$ inch wide from around the trunk. Before you know it, that tree will be churnin' out blossoms that'll knock your socks off—with lots of fruit to follow!

Grandma's GROW-HOW

Grandma Putt always grew foxgloves among her apple trees because, somehow, the foxgloves made the apples keep better in storage. Yours will, too, but it's important to store them the right way. They'll keep well in your refrigerator for up to six weeks, but to last through the winter, apples need temperatures of 30° to 32°F with a relative humidity of 90 percent. An unheated garage or shed is the perfect storage spot. And don't worry that you'll wind up with applesicles—the high sugar content will keep the fruit from freezing.

FRUIT TREE FRUSTRATIONS

Even though fruit trees need the same basic TLC that ornamental versions do, there are some diseases, pests, and cultural problems that plague only, or primarily, fruiters. The timely tips in this section will help you send trouble packing pronto—or, better yet, keep it from showing up in the first place.

No matter what kind of pest or disease you're battling (or trying to prevent), don't use any spray when your trees' blossoms are forming. If you do, you won't get a crop at all!

Dastardly Diseases

Fruit trees are not the giant germ magnets that some folks make them out to be. Still, you do need to keep an eagle eye out for a few maladies that could make for less than merry harvesting. Here's the scoop on the most common fruit tree diseases.

Brown rot. This fungal disease strikes peaches, plums, cherries, nectarines, and apricots. A small, round, brown spot appears and, in the blink of an eye, it grows to cover the whole fruit. It gets a toehold when the flowers first start to bloom, but you may not notice symptoms until picking time—and then it's too late. The key to saving your crop: Keep your eyes open. If the weather

---

No-Jive Chive Tea

This bracing brew is easy to make, yet it will put an end to brown rot—and any other kind of fruit tree fungi.

> **1 part chive leaves***
> **4 parts water**

Put the chives and water in a pan, and bring the water to a boil. Then remove the pan from the heat, let the tea cool, and strain it into a handheld sprayer bottle. Spray your fruit trees every seven days, and say, "Farewell, fungus!"

* Or substitute horseradish leaves.

---

is warm and wet in spring, when blossoms are developing, wait until three weeks before the harvest. Then spray your trees every seven days with my No-Jive Chive Tea (at left).

Fire blight. This bacterial disease strikes apples and pears, and it spreads like (yes) wildfire in warm, moist weather. First, reddish, water-soaked lesions appear on the bark of limbs and branches, and on warm days, an orangey brown liquid oozes out. Infected shoots look as though they've been scorched (hence the name fire blight). Branch tips wilt and turn under at the ends, like a shepherd's crook. Here's how to put out the fire:

> **BEWARE OF 'BARTLETTS'!**
>
> If fire blight is a problem in your neck of the woods, stay away from 'Bartlett' pears, or any pear that's related to them. (Any catalog description worth its salt will alert you to the family tree.) They attract fire blight like a picnic attracts ants!

☙ At the first sign of trouble, prune off all infected branches at least 12 inches below the wilted section. Then remove all suckers and water sprouts, where more bacteria could be lurking.

HELP!

Q My apple trees look healthy enough, but they seem to have an identity crisis—they think they're evergreens! They keep their leaves all winter long and never bloom in the spring. I live in California; could it be they don't like the climate? Should I just give up and plant orange trees?

A *In warm climates, apple trees (and pears, too) often keep their leaves when other plants drop theirs. Unfortunately, without a period of leafless dormancy, the trees can't bloom and bear fruit. Here's the simple solution: When the other trees and shrubs in your yard start losing their foliage, run your hand along each branch of your apple trees to strip off the leaves. The trees will then settle down for a long winter's nap. And come spring, they'll leaf out and bloom to beat the band!*

❧ To avoid spreading the disease, dip your shears or saw in a solution of 1 part bleach to 4 parts water after each cut.

❧ Finally, spray the tree from top to bottom with a solution of 4 parts vinegar to 6 parts water. Then apply the mixture again two weeks later.

❧ To head off more trouble, control insects, especially aphids (see Chapter 10) and psylla (see "Color Them Gone" on page 251), which spread the bacterium. Also, don't overfeed your trees, and avoid high-nitrogen fertilizers. They encourage exactly the kind of lush, leafy growth that fire blight bacteria seem to flock to.

Apple Maggots

Despite their name, these pests also target pears, plums, cherries, and blueberries. Your best apple maggot–control method is to trap the adults (small black-and-yellow flies) before they lay their eggs, just under the skin

GRABBY GRUBS

Folks generally think of white grubs as lawn pests, and most of them are. But one type—the larvae of June beetles—also munches on the roots of young fruit and nut trees, as well as blackberries and strawberries. The evidence: The plants just up and wilt when all else seems fine. Your best response: Douse the soil with beneficial nematodes to halt the attack. Then, for long-term protection, call up the troops, namely ground beetles, crows, robins, and starlings. (For the lowdown on hit-squad hospitality, see Chapter 10.)

Quick Fix

If you opt for quality over quantity when it comes to your homegrown apples, then this tip is for you: When the fruits are about the size of marbles, select those that are flawless, and slip a plastic sandwich bag over each one. Fasten the bag to the stem with a twist tie, but keep it loose enough to allow good air circulation. At harvest time, remove the "armor" along with the apples of your eye.

of the fruit. And here's a super-simple way to do it:

STEP 1. Before the blossoms on your tree turn to fruit, go to your local garden center and buy some red ball-shaped fake apples that are made just for this purpose.

STEP 2. Hang them in your trees or your blueberry bushes (yes, this works even if the target fruits are not apples). You'll need six to eight traps for a full-sized tree; two traps should do the trick for a dwarf tree (less than 9 feet high); and a single trap will work for a berry bush.

STEP 3. As the red orbs fill up with flies (and they will before you know it), take down the traps and replace them with new ones.

STEP 4. When the real fruit starts to appear, remove the traps. By that time, your maggot nightmares will have faded to a dim memory. If you forget and leave the traps in place, you'll zap good-guy bugs that are waking up from their winter naps—ready and willing to polish off any lingering flies and other destructive insects.

Garden Cure-All Tonic

When you need relief from bad-guy bugs in a hurry, mix up a batch of this rapid-acting remedy. It works like a charm every time!

> **4 garlic cloves**
> **1 small jalapeño pepper**
> **1 small onion**
> **1 tsp. of Murphy® Oil Soap**
> **1 tsp. of vegetable oil**
> **Warm water**

Pulverize the garlic, pepper, and onion in a blender. Then pour the puree into 1 quart of warm water and let it steep for two hours. Strain the mixture, and further dilute the liquid with 3 parts of warm water. Stir in the oil soap and vegetable oil, and pour the solution into a handheld sprayer bottle. Then take aim and polish off any bugs that are buggin' you.

Codling Moths

These culprits lay their eggs on the branches of apple, pear, quince, and walnut trees. When the eggs hatch, the larvae burrow into the fruit and feast on the core. But stopping codling moths in their tracks is easier than you might think. Just follow this season-by-season battle plan:

- In early spring, scrape off any rough bark from the lower 3 feet of the trunk. Underneath, you'll find cocoons filled with overwintering moths. Pull off the cocoons and drop them in a bucket of soapy water.

- In late spring, when the first infected fruit drops, pick it all up and destroy it. That way, you'll make a sizeable dent in the next generation.

- In early summer, wrap a band of corrugated cardboard around the tree trunk, about 3 feet off the ground. As the caterpillars crawl down the trunk to spin their cocoons, they'll be trapped in the paper. Then, either peel off the paper and drop it into a bucket of soapy water, or spray the 'pillars with my Garden Cure-All Tonic (see page 249). Either way, when you're sure the larvae are dead, toss 'em into the compost bin, cardboard and all.

Take 2

Codling moths have a sweet tooth the size of Texas, which is the secret behind my Drink of Death Traps. All you need are some 1-gallon plastic milk jugs and a solution that's made of 1 part molasses to 1 part vinegar. Pour 1 to 2 inches of the solution into each jug, tie a cord around the handle, and hang the trap from a branch. The moths will fly in for a drink, and that'll be all she wrote! Just one word of caution though: If you find that honeybees are visiting your sweet traps, take them down and stick with the other moth-riddance methods in this section.

Keep Birds at Bay

If you've ever grown cherries, you know that the number one challenge is guarding your crop from hungry birds. Well, I've got some advice on how you can say "Mine—*all* mine!" Here's all you need to do:

🐛 Wind black cotton thread among the branches; it'll confuse the wily wingers. When they see the thread against the sky, they can't judge the distance between strands, so they won't land. Just make sure that you string the thread *before* a mama bird builds a nest and fills it with eggs!

🐛 Put up a wren house near your cherry trees. Wrens eat no fruit or berries, only insects. And when they've got young 'uns in their nests—which is the same time you'll have cherries on your trees—they won't let any other

COLOR THEM GONE

Plastic bottles that once held liquid laundry products make terrific traps for all kinds of pesky fruit pests—and other kinds, too. Not only are these jugs sturdy and waterproof (with built-in handles for hanging), but they also come in colors that naturally appeal to bugs. To make your traps, just coat the appropriate bottles with corn syrup, petroleum jelly, or a commercial product like Tanglefoot®. Then either hang them from trees or berry bushes, or stick them, upside down, on stakes that you've pounded into the ground among your plants that are under attack. As for the shade of bottle to choose, let this chart be your guide.

BOTTLE COLOR	BUGS THAT FLOCK TO IT
Blue	Thrips
Green	Walnut husk flies
Red	Fruit flies (including apple maggot flies)
White	Flea beetles, four-lined plant bugs, plum curculios, rose chafers, tarnished plant bugs
Yellow	Most flying insects, including aphids, cabbage moths, leaf miners, psylla, squash beetles, webworm moths, whiteflies
Yellow-orange	Carrot rust flies

birds within 50 feet of the place. (Don't try this trick in your vegetable garden, though, because the wrens will chase off all the other insect-eating birds that you need for crop protection.)

🍃 Instead of full-size cherry trees, grow dwarfs or miniatures. They deliver a full-size, full-flavored crop on plants that are small enough to cover with a sheer curtain or two. The birds won't get so much as a nibble!

BERRY GOOD BERRIES

To my way of thinking, there is no finer luxury on earth than picking sweet, fresh, tender berries from your own bushes. But for reasons I've never understood, even many experienced gardeners panic at the mere thought of growing these fabulous fruits. Well, friends, if you're putting off growing the crops you crave because you've heard that raspberries, blackberries, and blueberries are just too much trouble, you've come to the right place. I've got tons of tips and tricks that'll help you grow the berry best berries ever—the fast and easy way!

If you're craving the taste of homegrown raspberries and blackberries, but just thinking about all those thorns makes you cringe, don't fret. Bramble fruits vary greatly in the number of thorns they wield. Good catalogs list the degree of spininess right along with disease resistance and cold tolerance.

Ramble with the Brambles

For an impatient gardener, the bramble fruits—raspberries and blackberries—are a godsend because they produce the biggest harvest with the least amount of effort of any other fruit crop. Not to mention the fact that because berries are so fragile, and therefore the mortality rate is so high in shipping, they cost an arm and a leg at the supermarket. Furthermore, you couldn't ask for an easier plant to grow. Here's your three-year ticket to success.

First year. Prepare the soil as you would for a vegetable or flower garden (see Chapter 9), and plant the little bushes 2 feet apart, following the basic directions in Chapter 2. Once the plants are in the ground, cut the tops back to 2 inches above soil level.

Second year. In early spring, cut the plants back to 2 inches above the ground. This will encourage maximum cane growth and ensure greater fruit production. In the fall, clip the plants back to a height of 4 feet or so, thereby enabling the canes to withstand the winter's snow and wind.

Third year and each year thereafter. During the summer, pull or cut out any sucker plants that grow in the rows, and cut off and destroy any wilted or sick-looking tissue (whether branches or whole plants) as soon as you spot the trouble. In late summer, remove and destroy any sick-looking canes, and thin out weak ones. Thin new, healthy-looking canes so that they're 6 inches apart. In the fall, cut the canes back to 4 feet, and cover the ground with an organic mulch like compost, leaves, or straw. If your raspberry bed gets too deep to harvest easily, or you get busy and don't prune at all for a year, don't worry about it. Just cut the whole shebang to the ground when you can and let it grow back.

> ## CAUTION: WINTER AHEAD
>
> Too much growth in late summer leaves your berry bushes—and next year's harvest—vulnerable to damage by Old Man Winter. So what can you do to prevent that from happening? It's simple; unless you need to get rid of diseased wood, halt all pruning at least a month before you expect the first frost. That way, new canes will have time to harden off before cold weather hits.

Grandma's GROW-HOW

No matter what you do, bramble fruits just won't stay put. New canes are always sneaking out from the base of the plants, and once they get started, they're tough to stop. So follow Grandma Putt's green thumb rule of planting: Place your raspberries and blackberries at least 12 feet away from the vegetable garden—or any other plants you don't want them to mix with. Then leave grass in the space in between. That way, any wandering canes can be mowed down before they get very far.

The Truth About Training

To hear some folks talk, you'd think that training raspberries was more complicated than putting a man on Pluto. Well, friends, it's not. The fact is that unless you want an ornamental effect, you don't need a trellis at all. Just let the canes grow naturally.

You say you've got no room to let your raspberries sprawl? Here's a simple, space-saving solution: Plant a bush on either side of a metal stake that's about 5 feet high. Then gather up the canes and tie them loosely together with old panty hose. You'll get a full-size crop in a fraction of the space. What's more, the stake and ties will attract static electricity from the air and give your plants a healthy dose of nitrogen (see the electroculture lesson on page 215). **Note:** This is also an excellent method to use when you're growing raspberries in containers.

Careful, They're Fragile!

There's no getting around the fact that raspberries (and blackberries) are delicate fruits. Especially in warm, moist climates, they're prime targets for

Chamomile Fungus Fighter

To help keep your bramble fruits free of mildew and other foul fungi, serve them a spot of this tea after each rainfall. **Note:** It works wonders on vegetables and perennial flowers, too!

> **4 chamomile tea bags**
> **2 tbsp. of Murphy® Oil Soap**
> **1 qt. of boiling water**

Put the tea bags in a pot, pour the boiling water over them, and let the tea steep for an hour or so, till the brew is good and strong. Let it cool, then mix in the oil soap. Pour the tea into a 6 gallon hose-end sprayer, and fire away! Try to apply this elixir early in the day so that your plants' fruits, flowers, and foliage can completely dry by nightfall.

all kinds of mold, rust, and mildew. But here are two quick and easy ways to keep your crop safe from foul fungi:

- Mulch your plants with plenty of compost. It helps guard against both fungal and bacterial diseases.

- After each rainfall, pick any ripe fruit ASAP! Then spray all the unripened berries with my Chamomile Fungus Fighter (at left) to fend off future trouble.

The Same Boring Story

When the canes of your bramble fruits wilt and die in early summer, or simply lack get-up-and-grow power, look beneath them. Most likely, the roots or crowns have been invaded by raspberry root, a.k.a. raspberry crown borers. Your best response? Cut off the infested canes below soil level, and destroy them. Then in late summer, look for patches of rust-colored eggs on leaves and destroy them, too. In the case of major infestations, drench the soil in early spring with Bt (*Bacillus thuringiensis*). Repeat the treatment the following spring, and your borer problems should be history.

HELP!

Q I've been growing blackberries for five years with no problems. But this year, something went haywire. The blossoms had too many petals, and there were tiny leaves in the middle of some of the flowers. The fruit—what little there was— was all hard and grainy. What's going on?

A *It's a fungal disease called double blossom rosette (Cercosporella rubi) that strikes blackberries and sometimes raspberries. No fungicide seems to get rid of it, but you can control it. The disease spreads from open blossoms, so before your plants flower next year, chop them clear to the ground. You won't get any fruit next spring, but after that, you should get a normal crop for the next four or five years because that's how long it takes this fungus to reestablish itself.*

Go for the Blue

The good news for impatient gardeners is that blueberry plants are hardy souls that can perform like troupers in just about any region in the country. Even if you live in an area where winter temperatures routinely fall below -20°F, or where you rarely get a touch of frost, you can find varieties that have been developed to thrive there. To zero in on the latest and greatest, check with your local Cooperative Extension Service and with nurseries that specialize in fruit plants.

Climate aside, though, blueberries are picky about a few aspects of their home, sweet home, namely sun, soil, and air.

NORTHWARD, HO!

If late spring frosts are common in your area, site your blueberries on a north-facing slope. This will delay blooming in the springtime, thereby lessening the chances of frost damage. The slope will also tend to dry the air, which will help fend off foul fungi.

Sunlight. Blueberries need at least eight hours of Ol' Sol's rays each and every day. If they don't get it, the result is spindly growth, reduced yield, and poor fruit quality.

Soil. The blues perform best in fertile, acidic soil that's rich in organic matter and has a pH between 4.5 and 5.6 (the same range that azaleas and rhododendrons favor). They also demand excellent drainage, with a water table that's no closer than 18 inches to the soil surface.

Grandma's GROW-HOW

To check your soil's drainage for its blueberry-pleasing potential, use Grandma Putt's simple test: Dig a hole that's about a foot deep, and fill it with water. Wait about an hour and a half, and check back. If the water is gone, you're good to go. If any remains, find another spot for your blueberries to put down their blueberry roots.

Good air circulation. Whatever you do, don't plant blueberries in an area that's completely surrounded by buildings or thick stands of trees, either of which will hinder air movement.

Say No to Sulfur

The quickest way to increase soil acidity (lower its pH) is to add powdered sulfur. That works just fine when you're growing turfgrass or almost any other kind of plant—but not blueberries. Since sulfur combines with water in the soil to form sulfuric acid, it kills off microorganisms that blueberry plants need for good growth. You'll save yourself a lot of time and trouble down the road if you opt for adding some organic matter that's high in acid instead.

Any of these sour treats will work like a charm to lower your soil's pH:

- **Aged sawdust**

- **Coffee grounds**

- **Composted leaves or bark (especially oak, beech, or chestnut)**

- **Pine or hemlock needles**

When It's Sweeter Than a Candy Store

If your soil's pH registers between 5.6 and 6.0, you should have no trouble getting it down to a blueberry-pleasing level. But anything sweeter than that will be darned near impossible to adjust successfully. So what do you do? Grow your blueberries in containers! That way, you can give them *exactly* the kind of soil they like best.

Although most blueberry plants are self-pollinating, you'll get a better yield if you choose two different varieties. Put them in half-whiskey barrels or similar-size pots. Fill the containers to within 6 to 8 inches of the rim with my Blueberry Potting Mix (see page 258), then add a 2-inch layer of mulch to retain moisture. (I use compost or pine needles.) Keep the plants well watered, and feed them every two to three weeks with an organic fertilizer that's high in nitrogen, such as cottonseed meal or fish emulsion. And, unless you live in a mild climate, move the containers to an unheated garage or enclosed porch for the winter.

Blueberry Potting Mix

You couldn't ask for an easier-to-please plant than a blueberry bush. Just give it a pot or a raised bed filled with this root-pleasing mix, and get ready for a fine, fruitful feast.

> **2 parts coarse builder's sand***
> **2 parts chopped, composted leaves**
> **2 parts good garden soil**
> **1 part compost**

Mix all of the ingredients together, then fill your containers.

* Don't use beach or "sandbox" sand. It's so fine that it'll harden up if it dries out. It also may contain a lot of ground-up shell fragments, which are highly alkaline.

Ready, Set, Plant!

Nurseries and mail-order companies sell blueberry plants in the same three forms that ornamental trees and shrubs come in: bare-root, potted, and balled-and-burlapped. In this case, go with either of the latter two if you can. You won't have to disturb the roots (which makes blueberries pout), so the plants will get off to a faster, stronger start.

First, clip off any flower buds and all weak, diseased, or broken wood. Then follow the basic tree- and shrub-planting guidelines in Chapter 2 (see "The Up-to-Date Planting Process" on page 80), with one difference: Set the plants into the ground 1 to 2 inches deeper than they were growing at the nursery or in their pots. If you're planting multiple bushes, space them 4 to 6 feet from each other in rows that are 8 to 10 feet apart.

The hard part is done because once they're snuggled sound in their beds, blueberries are easy keepers. All you need to do is feed them two or three times a year using ½ cup of 5-10-10 or 10-10-10 fertilizer per bush, give them a steady supply of water, and prune off any diseased or damaged stems as soon as you spot them.

Harvest Time

Don't rush out and pick your blueberries the minute they turn blue. It takes them a few days after the color changes to develop their best flavor. To tell for sure when they've peaked, just "tickle" a cluster with your fingers. If the berries fall right off the branch and into your hand, you've got yourself some delicious winners!

Simply Scrumptious Strawberries

On a hot summer afternoon, nothing tastes better than homemade strawberry ice cream made from your own homegrown strawberries. Or maybe you prefer strawberries swimming in a bowl of cream. No matter how you serve your berries, I have good news for you: Growing these tasty, versatile fruits is a piece of, um, shortcake—as long as you give them a good beginning. Read on for my simple secrets to a super start, strawberry style.

Buy the right stuff. Strawberries are prone to viruses, so always buy plants that are certified disease-free. And when you're shopping at a garden center, whether the plants are bare-root or potted, give 'em the old eagle eye. You want to see whitish roots, spotless green leaves, and a healthy neck with no sign of rot.

Get the soil just right. Strawberries need well-drained soil that's slightly acidic (6.0 to 6.5); chock-full of compost, humus, or well-cured manure; and absolutely free of weeds.

Give em' a bath. Before you plant your strawberries, dunk the roots into my Strawberry-Success Solution (see page 262).

Tuck 'em in just right. For each plant, dig a hole that's about 6 inches wide and a few inches deeper than the roots. Then mound up some soil in the center, set the crown on top, and spread the roots down over the slope. If any of them touch bottom, don't bend them to fit. Instead, snip 'em off with scissors. (Folding the roots stresses 'em out.)

Quick Fix

Got a lot of berries to pick and not much time to do the job? Get a small plastic bucket, and tie it to a rope around your waist. You'll pluck twice as fast with two hands. What's more, as the pail fills up, it'll tug at your tummy—reminding you to empty it before those tender berries start to squash each other.

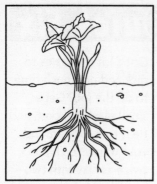

Too low . . .

Pinch, then pinch some more. For the first year, pinch off every single blossom that forms on your strawberries. That way, the plants will put all of their energy into forming strong roots, and strong roots equals bumper crops in the years to come.

Get the Depth Just Right

Strawberries need to be planted so that the crown is exactly at the soil level. If you set the seedlings in just a little too far, the roots rot; if the plants aren't in far enough, the roots dry out and shrivel up. Here's my tried-and-true method for planting strawberries at *precisely* the right depth: Set the seedlings into their holes, and water them thoroughly. Then keep close watch on the crowns. If they sink, dig up the plants and add more soil to the bottom of the hole. If the crowns are sticking up, add more soil to the ground surface. Then just to be extra safe, check again after the first steady rainfall.

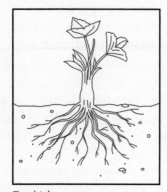

Too high . . .

Give 'Em a Safety Blanket

When a plant has all its vital parts lying on the ground, as strawberries do, the poor things are targets for every kind of trouble under the sun. So how do you defend your crop? Just lay down a good, thick mulch of pine, hemlock, or spruce needles. That scratchy blanket will fend off slugs and keep the leaves and fruit off the ground, away from soilborne pests and diseases. Plus, something in those evergreen needles actually improves the flavor of the berries. How's that for a triple-threat performance?

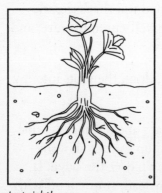

Just right!

It's Berry Confusing

Confused about which kind of strawberries to grow? This rundown will help you decide.

June-bearing. If you want a mountain of berries all at once for making jam, freezing, or serving at your annual strawberry social, this is your candidate. The plants form buds in the fall, then produce one big crop of fruit over six weeks or so in late spring. (Up North, that's usually June, but in warmer climates, it's earlier.)

Day-neutral. These are the plants for folks who just can't get their fill of strawberries. They flower and bear fruit pretty much nonstop for about five months, as long as temperatures stay between 35° and 85°F.

Everbearing. Don't be misled by the name. These plants don't keep churning out fruit the way day-neutral strawberries do. Instead, everbearing strawberries produce one crop in June and another in the fall. They're your best option if you want more than one crop a year, *and* you live where the weather gets too hot to suit the day-neutral weather wimps.

Grandma's GROW-HOW

Grandma Putt grew gladioli by the hundreds to use in the flower arrangements she made for her church, but she never put one of those bulbs within 50 feet of a strawberry plant. She said that'd mean certain death for the berries. If you're at all skeptical, you could experiment and see if that's true. But I'm not going to!

Birds home in on red more than any other color. So instead of red varieties, plant yellow raspberries or strawberries, green gooseberries, or white or golden currants. That won't necessarily guarantee safe passage for your crop, but it *will* lessen your problems with airborne diners!

Strawberry-Success Solution

Just before you plant your strawberries in their bed, give them a nice little bath in this root-ticklin' tonic.

1 can of beer
1/4 cup of cold coffee
2 tbsp. of mild dishwashing liquid*
2 gal. of water

Mix all of the ingredients together in a bucket. Then soak your berries' bare roots in the solution for about 10 minutes before you tuck the plants into their holes. When you're finished planting, dribble the leftover solution on the soil around your plants.

* Don't use detergent or any product that contains antibacterial ingredients.

Berry Bad Bugs

Most of the insects that go after berries also target other plants. (You'll find the full scoop in Chapter 10.) But two bugs raise major Cain in berry land.

Strawberry bud weevils, a.k.a. bud clippers. These pests are so tiny (just 1/12 to 1/8 inch long) that you may never see them, but they can stop your berry crop (strawberries, blackberries, and raspberries) dead in its tracks. The female drills a hole into a flower bud and inserts one egg. Then she slices into the stem just below the bud to halt further progress. The once-and-future flower may tumble to the ground or hang on the stem. Either way, a little grub grows up inside, eating the whole time. Your best response:

➤ Start watching for emerging adults when spring temperatures hit 60° to 65°F. At the first sign of trouble, get rid of all damaged buds.

➤ To catch any lingering weevils, douse your plants with my Peppermint Soap Spray (see page 226).

➤ In the fall, clean up all plant debris where the little devils hibernate.

Tarnished plant bugs, a.k.a. lygus bugs. You'll know these tiny terrors have arrived on the scene if your strawberries are smaller than normal with dark, sunken patches (known as catfacing). The bugs feed on buds and young fruit and in the process, inject them with a toxin that dwarfs and ruins the berries. What to do is this:

- Vacuum the pesky pests off your plants. Just put an inch or two of soapy water in the reservoir of a wet/dry vacuum cleaner, then get out there and sweep those beds! Empty the whole shebang into your compost bin.

GREAT GRAPES AND MIGHTY FINE MELONS

Not all fruit grows on bushes and trees, of course. In this section, I'll serve up a heaping harvest of quick and easy tips for raising two popular taste-tempting crops that climb up trellises and sprawl across the ground.

Although grapes are easy to please, the vines do get heavy. So before you set the plants into the ground, give them a strong, stout arbor to grow on.

Grape Success Begins at the Beginning

The secret to successful grape growing—whether you want to eat the fruits or turn them into wine or wine vinegar—lies in the planting process. Like a lot of other fruit trees and bushes, grapevines are usually two plants in one: a vine that produces flavorful fruit grafted onto hardy, disease-resistant roots. With grapes, the place where those two stems meet is especially sensitive. At planting time, always cover the graft union with a mound of sand to keep it moist while the roots take hold down below. After two months, remove the sandy blanket. Otherwise, roots could sprout from the upper stem, and you'll lose the benefit of your tough-guy rootstock.

One more thing: Before you plant your vines, soak them for about an hour in a bucket of my Manure Tea with a handful of bonemeal stirred in (see page 315). Those grapes'll be scrambling up their trellis faster than you can say "A glass of chardonnay, please."

Easy Does It

Grape roots are a mighty unthirsty bunch. So when you plant new vines, follow these rules of root:

- Water once a day for a week.

- Water once a week for a month.

- Water once a month for the rest of the growing season—but only if the weather is drier than usual.

- After the first year, let Mother Nature quench their thirst.

Look Twice

If you see ragged holes in your grape leaves that look like the work of Japanese beetles, but your vines are at the edge of a lawn, it's a good bet the culprits are rose chafer beetles. Once you've seen them, there's no chance of mistaken identity: Chafers are lighter in color and smaller in size than their Japanese cousins, and they have much longer legs. They're just as lethal, though: Left unchecked, chafers can destroy your whole grape crop in a hurry. So shout

THINK THIRDS

The way some folks carry on about pruning grapes, you'd think it was open-heart surgery. If you've been denying yourself all of this good eating (or drinking) because you thought you could never get the system down, think again. The fact is if you plant grapevines, you're gonna get grapes. Just choose the best, disease-resistant varieties for your region, then cut the vines back by a third of their length every year in late winter. (For the latest and greatest in grapes, call your closest Cooperative Extension Service office.)

uick Fix

As much as rose chafer beetles love grapes (and bramble fruits), they love rotten fruit even more. To turn your fruity garbage into a first-class chafercide, just fill some jars about halfway with soapy water, drop in chunks of over-the-hill fruit (any kind will do), and set the jars under your grapevines or berry bushes. The hungry hordes will hurry on over for a snack, fall right into the drink, and that'll be all she wrote!

"Checkmate!" and get to work. If you spot the invasion in its early stages, just pick the chafers off the plants, drop them into a jar of soapy water, and screw on the lid. When you're sure the beetles are dead, remove the lid, and set the jar on the ground among your grapes. (The more soap-and-chafer-filled jars you come up with, the better.) The sight—or, more likely, smell—of their decomposing comrades will make the chafers head elsewhere for dinner.

In the Black

For grape growers in humid climates, the most common grape gripe is black rot. It's a fungus that turns plump, pretty grapes into ugly, black, dried-up berries called mummies. Fortunately, as fearsome as this fungus sounds, it's really a paper tiger. To stop it dead in its tracks, you just need to understand how it operates. The fungus sleeps through the winter in the mummies, then wakes up in spring and produces spores galore. When it rains, the spores burst loose from the mummies, land on the new foliage, and the cycle starts all over again. So get out there and get rid of those mummies! Pluck 'em off the plants, pick 'em up off the ground, and send 'em off with the trash. Then when you prune the vines, destroy all the clippings, too.

Grandma's GROW-HOW

After you've cleaned up all your fungus-filled mummies, do what Grandma Putt did to protect her cherished grapes: Plant crimson clover (*Trifolium incarnatum*) under the vines, and keep it about 5 inches high. The clover will block any spores that are left on the ground and keep them from leaping onto the fruit.

Marvelous Melons

Melons crave heat, and most of them take their own sweet time maturing. But you can still get a great-tasting, juicy harvest, even if you live up North. You just have to know these green thumb tricks of the trade:

- Start with a variety that matures early and that's been bred to perform on your turf. The folks at your local Cooperative Extension Service can recommend some winners for your region. Good early-maturing varieties include 'Charmel' (78 days), 'Earli-Sweet' (70 days), and 'Fastbreak' (69 days).

🌿 Sow your seeds indoors, three weeks before you expect the last frost. And make sure you start those seeds in individual pots that can go right into the ground at planting time, because melons don't like to have their roots disturbed (see page 206 for more about travelin' pots).

🌿 While those seedlings are growing toward graduation day, get their bed ready to go, following my five-step Monster-Melon Master Plan (below).

🌿 Move the seedlings to the garden when the soil temperature hits 70°F, and cover the bed with floating row covers. They'll keep warmth in and bad bugs out. Just make sure to remove the covers as soon as the first blossoms appear—otherwise, bees and other good-guy bugs can't get in to pollinate the flowers, and you'll end up with no crop.

Quick Fix

When each melon is about half grown, slip a barrier between it and the soil to keep the fruit from rotting. In warm-summer climates, a board or a plastic milk jug cut in half will work just fine. In cooler regions, though, use a terra-cotta tile. It'll absorb and hold the sun's heat—and a growing melon needs all the warmth it can get! To find terra-cotta tiles for next to nothing, check places that sell used or surplus building supplies.

Monster-Melon Master Plan

There's really no secret to growing mighty marvelous melons—you just need to give 'em a root-pleasing home. Here's how to do that in five easy steps:

STEP 1. Dig a hole about 1 foot deep and 3 feet in diameter. In the center, dig a second hole that's about 1 foot wide and 2 feet deep.

STEP 2. Fill the smaller, deeper hole with compost and tamp it down firmly. It'll act as a water well that will draw needed moisture up to the plants.

STEP 3. Fill the larger hole with my Marvelous Melon Soil (at right), and mound it up so that the center is about 6 inches above ground level. Then if you live in a climate that's on the cool side, lay black plastic mulch over the whole bed so the soil can warm up.

STEP 4. Several days before planting, remove the plastic (if there is any) and soak each hill thoroughly with my Seed-Starter Tonic (see page 16). When the soil is dry enough to work, plant your seeds.

STEP 5. Once the seedlings have their second set of true leaves, thin the plants so that no more than three melon vines will grow from each hill.

Keeping On

As your vines start to grow, there are some key things to keep in mind to ensure a healthy melon crop. First, once the blossoms have turned to fruit, push an empty coffee can upside down into the soil until the bottom of the can is a few inches off the ground. Set the melon on top of it. The fruit will be protected from rot and soilborne pests. Plus, the metal will absorb and hold heat—thus making the melon ripen faster and taste sweeter. Then be sure to keep your plants evenly moist, especially from planting time through fruit set because melon plants will buckle under in a drought. Unless a prolonged dry spell strikes, stop watering when the fruits reach about the size of a tennis ball—they'll develop better flavor if they don't get too much moisture in the later growing stages. Finally, start feeding the plants fish emulsion when the fruits appear.

Marvelous Melon Soil

Melons are mighty particular about the ground they call home, and this marvelous mixture suits 'em to a T.

> **2 parts coarse builder's sand (not beach or "sandbox" sand)**
> **1 part compost**
> **1 part professional planting mix**
> **1 cup of Mouthwatering Melon Mix***

Mix all of the ingredients together in a bucket. Pour the soil mixture into each of your melon-planting holes per the Master Plan (at left). Then get ready to modestly accept your town's Most Mouthwatering Melon award!

* To make Mouthwatering Melon Mix, combine 5 pounds of earthworm castings (available in catalogs), $1/2$ pound of Epsom salts, and $1/4$ cup of instant tea granules. Store in a tightly sealed container.

When It's Melon-Pickin' Time

With melons, what you pick is what you get: They don't ripen off the vine the way a lot of other fruits and vegetables do. So make sure they're completely ripe before you harvest them. The clue to look for depends on the type.

Honeydews, casabas, Crenshaws, and true cantaloupes. These are ready when their skin turns either creamy gold or white, depending on the variety. Cut them from the vine using a sharp knife.

Muskmelons. These are ripe when it takes just a little pressure to pull the fruit from its stem. If you wait just a tad longer, they'll separate, or "slip," from the vine all by themselves. But by that time, they could be overripe.

Watermelons. These are tricky, and it seems everybody's got a different theory. My advice is to note the time the plants come into full bloom. Then about 35 days later, start looking for one of these signs:

- The part of the melon that sits on the ground is yellow.
- The tendril closest to the melon has turned brown.
- When you tap the fruit lightly, instead of a ping, you hear a lower-pitched thump or thunk.

Melon Marauders

If your otherwise healthy melon vines suddenly wilt from stem to stern, suspect one of these mischief makers.

Squash vine borers. These fat white caterpillars are closely related to the borers that target trees. If you look closely, you'll see small holes in the stems of your melon

SAY IT ISN'T SO!

If you think that cantaloupe is your favorite fruit in the whole world, you may be in for a surprise. The melons that go by the name of cantaloupe in grocery stores—and the ones most home gardeners grow—are not cantaloupes at all: They're muskmelons! True cantaloupes have a hard, warty rind. They're grown a lot in Europe, but almost never in North America.

plants, with stuff that looks like gooey sawdust piled up beside them. For fast-acting relief, slit the stem at each hole site, then reach in with a bent wire (a crochet hook works perfectly) and pull out the borer. Drown the culprit in a bucket of soapy water laced with alcohol, and pile soil over the opening in the stem. Or, if you're squeamish about the poke-and-drown technique and can get to a garden center quickly, buy Bt (*Bacillus thuringiensis*) and inject it into each hole, following the package directions.

Wireworms. For a positive I.D., poke around in the soil. If you see shiny orange worms, you've found your villain. The simple solution: Spear chunks of potato on sticks that are about 8 inches long, and bury them so that 3 inches or so of the stick shows aboveground. Then every day or two, pull up the tater bits, toss 'em in a pail of soapy water to kill the worms they harbor, then toss the whole shebang into the compost bin.

Quick Fix

All melons need room to roam, but some of them can roam *up* instead of out. Small-fruited varieties like 'Jenny Lind' will grow up happy as clams on trellises, so you can have fresh, sweet melons no matter how small your garden is. (Just be sure to put them where the trellises won't shade other sun lovers.)

HELP!

Q I planted several kinds of melons for the first time this year. The vines are all healthy and pest-free, and they're offering up a whole lot of fruit, but the overall quality is, well, just not what I'd hoped it would be. Is there something I could do to improve my crop next year?

A *There sure is! When the melons are about the size of walnuts, cut off all but four or five fruits on each vine. The plant will direct all its energy into those survivors, and they'll grow up big, sweet, and juicy. And don't feel bad about sacrificing all those baby melons—just rush 'em into the kitchen, peel them, and pickle them in your favorite sweet brine recipe.*

CHAPTER
8

HEROIC HERBS
Spice Things Up in a Hurry!

From an impatient gardener's standpoint, herbs deliver a bigger bang for the buck than any other kind of plant. Not only do they require little maintenance, but they also decrease your workload by repelling pests, fending off diseases, and generally making your other plants grow stronger and more productive. And that's in addition to their feats on the home front, which range from flavoring food and scenting rooms to amusing cats, and even curing the common cold. It's easy to see why herbs are known far and wide as "the wonder workers of the plant kingdom!"

Although most herbs require little maintenance, they still need care and attention. So heed the advice I've been repeating throughout this book: Decide on a garden size that you can handle comfortably, then reduce it by a third.

PLANNING WITH (AND FOR) A PURPOSE

Earlier in this book, I reminded you that while flowers, trees, and shrubs are beautiful accents in any landscape, they can also do some important jobs around the old homestead. Well, herbs turn that idea around: By definition, they're plants on a mission to perform some useful tasks—but they also make mighty attractive additions to your yard. And even though herbs demand much less TLC than most of their cohorts in the plant kingdom, the key to minimizing your workload and maximizing your enjoyment is the same as it is for any other plants—plan before you plant.

What's the Job Description?

Later on, we'll talk about many of the specific jobs herbs can do for you, indoors and out, as well as how to plant and care for them. But first, consider the general purposes of your herb garden. For instance, do you want:

🌿 Herbs and edible flowers to add flavor to your cooking?

🌿 A steady supply of leaves, petals, and flower heads to dry for craft projects?

🌿 Safe, gentle remedies for headaches, sniffles, aching muscles, and more?

🌿 A beautiful, fragrant garden that's great for rest and relaxation?

Home, Sweet Home

When it comes to putting down roots, you can chalk up another reason that herbs are a dream come true for impatient gardeners. It's because no matter what kind of growing conditions you have in your yard, you can find at least a few herbs that will thrive there with a minimum of time and effort on your part. But, of course, you do need to analyze those conditions before you start planning your garden or shopping for plants.

Soil. Most herbs prefer well-drained soil that's average to rich in fertility. But some, like lavender, put on their best show in the kind of dry, rocky soil that leaves other plants gasping "Food! Water!" And others, including many members of the mint family, actually love having wet feet.

HAPPY HERBS

These winners all grow well with four to six hours of sun a day in well-drained soil:

- Basil (*Ocimum basilicum*)
- Catnip (*Nepeta cataria*)
- Chives (*Allium schoenoprasum*)
- Feverfew (*Tanacetum parthenium*)
- Lemon balm (*Melissa officinalis*)
- Tarragon (*Artemisia dracunculus*)

This crowd loves partial shade and damp soil:

- Angelica (*Angelica archangelica*)
- Bee balms (*Monarda*)
- Parsley (*Petroselinum crispum*)
- Sweet woodruff (*Galium odoratum*)

Light. Many herbs, especially the most popular culinary ones, such as oregano, rosemary, and thyme, need full sun—that is, 8 to 10 hours of direct sunlight a day. Others are happy if they get 4 to 6 hours of sun a day (what gardening books generally describe as "partial shade" or "partial sun"). Beware, though: Their flavor and aroma won't be as intense as they would be if the plants grew in full sun.

Mints (*Mentha*) are by far and away the easiest-keeping champs of the herbal world. They'll thrive in any kind of soil and any kind of light, from full sun to just three to four hours of sunlight a day.

Spread the Wealth

If you don't have a single site that will please all the herbs you want to grow, congratulations! You've got the perfect opportunity to put a variety of plants to work throughout your yard. Here's a handful of possibilities:

- Combine them with annuals and perennials in beds and borders. (Lavender, sage, and artemesia are just a few prime candidates.)

- Plant low-growing herbs like creeping thyme, Corsican mint, or Roman chamomile between pavers or stepping stones, where you'll release their scent as you step on them.

- Edge pathways with herbs like rosemary or lavender, and enjoy the perfumed foliage and flowers as you brush by them.

- Make a small, easy-to-pick salad garden by combining herbs like basil and garlic with a tomato plant (or two) and your favorite greens.

From a plant's point of view, all sunlight is *not* created equal. For instance, in the South and Southwest, and at high altitudes anywhere, full sun translates into a maximum of four hours—preferably in the morning.

Pair herbs with specific plants to deter pests and diseases. (I reveal some of my dream teams on page 287.)

Plan on Pots

Even if you have acres and acres of planting space, plan on growing some of your herbs in containers. Not only do beautiful pots and tubs look attractive in any yard, but they also enlarge your plant palette. And because you can fill the containers with any kind of soil, you can grow varieties that could never survive in your home ground. Plus, they're easily portable, so you can grow plants that are too tender for your climate, then bring them indoors for the winter. Conversely, if you live in the sweltering South, you can move potted herbs to shady retreats during the hottest part of the day.

Super Stand-Ins

Next to tomatoes, cucumbers are the most-grown vegetables in American gardens. If you love the taste of fresh cucumbers, but lack the space to grow them—or you just don't want to fuss with all the cucurbit clan's pesky pest

HELP!

Q I plan to grow a lot of herbs in containers, and I love the soft, gentle look of old terra-cotta pots. But I just can't find any at my local antique stores. I did find some beautiful pots at the garden center, but they're so new-looking. Is there any way I can age those pots quickly?

A There sure is! Just "paint" the containers with some plain old unflavored yogurt, and set them outside in the shade. As the yogurt dries, moss and lichen will grow on the terra-cotta surface. Keep an eye on the pots, and when they've aged enough to suit you, gently hose them off. Generally, it takes only a week or so to produce an authentic-looking "antique."

problems—just plant one (or both) of these herbal cucumber taste-alikes.

Borage. This is an easy-seeding annual with long, fuzzy leaves, floppy stems, and pretty blue flowers—that all taste just like cukes. (If you don't care for the texture of the leaves only, use them to flavor your recipe, and then remove them before you serve the dish.)

Salad burnet. This is an old-time, rough-and-ready perennial that's hardy to Zone 3 and thrives in just four to six hours of sun a day. It's easy to grow from seed, and forms neat little clumps that stay evergreen in all but the coldest climates. In this case, it's the leaves you want, so keep a steady supply growing by clipping off flowers and old foliage.

BYE-BYE, BUZZERS

If you want a great-looking plant to grow anyplace you don't want bees buzzing around, consider feverfew (*Tanacetum parthenium*). It's a 2-foot perennial with light green leaves and daisy-like flowers from early summer to early fall. It's hardy in Zones 5 to 9, and bees won't go anywhere near it! On the flip side, you must keep feverfew far away from fruits and vegetables that depend on bees to pollinate their blossoms, or you'll end up with a nonexistent harvest.

Grandma's GROW-HOW

If you're looking for a top-notch pest-control agent, take a tip from Grandma Putt and plant plenty of dill. The blossoms attract and support beneficial bugs by the bucketful, including bees, good-guy wasps, and parasites that control tent caterpillars and codling moths. These super garden helpers also repel aphids and spider mites, draw caterpillars away from cabbages, and protect corn from diseases. Furthermore, at least according to Grandma Putt, dill improves the flavor of cole crops (which include broccoli, Brussels sprouts, cabbage, cauliflower, and kale) and is generally good for lettuce and onions. So don't just sit there—grab yourself a big old sack of dill seeds! (But don't plant dill near tomatoes or carrots because it may impact their growth.)

LAUNCHING THEIR CAREERS

Herbs are just like any other plants: The better start they get in life, the better equipped they'll be to thrive—and do the jobs they're supposed to do in your yard. Here's everything you need to know to give these hardworking heroes a first-class send-off.

To get the biggest bang for your buck, buy your plants from small growers who specialize in herbs. Not only do they generally propagate top-notch plants, but the best establishments are run by experts who love nothing better than sharing their enthusiasm, wisdom, and grow-how.

A Time to Sow?

Why the question mark? Because even though many herbs, both annual and perennial, are a cinch to start from seed, it usually makes more sense to buy transplants. After all, you probably need only one or two plants of each kind, so why go to all that time and effort (and waste all that seed, besides)? What's more, some perennial herbs, like tarragon, oregano, and lavender, simply don't come true from seed. So if you want to be sure of getting the precise flavor and aroma you desire, you have to propagate these plants from cuttings—or buy them from a reputable grower who did.

On the other hand, there are plenty of herbs that do come true from seed, and there are times—for instance, when you want to harvest big quantities to dry or freeze—when your best bet is to start them that way.

What You Smell Is What You Get

When you're shopping for herb plants—especially if you decide to shop at a big garden center or discount store—follow all the guidelines described in "Plants or Seeds?" on page 204. But I want you to take the process one step further: When you find a plant that meets all your other selection criteria, rub a leaf between your fingers, bring it up to your nose, and smell it. If you don't get a concentrated whiff of scent, put that plant right back where you found it. Then keep on looking until you find one that passes the sniff test. Don't take any herb home with the thought that it'll develop fragrance and flavor as it grows because the bottom line is that it won't. What you smell and taste now is as good as it gets.

Free and Easy

Just like many ornamental flowers, a lot of herbs reseed themselves freely. And when the parent plant is one that comes true from seed, this trait provides a great way to get a jump on the growing season without investing any time and effort in indoor seed-starting. There's just one problem: Quite often, the baby plants pop up in all the wrong places, and you have to dig up the seedlings and move them to locations of your choice. But that's not a problem if you use this little trick:

✤ In the fall, get the planting bed all ready to go, following my Super Soil Sandwich recipe in Chapter 9 (see page 312). Then pound two stakes into the ground and run a string between them, a foot or so above the soil surface.

✤ When the seed heads begin to turn brown, cut the flowers from the plants, leaving 6 inches or so of stem.

✤ Tie the flower stalks to the string so that the seed heads are hanging upside down a few inches above the soil. When the seeds are good and ready, they'll drop to the ground exactly where you want them to grow.

SEEDTIME

These herbs are a snap to start from seed (or bulbs, in the case of garlic), sown either right in the garden or indoors, following the guidelines in Chapter 6 (see "Life in the Great Indoors" on page 205):

- Basil (*Ocimum basilicum*), annual

- Chives (*Allium schoenoprasum*), perennial, Zones 3 to 10

- Cilantro, a.k.a. coriander (*Coriandrum sativum*), annual*

- Dill (*Anethum graveolens*), annual*

- Garlic (*Allium sativum*), perennial, Zones 3 to 9

- Parsley (*Petroselinum crispum*), perennial, Zones 6 to 10*

* Either sow these seeds in the garden when the soil has warmed up, or start them in individual traveling pots to avoid disturbing the roots.

They Sure Don't Look Like Strawberries!

Few containers are finer-looking than a terra-cotta strawberry jar with healthy herbs spilling out of its pockets. This is a great way to grow low, spreading plants like creeping thyme and mint. It keeps the herbs from spreading too far, and lifts them off the ground, away from soilborne pests and diseases. There's just one problem: Those pots dry out fast, and when you water, it's hard to get the soil evenly wet. But here's how to solve that dilemma:

STEP 1. Gather your supplies. You'll need a pot that's at least 16 inches high, a piece of 1- to 2-inch-diameter PVC pipe, a cap to cover one end of the pipe, a saw, and a drill with a ½-inch-diameter bit.

STEP 2. Cut the pipe to be even with the pot's rim when it's standing up inside. Cap one end.

STEP 3. Drill holes about 1 inch apart on both sides of the pipe.

STEP 4. With the capped end pointing downward, insert the pipe in the center of the pot so that the top is even with the rim. Then fill the container with potting mix.

STEP 5. Starting at the bottom of the jar, tuck an herb seedling into each pocket, soaking the soil as you go. Then set several more seedlings into the top of the container.

STEP 6. Every time you water, slip a funnel into the top of the pipe, and pour water into it. The holes will distribute moisture evenly throughout the pot.

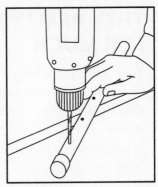

Drill holes in both sides of the capped pipe.

Insert the pipe in the center of the container, and add potting mix, filling the jar to the brim.

When it's time to water, slip a funnel into the pipe and pour the H_2O into it.

277

THEY REALLY DON'T ASK FOR MUCH

Your herbs labor long and hard for you, and they ask very little in return. But, like any other living thing, they do need *some* attention during the growing season. These tips and tricks will help you keep your heroic herbs in the pink of health without a lot of labor on your part.

Stop feeding your perennial herbs at least one month before you expect the first frost in your area. Feeding too late in the season tends to weaken the plants and makes them more susceptible to winter's cold.

Healthy Eating Habits

Despite all the hard work they do, herbs are not what you'd call heavy eaters. After a lot of practice, patience, and persistence, I've found that mine do their best when I give them a light meal of punched-up compost two or three times during the growing season. This concoction is bona fide super chow as far as they're concerned, and it couldn't be simpler to make: It's a mixture of fresh, good-quality compost and either rabbit, chicken, or sheep manure. Why those three? Because those critters' waste material has a higher concentration of the nutrients that herbs need than either horse or cow manure has. Use about 2 parts compost to 1 part manure. Let it sit for a week so the hot compost can kill any lingering weed seeds, then spread it around your plants, gently working it into the top inch or so of soil. You'll almost hear your herbs shout "Hooray!" before they dig in.

Quench Their Thirst

Herbs differ greatly in their need for moisture, so check catalog descriptions or a comprehensive herb book for specific requirements. Just remember that even the most drought-tolerant herbs need a steady supply of water while their roots are getting established. Generally, that's about an inch of H_2O each week, from either the sky or your garden hose. After that, my basic rule of thumb is to let the top inch of soil dry out before you add any more life-giving sustenance. And every six weeks or so during the growing season, treat your plants to a drink of my Herb-Refresher Tonic (at right).

Herb-Refresher Tonic

Herbs are like any other plants—and people, too, for that matter. When the temperature really starts rising, there's nothing they enjoy more than a nice cool drink. So quench their thirst with this oh-so delicious pick-me-up concoction.

1 can of beer
½ cup of ammonia
½ cup of corn syrup
½ cup of Murphy® Oil Soap

Mix all of the ingredients in a bucket, then pour the solution into your 20 gallon hose-end sprayer. Spray your herbs to the point of runoff every six weeks or so during the growing season to freshen them up.

Southern Exposure

Even heat-loving herbs call it quits when both temperature and humidity skyrocket. Especially in the Deep South, plants' stems, leaves, and roots are all prime targets for fungal diseases—not to mention simple heatstroke. But don't despair! This routine will keep your herbs fit as a fiddle whenever—and wherever—steamy weather strikes:

- Grow your herbs in raised beds or large pots. That will improve both drainage and air circulation, which are crucial for fending off the fungus among us.

- Add heaps of compost and composted manure to the soil. In addition to giving off chemicals that destroy fungi, this duo provides steady, balanced nutrition that keeps plants free of stress. And in brutal heat, a stressed plant can become a dead plant in the blink of an eye.

- Cast some shade on the scene. Down South, all herbs need shade from 2:00 p.m. on, and some—including chives, parsley, sorrel, and the mint clan—require permanent shelter. So either grow them in the shade of taller plants, or cover their raised bed with a lattice roof or an awning made of greenhouse shade cloth (available in catalogs and some garden centers).

✎ Avoid gray-leaved herbs, such as artemisia, woolly thyme, and gray santolina. They're very difficult to grow in a hot, humid climate—and when they get rained on.

Give It a Shot

If you live in a hot, humid climate and you have your heart absolutely set on using some beautiful silvery leaves in your craft projects, use this trio of tricks. They'll give your gray guys their best chance of performing well, even in steam-bath territory.

Say no to organic mulch. It encourages moisture retention, which you don't want in this situation. Instead, mulch your gray- and silver-leaved plants with pebbles, gravel, or coarse sand. That way, you'll keep the leaves and stems dry at soil level and also allow for better air circulation.

Quick Fix

Some herbs—chervil and coriander are two examples—won't survive a southern summer no matter how much you baby them. The simple solution: Grow them in the winter or early spring. The ideal time frame varies from one area to another. If you're not sure what grows when in your neck of the woods, check with gardening friends, your local garden club or herb society, or the closest Cooperative Extension Service office.

HELP!

Q I grow woolly thyme in pots, and recently I moved them to a partly shady area because I was concerned that the plants were suffering from too much sun. They're growing well, but the beautiful silvery leaves have turned green. What went wrong?

A In a word, nothing. If you move silver-leaved herbs into the shade, in any climate, the foliage will turn green. It's not a permanent change, however; if you put them back in the sun, the leaves will revert to their normal silvery gray color fairly quickly.

Lift 'em up. If you want to grow low, spreading plants, such as creeping thyme, plant them in tall containers to keep the stems and foliage off the ground. (A strawberry jar or a tall clay flue tile is perfect.)

Give 'em shelter. When a rainstorm threatens, whisk your container-grown herbs under a roof, and cover up any in-ground plants. Remove the topcoats the minute the rain stops, so fresh air circulates in and around the plants.

Chilling Challenges

Folks in the snowy North may not have to cope with the sweltering southern heat, but they have to face a challenge that's just as trying—namely, those long, cold winters. Fortunately, there's an ultra-simple solution to cold and other herbal woes, and it's called kelp. This sensational seaweed provides essential nutrients, helps plants absorb water better, and keeps all kinds of pests at bay. What's more, it even helps herbs stand up and say "Boo!" to Old Man Winter—indoors or out. Hardy perennials that get regular sprayings of kelp tolerate cold temperatures better than their unsprayed counterparts. And tender perennials spending the winter indoors hold up better under the low light and dry air that most houses offer up. So how do you deliver this miraculous gift? Just spray your herbs (and all your perennial plants) with my Perennial Wonder Drug (below).

Perennial Wonder Drug

To keep your herbs and other perennial plants in the pink of health year-round, give them regular doses of this terrific tonic from spring through fall.

> **1 tbsp. of liquid kelp, a.k.a. seaweed extract**
> **⅛ tsp. of mild dishwashing liquid***
> **1 gal. of water**

Mix all of the ingredients together and pour the solution into a handheld sprayer bottle. Then mist-spray your plants from top to bottom every two to three weeks throughout the growing season.

* Don't use detergent or any product that contains antibacterial ingredients.

Crucial Cuts . . .

And pinches, too! These two routines will help keep your herbs healthy and lush all season long:

🍃 Start by pruning perennial herbs back hard in early spring, when the first shoots come out. Cut each plant back to one-third of its original size, and it'll burst forth with a glorious crop of new, leafy branches. French tarragon, thyme, winter savory, and lavender respond especially well to a spring crew cut.

🍃 Each week during the growing season, pluck or cut off the growing tip of every single shoot on both annuals and perennials. If you can't manage to do the job every week, do it as often as you can. The more you pinch, the more new leaves (or flowers) the plants will churn out.

Separate Quarters

If you've ever shared space with so much as a single mint plant, you know that its roots travel faster than Superman flying to the rescue. The same holds true for a number of other herbs, including catnip, lemon balm, and pennyroyal (to name only a few). The surest way to keep these hard chargers in their place is to plant them in pots. That way, their roots can't possibly escape. But that's not the only containment policy in your arsenal. Here are several other ways to keep these rambunctious roving rooters from rambling too far.

Take 2

After you've pruned your perennials in the spring, either toss the clippings into your compost bin, or let them dry and use them as scent-sational kindling in the fireplace or barbecue grill. As for what to do with all those little growing tips from your weekly pinching sessions, here are some dandy options:

• Toss 'em into salads, casseroles, or stir-fries.

• Dry them to make potpourri or to use in other craft projects.

• Freeze them whole in ice cube trays, then use the cubes in drinks.

• Scatter them here and there—indoors or out— wherever you need to repel pests like mice, moths, or fleas.

Fence them in belowground. Sink terra-cotta flue tiles or other bottomless containers into the soil, and plant your rovers inside. You won't have to fuss with special potting soil, and for the most part, the roots will lose their wanderlust.

Don't grant their wishes. Most mints will grow just about anywhere, but they feel most at home in rich, moist soil in full sun to partial shade. So give your plants average soil that's on the dry side. They'll still thrive, but they'll stay more or less within bounds.

Give them tight quarters. Potential ramblers can't get far if you put them in a small, hemmed-in plot of ground—say, between a walkway and the walls of your house or garage.

TOODLE-OO, TROUBLE!

When you grow plants that are as problem-free as herbs, trouble rarely comes knocking at your door. Still, there are times when even these easy keepers can hand you a challenge or two. In these pages, I'll fill you in on my tried-and-true tricks for waving good-bye to whatever woes may dog your herbs. I'll also share some quick and easy ways for using your herbs to fend off problems all through your yard.

Most disease organisms and destructive insects give healthy herbs the cold shoulder—so as long as you deliver basic TLC, you stand a first-class chance of barring the door to trouble and woe.

Wretched Rot

When herbs fall prey to root rot fungus, it's all but guaranteed that you have one of two problems: Either your plants are getting too much water, or they're sitting in poorly drained soil. Here are your best courses of action:

- If you catch the problem when the plants are just turning yellow—a sure sign of overwatering—ease off on the hose trigger. How do you know when to water again? Stick your index finger into the ground. If it's dry from your fingertip up, reach for the hose.

🐚 When drainage is poor, even if you're keeping a tight rein on the water supply, it'll hang around the roots too long and cause trouble. In that case, you need to improve the soil pronto (for the lowdown on that, see Chapter 9), or grow your herbs in containers.

Lush Life

If your herbs are looking a tad too soft and lush aboveground, and pests are traveling from near and far, the trouble lies below the soil: The roots are getting too much to eat. In particular, they're getting an overdose of nitrogen, which encourages mountains of leafy growth. That, in turn, makes the plants sitting ducks for slugs, snails, rot, and other diseases. Your first response: Clip away the lush foliage, and lay down a blanket of compost. It'll help balance the nitrogen overload and fight off pests and diseases. From then on, feed those plants according to the guidelines in "Healthy Eating Habits" (see page 278).

Battered Basil

Several things can cause spots on basil leaves, and your reaction depends on the diagnosis. Here are the possible problems.

Dark spots. These indicate that either the plants caught a chill or there's a fungus among us. Although it's hard to tell cold injury from a fungal disease,

Quick Fix

Foul fungi—whether they're causing trouble in the soil or on plants' leaves—can move from sick plants to healthy ones by way of gardening tools. So when you're working with ailing herbs (or any other plants), disinfect your tools between cuts by wiping them down with a solution made from 1 part antiseptic mouthwash to 3 parts water. After your chores are done, mix 1 cup of antiseptic mouthwash per gallon of water in a bucket, and soak your tools (including shovels and trowels) in the solution for an hour. Rinse the gear with clear water and dry it thoroughly before stowing it away.

the weather is a dead giveaway. First, pluck off all of the spotty leaves. Then respond as follows:

Take 2

 If the temperature is below 40°F, your culprit is the cold air. So just toss the plucked leaves into the compost bin, or bury them in the garden. In the case of a late-spring cold snap, cover your plants pronto, and keep the blankets in place until the temperature rises. If it's the end of the growing season, harvest your crop and rush it into the kitchen. Don't dawdle—even a light freeze will turn basil black faster than you can say "Jack Frost."

 When spots appear in warmer weather, you've got fungus. But most likely it's not deadly. First, destroy the leaves that you plucked off (don't compost them!). Then spray your basil with my Compost Tea (see page 315) every two weeks for the rest of the growing season.

When cold weather strikes, plastic bottles and jugs—whether they formerly held soda pop, milk, water, or juice—make dandy "jackets" for basil or any other tender plants. Just slice off the bottom of each container, plop it over a plant, and sink it an inch or two into the soil so it won't blow off in the wind.

Flower and Foliage Flu Shot

There is no absolute cure for plant viruses, but this "vaccine" could help your herbs fend off attacks.

> **2 cups of leaves from a healthy green pepper plant**
> **½ tsp. of mild dishwashing liquid***
> **4 cups of water**

Put the leaves and 2 cups of water in a blender and liquefy. Then dilute the mixture with the remaining 2 cups of water, add the dishwashing liquid, and pour the solution into a handheld sprayer bottle. Spray generously to drench your plants from top to bottom.

* Do not use detergent or any product that contains antibacterial ingredients.

Yellow spots. Basil leaves that are splotched or mottled in yellow, with turned-down edges, *do* have a serious problem: cucumber mosaic virus. If the infection is advanced and widespread, pull up and destroy the plants. If you catch it in the early stages, pluck off and destroy all of the infected foliage. Then follow up with my Flower and Foliage Flu Shot (see page 285). And to head off further attacks, you need to control cucumber beetles, which spread the virus like crazy (see page 226 for my cuke beetle battle plan).

A Dilly of a Duo

Although it's true that few insects cause harm to healthy herbs, there are a couple of caterpillars that you may see on your dill plants. Your plan of action depends on which one you're dealing with.

Tomato hornworms. (Yes, these are the same giant-size caterpillars that target tomato family crops.) Pick them off your plants, drown them in a bucket of soapy water, and empty it into the compost bin. In the case of a major invasion, blast the bad guys with my Orange Aid (see page 338).

Parsleyworms. These are about 2 inches long and green with a yellow-dotted black band over each body segment. When disturbed, they send out a pair of orange horns to scare the enemy. Your best response: Leave 'em be. Parsleyworms almost never eat enough to cause real damage, and their tough-guy act is fun to watch. Plus, they grow up into beautiful swallowtail butterflies that will flit around your garden, sipping nectar and pollinating your posies.

If the parsleyworms are causing too much destruction, gently pick them off your dill and move them to a clump of Queen Anne's lace (*Daucus carota*). Chances are they'll never give your dill—or your parsley—another thought.

DON'T HURT THAT HORNWORM!

If you spot a tomato hornworm with little papery cocoons on its back, its days are already numbered—those baubles are the eggs of braconid wasps, natural parasites of tomato hornworms. Move the worm away from your garden, but let it live so the wasps can reproduce and continue their good work. Tomato hornworms have hordes of other natural enemies, too. See Chapter 6 for the complete roster.

SCAT!

Grandma Putt and generations of gardeners before her put herbs on pest-control duty all through their yards for one simple reason: They worked! Now, thanks to modern science, we know why. The roots, leaves, and flowers of all plants send out chemicals, and some of these substances repel particular insects and even big four-legged critters. Here are some examples of how you can put herbs to work preventing pests in your yard.

TO KEEP THESE AT BAY	PLANT THESE AMONG THEIR TARGETS
Ants	Pennyroyal, southernwood, spearmint, tansy
Aphids	Chives, garlic, mint
Borers	Garlic, tansy
Cabbage moths	Hyssop, mint, rosemary, sage, thyme
Cats	Rue
Colorado potato beetles	Catnip, horseradish, tansy
Deer	Catnip, chives, garlic, lavender, rosemary, spearmint, thyme, yarrow
Japanese beetles	Garlic, rue, tansy
Mice	Mint
Mosquitoes	Southernwood, wormwood
Rabbits	Garlic
Slugs and snails	Prostrate rosemary, wormwood
Tomato hornworms	Borage, opal basil

HAPPY HARVEST!

Although lots of folks grow herbs only as ornamental plants or as in-ground companions to flowers and vegetables, most gardeners want to use their herbs in other ways around the old homestead, too. In this section, I'll share some super secrets for harvesting and storing your herbs so they'll be able to work wonders, whether you intend to eat them, turn them into health and garden aids, or make them part of your creative crafting arsenal.

Cooking-supply stores and catalogs sell special containers that can increase the storage life of fresh herbs by three times or more. They're not cheap, but if you want to enjoy your bounty for as long as possible, they're well worth the investment.

Helpful Harvesting Hints

If you're anything like me, harvesting herbs is an ongoing process—you just clip off whatever you're planning to cook with that day, or whatever strikes your fancy as you're strolling through your garden. It's another matter, though, when you want larger quantities, either to use fresh or to store for use sometime in the future. At those times, you'll get the biggest bang for your buck if you follow these guidelines.

Beat the flowers to the finish line. Most herbs reach their peak of flavor, fragrance, and quantity just before the flower buds open. If you cut them way back at that time, the plants will often regrow and give you a healthy second harvest.

Make it morning. Try to harvest your herbs early in the morning, after the dew has dried, but before the sun gets hot. That's when the volatile oils that give herbs their flavor and aroma reach their highest levels. The plants are also cool then, so they'll stay fresh longer. If you can't get to them that early, aim for an overcast day.

Don't overdo it. Once they're cut, herbs go downhill fast, so harvest only as much as you're sure you can handle before the cuttings start to wilt. (You can always go back for more the next day.)

Fabulous Freshness

Just like vegetables and fruits, herbs deliver their best flavor and aroma when you rush them straight from the garden to the kitchen. But that's not always possible, especially when Old Man Winter is bearing down and you need to harvest your treasures pronto. How long fresh herbs retain their full flavor (or at least most of it) varies. But most of them will last for up to two weeks in your refrigerator's crisper drawers. Just rinse the herbs well, wrap them loosely in paper towels (one type of herb per bundle), and put them into individual ziplock plastic bags. One notable exception is basil, which goes belly-up almost immediately in the refrigerator. But it will stay fresh for up to a week if you put it into a glass of water, set it in a sunny window, and keep the container filled to the brim with H_2O.

Freezing Is Finer

At least it's a more effective method than drying for many culinary herbs. In particular, *(continued on page 292)*

WHOOPS—I MISSED!

Nobody's perfect. If you went away on vacation and missed the peak herb harvest season, don't fret. You still have some fine treats in store. All you need to do is shift your sights. For instance:

• Harvest the seeds instead of the leaves.

• Clip the flowers. Then use them in salads or desserts, add them to homemade herbal vinegars, or dry them for use in your arts and crafts projects.

• Let some of the seed self-sow and give your herb garden a jump-start on next year.

Quick Fix

As eager as you may be to bring in your garden-fresh herbs, be patient long enough to perform one preliminary chore: About an hour before you plan to harvest them, hose the herbs off with a light spray to remove any lingering soil or bugs. The leaves and stems will retain more of their fresh color and fragrance if you rinse them while they're still on the plants. Then as soon as the leaves are dry, grab your shears, and start harvesting to your heart's content.

DIRECTIONS FOR DRYING

Grandma Putt dried her homegrown herbs in the attic, which had exactly the conditions they needed to retain their volatile oils (the secret of their health-giving, housecleaning, and pest-defying power). What are those conditions? Low humidity, good air circulation, and near-total darkness. But you don't need an attic in order to dry herbs. Any of the easy alternatives in this chart will work just fine. The best method for you is strictly a matter of personal preference.

One important note: To make sure your dried herbs retain as much fresh-from-the-garden taste as possible, store them in airtight glass containers in a cool, dark place. Whatever you do, don't keep them anywhere near the stove! If you do, the heat and light will send their flavor and aroma downhill fast.

IF YOU'RE DRYING YOUR HERBS HERE	GO ABOUT IT THIS WAY
In a dark room	Set old window screens or hardware cloth on bricks, boxes, or other supports, and spread the herb stalks on top. Leave a door or window open a crack, and unless you live in a very dry climate, turn on a fan or two so that air circulates through the room and keeps humidity from building up.
In a room where light penetrates	Gather the sprays into bunches of 5 or 6 stems each, and tie the stems together with twine. Then put each bunch upside down in a brown paper bag (making sure the herbs aren't touching the bottom), fasten the top with a rubber band, and hang the bundles from anything that'll hold them. A clothes-drying rack works well for this purpose.

In an electric oven*	Heat the oven to 200°F, then turn it off. Spread your herbs in a single layer on a baking sheet, leaving half an inch or so between the sprigs. Set them in the oven, and leave them for 6–8 hours, or until the leaves and stems are crisp.
In a gas oven*	Spread your herbs in a single layer on a baking sheet. Then turn the oven to the lowest temperature that will keep the pilot light on, and heat it, with the door open, for 2–3 minutes. (This will get rid of any moisture, which would make the herbs bake, rather than simply dry them.) Turn off the oven, set the tray of herbs inside, and close the door. They should be dry in 6–8 hours.
In a microwave oven*	Put a single layer of herbs between two paper towels, and nuke 'em for 2–3 minutes. Then check for "doneness" and give them additional 30-second jolts as necessary until they're crisp. (But keep a close watch to make sure they don't burn!)
In a food dehydrator*	Set the temperature between 95° and 100°F. Spread your herbs in a single layer on a tray, and put them in the dehydrator. Depending on the fleshiness of the leaves, the drying process can take anywhere from 4–18 hours, so be patient, and keep checking! Tip: For future reference, jot down how long it took for each variety.

To keep flavors and scents from mixing and mingling, dry only one type of herb at a time.

Quick Fix

Basil turns black when it's frozen. The color change doesn't affect the flavor, but who wants to eat black leaves? To keep them green, you just need to blanch the leaves before freezing by putting them in a strainer and pouring boiling water over them for a second. Then lay the leaves on paper towels and let them cool naturally. Don't dip basil into ice water, as you do when you blanch vegetables, because that'll dilute the flavor.

basil, chives, mint, and parsley retain little flavor when they're dried. Of course, frozen herbs don't keep their natural good looks, but they do retain a lot more of their fresh-from-the-garden taste. There are several quick and easy freezing methods, and no matter which one you use, the advantage of freezing your herbs is that you simply pull out whatever quantity your recipe calls for, and put the rest back in the freezer. Use any of these methods:

- Wrap bunches of herb sprigs (one kind per bunch) in aluminum foil, and pop them in the freezer.

- Coarsely chop fresh herbs, put them in plastic containers with tight-fitting lids, and freeze.

- Puree chopped herbs with water, butter, or olive oil. (The exact amount is your call.) Then pour the mixture into ice cube trays. When the cubes are frozen, pop them out of the trays and store them in ziplock plastic freezer bags or plastic containers with tight-fitting lids.

HERBS ON THE JOB

There are literally thousands of ways you can use herbs in cooking, crafting, health-care preparations, and garden tonics. In this book, I can't even begin to scratch the tip of the iceberg. But I will clue you in on some of my—and Grandma Putt's—favorite, fast, and fun herbal recipes and projects that will add spice to your life and oomph to your garden.

To make herbal potpourri, combine 13 cups of your favorite dried herbs with 1 ounce each of orrisroot and sweet flag powder. Pour into plastic food-storage containers with tight-fitting lids, and store in a cool, dark place.

Simple Elegance

Or maybe elegant simplicity. I'm talking about one of my favorite homemade gifts: herbal vinegar. It packs a flavor punch you'll never find in store-bought vinegars, and it's as easy to make as a pot of tea. Why, in just a few hours, you can whip up a year's worth of Christmas, birthday, and hostess gifts. What's more, the final product looks as grand as anything you'd buy at a fancy-food boutique—for a small fraction of the price. For each bottle, you'll need six to eight fresh herb sprigs and 1 quart of good-quality vinegar. Here's the simple procedure:

STEP 1. Wash and dry the herbs, then pack them into clean, quart-sized glass canning jars.

STEP 2. Heat the vinegar until it's warm (don't let it boil!), pour it over the herbs, and close the lid. **Note:** If you're using jars with metal lids, cover the jar openings with plastic wrap or waxed paper before you screw the lids on. The inner wrap will keep the metal from reacting with the vinegar.

STEP 3. Put your filled jars in a dark place at normal room temperature, and let them sit for a couple of weeks.

STEP 4. Open the lid and sniff. If you detect a rich herbal aroma, it's ready. Otherwise, close the jar, and check again every week.

STEP 5. When the scent is just right, strain out the solids, pour the flavored vinegar into a pretty bottle, and tuck in a fresh herb sprig or two. Get ready for a lot of oohs and aahs!

Pack six to eight sprigs of herbs into each glass canning jar.

Store the filled jars in a dark place at room temperature for two weeks or so.

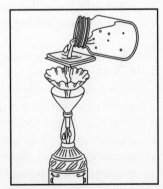

Strain the finished vinegar into attractive bottles.

Secrets to Very Fine Vinegar

When you make an herbal vinegar, there are several tips you should keep in mind for the best results.

Let your taste be your guide. Use whatever kinds of vinegar and herbs that appeal to you. If you need inspiration, check books or websites devoted to herbal cooking and crafts. (There are many of them, including ones that specialize in herbal vinegars.)

Use the good stuff. Don't try to economize by using bargain-basement vinegars. If the vinegar you start with doesn't taste good to you, the finished product won't either—no matter how much herbal flavoring you pack into it.

Don't put 'em on display. Decorative bottles filled with herbal vinegar look beautiful on a windowsill with the light streaming through them. But that light will make the flavor fade fast. So make a few just-for-show

HELP!

Q My grandmother used to make herbal vinegar to use as a facial skin tonic. As a teenager, I (of course) thought she was extremely eccentric. But now that I recall what soft, beautiful skin she had all her life, I think maybe she was on to something. How can I make my own supply?

A *Just follow my basic recipe for culinary herbal vinegar (see "Simple Elegance" on page 293), using 1 cup of fresh flower petals or leaves for each 2 cups of vinegar. To use it, dilute the vinegar with six parts of spring water, rose water, or orange flower water. Then either splash the mixture onto your face, or dab it on with a cotton ball. Flowers such as lavender, jasmine, roses, pinks, and orange blossoms are especially popular for cosmetic vinegars. But many culinary herbs, including spearmint, rosemary, and sage, are also good for the skin.*

batches if you want to, but keep your cooking and gift-giving supply in a dark place at room temperature.

Double-Duty Herbs

If your herb garden's job description includes providing both safe, gentle remedies and tasty leaves and flowers for cooking, but you don't want to fuss with two separate gardens, you're in luck. Most of the same plants that spice up your cooking do double duty as health-care workers. Here's a small sampling of the cream of the crop:

- Basil fights cold and flu infections, eases migraines, relieves stress, helps cure depression, removes warts, and stimulates the flow of milk in nursing mothers.

- Bay helps prevent tooth decay and eases the pain of headaches and stomachaches.

- Dill soothes upset stomachs, relieves muscle spasms, freshens breath, and stimulates the flow of breast milk in nursing mothers.

- Garlic kills bacteria, clears lung congestion, lowers blood sugar and cholesterol levels, boosts circulation, and acts as an antihistamine.

- Peppermint energizes mind and body and relieves nausea and upset stomachs.

- Rosemary stimulates memory, boosts energy, and helps chase the blues away.

Take 2

Olive oil and many other kinds of cooking oils come in fancy glass bottles that make perfect containers for homemade herbal vinegar. To get those vessels crystal clear, even if they have hard-to-reach "shoulders," use this old-time trick: Pour $1/2$ teaspoon or so of salt into the bottle, and plug the top with a cork or a wad of paper towel. Shake, rattle, and roll the bottle until it's spotless, and rinse well with clear water. Then pour in your vinegar, insert a fresh cork, and enjoy your creation!

🍃 Sage restores vitality and strength, fights fevers, and soothes mucous membrane tissue—thereby curing mouth ulcers, sore gums and throats, and even laryngitis.

Note: If you're pregnant, on medication of any kind (even aspirin), or suffering from high blood pressure, diabetes, or any other chronic condition, check with your doctor before you dose yourself with any of these herbs.

Ways and Means

Once your herbal medical team is up and growing, you've got several options for turning the leaves, flowers, and/or roots into handy health-care workers. The best choices depend on the jobs you want them to do—and on your own personal preference. Here are some of the most common ways to use medicinal herbs for good health.

Teas. To Grandma's way of thinking, there was almost nothing that a cup of herbal tea couldn't cure. You'll find her super-simple tea recipe below.

Grandma Putt's Herbal Tea

This was the simple recipe Grandma used to make both medicinal and garden-variety teas. It makes 1 cup of brew. For some of Grandma's favorite ingredients, see "Double-Duty Herbs" on page 295.

> **1–2 tsp. of herbs (dried or fresh)**
> **1 cup of fresh spring water**
> **Honey (optional)**

Put the herbs into a ceramic teapot or mug that you've preheated by pouring boiling water into it, then dumping it out. In a pan or teakettle, bring 1 cup of water to a boil, and pour it over the herbs. Let the mixture steep for three to five minutes, and strain it into a fresh cup or mug. Add honey to taste, if you'd like, and drink (or pour) a toast to good health and a long life!

Infusions. An herbal infusion is simply an extra-strong tea that's ideal for topical or garden use—although you can also drink it, provided the herbs are edible and you prefer your tea on the strong side. You make an infusion the same way as a tea, but use 1 to 2 tablespoons of herbs per cup of water. If you need a larger quantity, use 1 to 2 cups of herbs per gallon of H_2O. Let the brew cool before you use it on your skin or your plants, but sip it at whatever temperature suits your fancy.

Tinctures. These are concentrated formulas that you take in the same way you would take cough syrup or any other liquid medicine. You can down it straight from a spoon, or mix it in warm water or fruit juice.

It's Teatime!

Grandma Putt's Herbal Tea (at left) can work wonders for the inside and outside of your body. Check out this fistful of ways it can make you feel—and look—better on the double:

If the thought of making cup after cup of tea tries your patience to the limit, make your brew by the quart instead. Then put it in the refrigerator, where it'll keep for three to four days, or freeze it in ice cube trays or plastic cups. When teatime comes, your potion will work the same magic, whether you warm it up, drink it cold, or eat it like an ice pop. Whatever you do, though, don't let herbal tea sit at room temperature for any length of time because within a few hours, it'll start to go sour.

☙ Call it quits on car sickness. If your children or grandchildren are prone to the automotive queasies, serve them each a cup of peppermint tea 5 to 10 minutes before you hit the road. Your trails will be happier—guaranteed!

☙ Fend off infection in cuts by washing them several times a day with rosemary tea. It's a mild antiseptic that makes wounds dry out quickly, and it also helps hasten the healing process.

☙ Soothe and cleanse your skin—and reduce any kind of inflammation— by gently swabbing it with lavender tea.

🍃 Tone and refresh dry, oily, or normal skin by treating it to frequent splashes of your favorite mint tea.

Note: In each case, let the tea cool to room temperature before you apply it to your skin.

Incredible Infusions

As I said earlier, an herbal infusion is an extra-potent tea that can make quick work of some of your most annoying health—or common house and garden—problems. Like these, for instance.

Bad blisters. Prevent infection by dipping a soft cotton cloth into a brew made from equal amounts of dried rosemary and thyme. Hold the cloth against your blister for 20 minutes or so. Repeat the treatment twice a day until the blasted bump is history.

Doggone itchy skin. Soothe your pup's dry, itchy skin with a rinse made from calendula flowers. While the infusion is still warm (not hot!), soak a hand towel in the solution, and lay it on Fido's back. Repeat all over his body until you've used all of the potion. Then let his fur air-dry.

Sore eyes. When a cold, flu, allergy attack, or night on the town leaves your eyes swollen and inflamed, brew up a catnip eyewash. Then soak a terry-cloth towel in the solution, and put it over your eyes for half an hour—repeating the process until you feel soothing relief.

Tired tootsies. Relax your sore, aching feet by soaking those dogs in a peppermint infusion once or twice a day—or as often as you can—until you feel perky enough to go out and dance the night away (or at least stroll around the block).

ZZZZZZ . . .

If you have trouble falling asleep at night, try this easy herbal project—it'll send you off to dreamland in a flash. Grab two washcloths, and sew them together on three sides, front to front. Flip them inside out, and stuff the pouch with equal amounts of dried leaves of catnip, rabbit tobacco, a.k.a. sweet everlasting (*Gnaphalium obtusifolium*), mint, and sage. Sew the fourth side shut, and lay this little pillow beside your head at night.

The Truth About Tinctures

If you've never made an herbal tincture, you might think you'd need a degree in pharmacy just to understand the procedure. The fact is, though, it's as easy as 1, 2, 3, 4. Just gather up ½ cup or so of fresh herbs (leaves, flowers, or both), a bottle of vodka, gin, or brandy (80 to 100 proof), and a clean glass jar with a tight-fitting lid. Then follow this four-step routine:

STEP 1. Harvest your herbs. Then rinse, towel dry, and chop them finely.

STEP 2. Put the herbs in the jar, and pour in the alcohol until it reaches 2 to 3 inches above the top of the herb layer.

STEP 3. Cover the jar with the lid, and put it in a warm, dark place. Let the mixture sit for at least four to six weeks—the longer, the better. During that period, shake the bottle every now and then to keep the herbs from packing down on the bottom.

STEP 4. Strain out the solids, and pour the liquid into clean, fresh bottles. Label them, and store your tinctures in a cool, dark place well out of reach of children and pets.

If you're sensitive to alcohol, or you're making a tincture for children or pets, substitute warmed (not boiled!) vinegar or a half-and-half mixture of glycerin and distilled water. The result will be less potent than the alcoholic version, but it'll still work.

Grandma's GROW-HOW

Grandma Putt's pantry shelves were stocked with tinctures that she made from all kinds of herbs, but one she reached for most often was her catnip tincture. It was, well, the cat's meow for relieving both muscle spasms and nagging coughs. To treat either condition, just put 2 to 4 ml of the potion in a glass of water or juice, give it a stir, and drink to your good health.

CHAPTER
9

GREAT GROUNDWORK
Secrets to Green Scene Success

**For an impatient gardener, the key to satisfaction—
that is, a low-maintenance yard that hands you as few
problems as possible—is to apply the philosophy that
works in just about every other aspect of life as we know
it: The best defense is a good offense. In this chapter,
I'll let you in on some of my tried-and-true secrets for
building strong, healthy soil, which is the basis of
any easy-care landscape. I'll also pass along a passel
of tips and tricks for growing plants in containers
(one of the very best trouble-avoidance strategies).**

LAYING THE FOUNDATION

When you're in a hurry to get growing, analyzing
your soil may seem like a colossal waste of time.
But actually, it is the beginning of life in the fast
lane—yard and garden style. That's because your
soil's basic character determines which plants,
including turfgrasses, will grow best in your little
piece of paradise. Yes, it is true that you can alter
your home ground to a certain extent (and later
on I'll share some simple ways to do just that).
But the bottom line is that the happier your plants
are in the soil you already have, the less time
you'll have to spend fussing with them.

If you think soil is just
plain old dirt, think
again. Healthy soil is
actually a miniature
world filled with billions
of the earth's tiniest
creatures, going about
the business of life, and
in the process, giving
plants sustenance.

Soil Lingo 101

The first step in analyzing your soil is to understand a few terms that gardeners and soil scientists toss around. (Be patient—I'm not going to get too technical here!)

Texture and structure. These words refer to the relative amounts of various mineral particles found in your soil. These are sand (large particles), silt (midsize), and clay (tiny). Sandy, or light, soil drains quickly and doesn't hold nutrients well. Clay, or heavy, soil holds nutrients like a dream, but it also holds water too well. When it gets wet, it sticks together like two sides of a peanut butter sandwich. And you can imagine what that can do to a plant's roots! The answer to a gardener's—and most plants'—prayers is loam: a nicely balanced mixture of sand, silt, clay, and organic matter. Loam holds a good supply of nutrients, doesn't dry out too fast, but doesn't stay soggy either.

pH. This is short for potential of hydrogen. It measures acidity and alkalinity on a scale that runs from 0 (pure acid) to 14 (pure alkaline), with 7 being neutral. While there are many exceptions, the majority of plants, including most turfgrasses, tend to perform best when the pH is close to neutral because that's when nutrients in the soil are most available to the roots. Beneficial soil bacteria also seem to be most active in the 6.0 to 7.0 pH range.

Rich and lean. These terms have to do with fertility. Rich soil is chock-full of all the nutrients, including trace elements, that plants need for healthy growth. Soil that's lean has a low supply of nutrients.

SWEET OR SOUR?

Although most plants prefer a near-neutral pH, some perform best in soil that's either extremely sweet or extremely sour. To learn whether your soil falls into one of those categories, use this simple test:

• To check for severe acidity, put about a tablespoon of wet soil on a plate, and add a pinch of baking soda. If the soil fizzes, then the pH is most likely below 5.0, which means it's sour.

• To check for high alkalinity, use about a tablespoon of dry soil, and add a few drops of vinegar to it (any kind will do). In this case, fizzing indicates a pH that's above 7.5, which means it's sweet.

H E L P !

Q I don't understand all this fuss about the pH of my soil. I'm in a hurry to get my new lawn started and plant a nice perennial garden. To me, this testing business seems like a major nuisance. Why can't I just load the dirt up with fertilizer and be done with it?

A *I'll tell you why: You can work all of the fertilizer in the world into your soil, but if the nutrients it contains can't dissolve in water, they can't get to the plants' roots. One of the factors that determines how well the nutrients dissolve is pH. If your soil is either too acid (sour) or too alkaline (sweet), the nutrients in it have no way of getting into your plants. And that means you might as well pour all that good fertilizer right down the drain!*

Test Time

There are two ways to test your soil. One is to use an inexpensive kit that you can buy at any garden center. Just follow the simple directions, and almost instantly, it will tell you the soil's pH and how much phosphorus, nitrogen, and potassium are in it. This is a fine way to go if you're growing annual flowers or vegetables. But if you're starting a new lawn or planting trees, shrubs, or long-lived perennials, you're better served by sending your sample to your local Cooperative Extension Service or a private testing lab for a thorough analysis. It will take longer to get the results, but it will be well worth the wait. A full-blown test gives you the skinny on soil texture, pH, both major and minor nutrients, as well as organic matter, and even the presence of toxic materials, like lead. All of these are important factors for the long-term health of your plants.

If you're using a DIY kit to test your soil, when you get to the step that calls for mixing your samples with water, make sure you use the distilled variety. Tap water and bottled spring water both contain minerals that can sometimes alter results.

Super-Simple Sampling

Whether you take the do-it-yourself approach or have your soil tested by a laboratory, here's the six-step process for taking your sample:

STEP 1. Remove any sod, mulch, or surface litter in the test area.

STEP 2. Dig a circular hole that's about 5 inches in diameter and as deep as the soil your plants' roots will be growing in. For vegetables and most flowers and herbs, stay within the top 5 to 6 inches of soil.

STEP 3. With a trowel, slice off about a ½-inch strip of soil from the side of the hole, and slide the slice into a clean plastic bucket. Repeat the process from at least nine more areas of your future lawn or garden.

STEP 4. Mix all of the soil slices thoroughly. Be sure to break up soil clumps and remove any sticks, stones, and other litter because they could skew the test results.

STEP 5. Scoop out a cupful of the mixed soil, spread it on a clean baking sheet, and let it air-dry for a day. If you're using a DIY kit, you're good to go at this stage. Just follow the directions that came with the kit.

STEP 6. Otherwise, prepare the sample for shipment following the instructions you received from the testing lab. If you're having more than one area of your yard tested, label each sample you're sending off, and make a note to yourself of where you took it from.

Slice off a ½-inch strip of soil from the side of each hole.

Mix the slices thoroughly, removing any and all debris.

Prepare the samples for shipment, and label each one.

Place and Time

As we all learned in high school chemistry class, the accuracy of any scientific test depends on the quality of the sample. In this case, that quality depends in large part on where and when you dig up the soil slivers that you'll be sending to the lab. With a little practice, you can do this job like a pro. For now, though, just remember to think "normal" in terms of location— that is, don't include soil from an atypical spot, like the site of a former compost pile, or a low area that puddles up after a rain. As for the timing, keep these tips in mind:

🌿 Test your soil in early fall, if possible.

🌿 Choose a day when the soil is warm and neither bone-dry nor sopping wet.

🌿 Take your samples *before* you work the soil or add anything to it.

🌿 If you have added fertilizer or other amendments to the soil, wait a month before you collect your sample.

YOU'LL HAVE A BALL!

Although a good professional lab test will tell you the texture of your soil, it's easy—and fun—to perform this do-it-yourself experiment. Simply roll a handful of moist (not wet and not dry) soil into a ball, just like a snowball. Then squeeze it hard. If it crumbles into a pile that looks like leftover cake crumbs, lucky you! You've got loam. If the ball just packs together more solidly, like a billiard ball, your soil is mostly clay. And if you can't even form a ball with your soil, it's too sandy to suit all but the most desert-loving plants.

Quick Fix

Order separate soil tests for areas where you'll grow plants that have very different nutrient requirements, such as tomatoes in the vegetable garden, azaleas in the shrub beds, and turfgrass on the lawn. Yes, that may entail more time digging, sifting, and packing. But your patience will pay off in healthier—and therefore less troublesome—plants for many years to come.

When you send in your sample, include a list of the plant(s) you intend to grow in each area. That way, the lab folks can give you specific recommendations for giving each plant the nutrients and pH range it needs.

While You're Waiting

No matter how eager you are to get your plants up and growing, it's important that you *don't* amend your soil or do any planting until after you receive your test results. If you do, you'll defeat the whole purpose of analyzing your soil! But that doesn't mean you need to just sit back and cool your heels until your lab report arrives. If you haven't followed my advice in earlier chapters to decide exactly what you and your family want from your new planting venture, now's the time to do it. More importantly, ask yourself how much time, energy, and money you really want to spend on your new planting venture—whether you're re-doing your whole yard or just starting a small herb garden.

There is one exception to the don't-add-anything-to-your-soil rule: It's okay to bury any organic matter that you have on hand, ranging from used tea bags to tree and shrub prunings.

Take a Census

Another constructive—and fun—project that will help fill your waiting time is one that folks used before there were soil-testing laboratories or do-it-yourself test kits: an old-fashioned worm count. This census-taking routine won't give you a scientific profile, but it's still the fastest, simplest way to find out whether your soil is healthy and productive.

Although earthworms may appear to be just about the lowliest beings on earth to human eyes, they're actually some of its most important caretakers. And when a large number of them are present in the soil, it means that (thanks to their work) the soil is well drained and aerated, has a pH between 6.0 and 7.0, and contains a big stock of organic matter—in other words, exactly the conditions most plants prefer. Here's how to find out how your soil stacks up:

Take 2

To really lure worms to your yard, dish up frequent servings of a fantastic fruit and veggie scrap soup. And best of all, it couldn't be easier to make. After dinner, simply whirl up your leftovers and any peelings in a blender or food processor (minus meats, bones, dressings, and sauces). Then dig a hole anyplace in your yard or garden, pour in the soup, and cover it up with soil. Hordes of worms will charge in and eat hearty!

- Dig out a block of soil that's roughly 1 foot square by 7 inches deep, and ease it onto a board.

- Very gently break up the clumps with your fingers, lift out the worms, and count them. Just be quick about it, so the little guys can scurry back underground before they dry out.

- Do the math, and if your block of soil contains 10 or more earthworms, congratulations! That means your soil is healthy and productive. The higher the head count (so to speak), the better the soil. A count of fewer than 10 means you've got work to do. You'll need fancier tests than this one to figure out exactly what the problem is, but one thing is certain: You can make any soil healthier by adding big helpings of organic matter to it.

Grandma's **GROW-HOW**

When you take your worm census, it's best to follow Grandma Putt's example by choosing a day in the spring or fall when the soil temperature is about 60°F. When it's either cooler or warmer than that, worms head deep into the soil, where your shovel won't be able to reach them. So don't try to rush this chore; just be patient and wait for the ideal weather.

KNOWLEDGE IS POWER

When your soil test results come back, they'll tell you how your soil stacks up in terms of the three categories we talked about earlier: pH level, fertility, and texture. Your mission then depends on the numbers in the report and on what plants you intend to grow. In earlier chapters, we talked about some of the special requirements of various kinds of plants. But here—in one handy spot—are the general guidelines you need to follow.

When it comes to adding lime or sulfur to adjust the pH of your soil, more is not better. Use only as much as you need to achieve the desired results.

Ups and Downs

The quickest way to change your soil's pH is to add either ground limestone (generally referred to as "lime") to raise the pH, or sulfur to lower it. Your test results will tell you which of these two miracle workers you need to use and in what quantity. Whichever one the results call for, apply it with a handheld broadcast spreader. And for the best outcome, keep these tips in mind:

- Apply your pH soil-adjuster only in the spring or fall, *not* during the hot days of summer.

- Don't apply more than 1 pound of sulfur or 5 pounds of lime per 100 square feet at any one time. If you need to add more than that, be patient and do it over two or more seasons, so the pH change is gradual.

- Do the job on a nice calm day, and be sure to wear a mask, gloves, and protective eye gear. (You want that stuff in the soil, not in your mouth, eyes, and skin pores!)

The Main Menu

In addition to altering the pH of your soil, your test results may call for adjusting its fertility by amending it with various nutrients. Here's a quick rundown of the major ones—what gardeners call "The Big Three." These

FOR THE LONG HAUL

When you need to change your soil's pH, lime and sulfur are good quick fixes, but they don't last forever. Furthermore, they do nothing to nourish all those tiny, living things that keep the soil strong, healthy, and productive. You'll get longer-lasting results—and give those underground workers a helping hand at the same time—if you add the right kind of organic matter to the soil.

Here are some of my favorite sweet-and-sour condiments. Just keep in mind that they won't get the job done quite as fast as lime and sulfur will, so you'll need a little patience.

SWEET (TO RAISE THE pH)	SOUR (TO LOWER THE pH)
• Bonemeal* • Ground clam or oyster shells • Ground eggshells • Other seashells • Wood ashes	• Aged sawdust or wood shavings • Coffee grounds • Cottonseed meal • Fresh manure** • Oak leaves • Pine needles

A word of caution: Most dogs find bonemeal irresistible, so if you share your yard with a canine companion, do yourself a favor and amend your soil with something else!

** *If you're making a new rose bed, this is your best choice, bar none. Roses love manure. But don't use the fresh stuff on an established rose bed—or any other planted area—because it will burn the plants' roots.*

are the elements represented by the triple-digit numbers like 12–4–8 on fertilizer labels. They stand for nitrogen (N), phosphorus (P), and potassium (K), and each one works in a specific way to nourish your plants. Note that while all plants need this trio of nutrients, they need them in different quantities.

Nitrogen. This nutrient provides the get-up-and-grow power for leaves and stems. That's why lawn fertilizers are so high in nitrogen—and why an overdose of it can make other plants become too lush and leafy.

Phosphorus. This promotes the growth of strong, vigorous roots and the formation of flowers, fruits, vegetables, and seeds.

Potassium. The Big K supports all phases of growth and helps plants stand up and fight back when pests or diseases strike.

The Second Course

In addition to The Big Three, plants need a small, but steady supply of five other basic food groups. If your soil testers are up to snuff, your results will include readings for these nutrients, too:

- Calcium

- Iron

- Magnesium

- Manganese

- Sulfur

Plants also require very small amounts of boron, copper, and zinc (a.k.a. micronutrients). In most cases, your soil will contain enough micronutrients to suit whatever plants you want to grow, but there are exceptions. For instance, in some regions, the soil tends to be deficient in boron, which is essential for both root and cole crops. And too much zinc or copper can harm some plants. As long as you've told the lab folks what you intend to grow in which spots, the report should tell you whether your soil has too little, too much, or just enough of these tiny tidbits—and how to correct any discrepancies.

Quick Fix

If you're lucky, any problems your soil test reveals about the texture of your sample—and therefore drainage—can be solved simply by adding plenty of organic matter to your soil. But if you do that and find that water still hangs around for hours after a short, heavy rain, stronger measures are called for. How strong? That's a question best answered by a professional. Before you try any more do-it-yourself tactics, get an opinion from a landscape architect or landscape contractor first. A short consultation now, at an hourly rate, could save you a lot of time, trouble, and money down the road.

THE TRANSFORMATION PROCESS

No matter what kind of soil you're starting out with—even if it's little more than rocks and rubble—there's a simple ingredient that can help you transform it into rich, productive earth. What is it? Organic matter. As it breaks down (with the help of the little underground helpers we talked about earlier), it makes soil drain well and retain just the right amount of water, and it helps deliver wholesome, well-balanced meals to every plant in your yard. Take it from me, the more practice you have in tending your yard and garden, the more you'll appreciate this miraculous matter! Here are some of my best tips for getting the most out of it in your yard.

Whatever you do, don't ever till or dig up soil when the ground is wet—that will give you hard, compacted soil faster than you can say "Step on it"!

Dig In?

Maybe. The fastest, most efficient way to improve your soil is to spread a thick layer of organic matter across the surface and till it in deeply, using either a shovel or a tiller. Just don't repeat the process too often. Why not? Because tilling soil can compact the pores so that air, water, and the underground breakdown squad can't move through it. Repeated tilling, especially in clay soil, can actually cause hardpan to form. That's a layer of soil that's so compacted, it's almost the consistency of concrete. Because neither roots nor water can penetrate it, both of them just sit there—with the roots rotting away in the process.

If you decide to till organic matter into clay soil, use material that's on the chunky side, like straw, pine needles, wood chips, or mature plant stalks. These things take longer to break down than finer-textured stuff, like grass clippings or leaves, and during the waiting period, they'll open up the soil so that water, nutrients, and earthworms can move through it freely.

The Hole-Improvement Plan

If you already have hardpan, and you want to start a new lawn or planting bed, whip up one of my Super Soil Sandwiches (see page 312). But to soften up the hardpan in your whole yard over time, go at it piece by piece this way: Every time you have some organic matter on hand, dig a hole, toss in your stash, and refill the hole. It's best if the hole reaches down to the hardpan layer, but if you don't have time to dig that far, don't worry. Just go deep enough to cover whatever material you're planning to bury. The depth could range from an inch or so for a couple of tea bags to a foot or more for tree and shrub prunings. As the material decomposes, it will eventually break up the hard stuff—and keep it broken up.

Rise Up or Dig Down?

It seems that every time you turn around, you hear somebody (including yours truly) raving about raised beds as the answer to all kinds of garden-variety soil problems. Well, these elevated planting sites can work wonders, all right, but there actually are times when you want to sink your beds, not raise them. So how do you make the call? It's simple: You just need to understand how each type works.

Take 2

The hole-improvement method isn't just for soil with hardpan. It's a simple way to add get-up-and-grow power to any kind of soil, using all kinds of stuff that you toss out every day. Take these castoffs, for instance:

- Feathers

- Hair from your (or your pets') brushes

- Newspaper

- Paper egg cartons

- Paper towel and toilet paper rolls

- Scraps of cotton, linen, or wool (no synthetic fabrics!)

- Shredded bulk mail

- Wine corks

Raised beds. These improve both drainage and air circulation and make the soil warm up faster in the spring. This is the way to go if you have heavy and damp soil, you live in a humid climate, or you want to grow plants that need all the warmth they can get for as long as they can get it.

Sunken beds. These beds capture and hold moisture and provide some protection from the wind. They're your answer if you have very sandy soil, or your climate is hot, dry, and windy.

Super Soil Sandwich Time

Throughout this book, I've been telling you that the best and easiest way to make a planting bed in any kind of soil—or even on a hard surface like a patio or driveway—is to whip up one of these sandwiches. Well, finally, here's the easier-than-pie recipe. If possible, start in the spring, a year before you intend to plant anything. Then follow this process:

If you can't wait months for a soil sandwich to cook, just make the top layer 4 to 6 inches of good-quality topsoil, or a half-and-half mixture of compost and topsoil. Then saturate it with my Super Soil Sandwich Dressing (below), wait two weeks, and plant to your heart's content.

STEP 1. Mark off your planting beds or lawn area. If you have hardpan, puncture the layer in a few places, using a garden fork or even a hammer and metal rod. This may take some persistence, but it will enable

---

Super Soil Sandwich Dressing

When you've got your ingredients all stacked up, top off your "sandwich" with this zesty condiment. It'll kick-start the cooking process, and by the following spring, your soil will be rarin' to grow!

> 1 can of regular (not diet) cola
> ½ cup of ammonia
> ¼ cup of instant tea granules
> 1 package (2 ¼ tsp.) of active dry yeast

Mix all of the ingredients in a bucket, and pour the solution into your 20 gallon hose-end sprayer. Then spray your Super Soil Sandwich until all the layers are thoroughly saturated.

earthworms to penetrate the nasty stuff and eventually help soften it up.

STEP 2. Lay a 1- to 2-inch-thick layer of newspaper over the bed, overlapping the edges as you go and trampling down any tall weeds. (Just ignore the turfgrass and short weeds.) Then soak the paper thoroughly with water.

STEP 3. Spread 1 to 2 inches of compost over the paper. Then cover the compost with 4 to 6 inches of organic matter. Leaves, pine needles, dried grass clippings, seaweed, and shredded paper will all work like a charm. Add alternate layers of compost and organic matter until the stack reaches 12 to 24 inches high.

STEP 4. Saturate the bed-to-be with my Super Soil Sandwich Dressing (at left), then go about your business. The "dish" will cook by itself, and by the following spring, you'll have 6 to 8 inches of loose, rich soil, just ripe for the planting.

HAVE YOU HEARD THE NEWS?

Whether you choose to plant while your sandwich is still cooking, or let it simmer slowly until all the ingredients have blended together, the secret to success is the thick bottom layer of newspaper. First off, it smothers any existing weeds and unwanted grass. More importantly, it attracts throngs of earthworms, and they will quickly perform the job for which (I'm convinced) they were created: breaking down the organic matter into fertile, fluffy, plant-pleasing soil.

Black Gold

When it comes to improving any kind of soil, compost is the greatest gift a gardener could ask for (which, of course, is how it got the nickname *black gold*). But it's really far more than a valuable soil amendment—it's nature's way of turning once-living matter, such as fallen leaves, grass clippings, and decaying fruit, into a substance that makes living plants thrive in a manner that no commercial fertilizer can. In fact, compost has even been proven to prevent many plant diseases. You can buy compost at most garden centers, but it's a snap to make your own.

The bin system. This method produces hot compost, just like the kind you'd get from an old-fashioned compost pile—but in a much neater and easier way. To get started, buy a commercial compost bin at a garden center or from a catalog. (I prefer the bins that look like big, fat, black wheels, mounted on a turning mechanism.) Then throw in your raw ingredients, and give the wheel a spin every week or two, so air can get into the mixture (the sides are perforated, so the more you twirl the wheel, the more oxygen gets in, and the faster the stuff inside breaks down). As for what to put inside, you want roughly three parts high-carbon ingredients—the "browns"—for every one that's high in nitrogen—the "greens" (see "The Composting Menu" below). If you have too much carbon, the compost could take years to cook. Too much nitrogen, and it'll give off an odor that would outperform a startled skunk.

The bag routine. In this method, known as cold composting, anaerobic bacteria break down the organic material without the help of oxygen, so there's no turning required. The process takes longer than the bin method,

THE COMPOSTING MENU

When you're making your compost in either a bin or an old-fashioned pile, include roughly three helpings of browns to each one of greens.

THE BROWNS	THE GREENS
• Chipped twigs and branches • Dead flower and vegetable stalks • Dry leaves and plant stalks • Hay • Pine needles • Sawdust • Shredded paper • Straw	• Coffee grounds • Eggshells • Flowers • Fruit and vegetable scraps • Grass clippings • Green leaves or stems • Hair (pet or human) • Manure • Tea bags

Compost Tea

One of the best things you can do for the plants in your yard is to serve up frequent drinks of Compost Tea. It delivers a well-balanced supply of all the nutrients—major and minor—that keep your plants looking their best and producing heaps of fruits, flowers, or vegetables. And it's far more than just a good fertilizer; applied every two to three weeks throughout the growing season, it's also one of your best defenses against diseases.

1 gal. of fresh compost
4 gal. of warm water

Pour the water into a large bucket or tub. Scoop the compost into a square of cotton or burlap, or a panty hose leg, and tie it closed. Put the super-sized "tea bag" in the water, cover the container, and let the mixture steep for seven days. Pour some of the finished tea into a watering can and sprinkle it around the base of your plants. Put the rest in a handheld sprayer bottle and spritz it onto the leaves.

To make Manure Tea—another garden-variety wonder drug—simply substitute 1 gallon of composted manure for the compost, and use the finished product in the same way.

but there's no special equipment to buy. All you need are some plastic garbage bags and whatever yard waste or kitchen scraps (minus meats and sauces) that you have on hand. Just one word of warning: When you open the bags, you'll be hit with a potent odor, but it'll disappear as soon as the compost is exposed to the open air. Here's the process:

🌱 Fill a large, black plastic garbage bag with a mixture of chopped leaves, grass clippings, and vegetable scraps. For every couple of shovelfuls of bulky, carbon-rich material (see "The Composting Menu" at left), add a few cupfuls of my Super Soil Sandwich Dressing (see page 312).

🌱 When the bag is nearly full, sprinkle a couple quarts of water over the contents, and mix until all the ingredients are moist. To do that, shake small or light bags and roll large or heavy ones.

What a bummer! It's time to make compost tea, and you have no scoop on hand. Well, don't run out and buy one! Just grab an empty 1-gallon bleach or detergent jug. Cut diagonally across the bottom, set aside that bottom piece, screw the top back on, and bingo! You've got the perfect tool for scooping up compost, fertilizer, potting soil, or just about any other nonedible substance around the old homestead.

Tie the bag shut, and leave it in an out-of-the-way place where the temperature will stay above 45°F for a few months. **Note:** You'll get dandy compost if you ignore the bags, but faster results if you roll them around every few days.

CONTAINERS ON PARADE

I've sung the praises of growing plants in containers as simple solutions to problems ranging from poor soil to pest invasions. There is one minor catch: In exchange for helping you avoid trouble, potted plants demand slightly different kinds of care than their counterparts in the ground. But don't worry! Armed with the tips, tricks, and tonics in this section, it's a cinch to keep contained plants happy and healthy.

If you're planning to sell your home in the near future, one of the fastest and easiest ways to increase its curb appeal is to deck your front and back porches with thriving plants in big, beautiful pots.

Why Bother?

Even if you have a grand and glorious yard and garden, there are still plenty of good reasons to grow plants in containers. Here's a sampling:

Container plants are safe from most of the soilborne pests and diseases that thrive in open ground. Even hostas—prime targets of slugs and snails—are much easier to protect when you grow them in pots.

Some plants have a roving spirit that just won't quit. Planted in the ground and left to their own devices, these gypsies will take over an entire garden in a single season. But with their roots in pots, even the most enthusiastic ramblers stay at home.

Containers enable you to grow plants that could never survive in your in-ground garden. When the weather turns too hot or too cold, all you need to do is whisk both plant and pot to shelter. And you can amend the potting mix to suit the needs of any plant—which is not always possible to do in your garden.

No matter how patiently you plan and tend a flower garden, the great wheel of life keeps on turning—which means gaps are bound to appear every now and again. But you can keep the parade going with pots of colorful annuals or bulbs.

Measure Up

You might think you're doing a plant a favor by tucking it into the biggest container you can find. Not so! In fact, potted plants are like Goldilocks: They prefer accommodations that are not too big and not too small. Without ample room to spread out, a plant's roots quickly deplete the oxygen and nutrients in the soil. On the other hand, using a container that's too large can cause trouble ranging from delayed flowering and fruiting to deadly root rot.

To find a pot that's just right, consider the mature size, root structure, and growth rate of the plant(s) you intend to put in it. That last factor is important

Grandma's GROW-HOW

When you're choosing container candidates, take some friendly advice from Grandma Putt: Although it is true that you can fill a pot with any kind of soil under the sun, you still need to consider many of the other factors that affect in-ground plants. So before you run down to the garden center or send off a catalog order, assess prevailing winds, temperature ranges, and humidity levels in your potential potting site(s).

SIZE 'EM UP

Standard, commercially made pots are measured by their top diameter. There are no clear-cut rules for determining what kind of plant needs which size pot, but here are some basic rules of thumb.

DIAMETER OF POT (INCHES)	WHAT IT WILL HOLD
6–8	Dwarf annuals, some succulents, young plants in temporary quarters
8–12	Most flowering annuals, perennials, and herbs; many vines; some dwarf shrubs
14–18	Small shrubs, young trees, multiplant groupings*
20 or more	Trees and shrubs, vegetables, multiplant groupings**

An 18-inch container will hold two perennials that have been grown in 1-gallon pots.

**A 20- to 24-inch container will hold four to five perennials that have been grown in 1-gallon pots.*

because often a fast grower will fill a too-large container before trouble sets in. As a general rule, though, plants perform their best when they have 1 to 2 inches of soil all the way around the root-ball. In the case of permanent plantings, this will mean repotting every couple of years to maintain that margin of comfort. Your attention to detail now will pay off in a healthier container garden—and therefore, less maintenance time for you later on.

Material Matters

A plant couldn't care less about what kind of container you put it in. It'll happily send out roots in anything that holds soil, from a custom-made cast-iron planter to a worn-out old boot. From a plant tender's standpoint, though, the right choice of container materials can spell the difference between a scene that's a joy to look at and a breeze to care for—and one that demands all the patience and persistence you can muster up just to keep it going. Each type, however, has its pros and cons. The right ones for you depend on your climate, the kinds of plants you're growing, and the time and inclination you have for maintenance.

Terra-cotta. Unglazed clay is porous, which all but guarantees good drainage. That makes it the perfect material for a cool, rainy, or humid climate, or when you want to grow dry-soil lovers—but it does mean you have to be especially diligent about watering.

Terra-cotta is heavy, so it's an excellent choice for trees, tall shrubs, or any plants

COLOR IT HAPPY

Believe it or not, the color of your pots can play a crucial role in the success or failure of your garden. This is particularly true with black containers, which capture and hold heat. That can be a big advantage in a cool climate, especially if you're growing heat-loving vegetables like tomatoes. But in a hot summer, the sun's rays will turn the pot into an oven that will bake your plants' roots before you know it. So if you live where the weather gets steamy, stick with white or pale-colored pots.

Quick Fix

When it comes to ensuring the health (and good looks) of your potted plants, the shape of their containers is just as important as the size. For example, violets or spring crocuses have shallow roots and short top growth, so they'll look good and perform well in a pot that's only a few inches high. On the other hand, dill, which has a long taproot and tall foliage, needs a container that's deep enough to not only hold the roots without bending, but also visually balance the upper portion of the plant.

in a windy location. But it does have one major drawback: A large terra-cotta pot filled with soil is hard to move and may end up being too heavy for a deck, rooftop, or balcony.

Wood. Untreated lumber is somewhat breathable, but when it's coated with a waterproof sealer, it becomes nonporous. Wood is naturally insulating, so the soil inside remains at a fairly even temperature if the walls are at least 7/8 inch thick. Wooden containers are also durable, especially if they're made of rot-resistant redwood, cedar, or cypress.

Whether you choose terra-cotta, wood, or plastic containers, it's the same old story: Although there are bargains to be had, by and large, you get what you pay for. So if you want durable, long-lasting homes for your potted plants, don't pinch pennies at shopping time.

Plastic. Because all plastic is nonporous, water remains in the soil longer. This is a major advantage if you live in a hot, dry region or want to grow moisture-loving plants. In a wet climate, however, or for plants that need good drainage or soil that's on the dry side, plastic can be a big drawback. It also provides little protection from heat or cold. On the other hand, plastic is lightweight, which means you can use it in places where other materials might be too heavy. But it may be too light for a windy or exposed location.

A Word About Water

Waterlogged soil is the most common cause of death for container plants. To avoid that problem, make sure each pot you use has at least one opening in the bottom. If you fall in love with a container that has no drainage hole, plant in a smaller container that does have holes, and set it inside the larger one. Then raise the inner pot up on bricks or stones so that it never sits in water.

Putting Down Roots

You might think that good topsoil, straight from the garden, would be just the ticket for outdoor container plants. Not so! Even the best loam is too dense to use by itself in containers. It will quickly harden into a rock-like mass that's impossible for plants' roots to penetrate. Your best bet for most plants is a standard commercial potting mix. You can also buy specialty blends for finicky eaters like roses, orchids, cacti, succulents, aquatic plants, and acid-soil lovers, such as azaleas, rhododendrons, and camellias.

Most garden centers carry a mind-boggling assortment of potting mixes, but just like fertilizers, they all fall into one of two broad categories.

Soil-based mixes. As the name implies, these contain real, garden-variety loam (sterilized, of course) along with varying amounts of plant food and additives such as peat, sand, bark chips, vermiculite, or perlite. Soil-based mixes are heavier than soilless versions, and they tend to be messier to use. On the plus side, they retain water and nutrients better and provide greater stability for plants. They are, by far, the better choice.

Soilless mixes. The main ingredient in these products is peat moss or a peat substitute such as coir, which is made from shredded and composted coconut husks. Depending on the formulation, these mixes contain the same kinds of additives you'll find in the soil-based types. Soilless mixes dry out and lose nutrients fairly quickly, but their light weight and ease of handling make them godsends for use in hanging baskets, window boxes, and short-term plantings of all kinds.

TRANSLATION, PLEASE

Until you've had a fair amount of practice, knowing how much potting mix to buy can be tricky. That's because it's generally sold by the cubic foot, while standard containers are labeled in inches. (I have no idea why that is—maybe the manufacturers just like to keep us gardeners on our toes!) As a handy translation, here's what you can fill with a 2-cubic-foot bag of either soil-based or soilless potting mix:

- 1 window box or a planter that measures 36 x 8 x 10 inches

- 2 pots that are 12 inches in diameter and 15 inches deep

- 8 to 10 standard-depth 10- to 12-inch pots

ⒽⒺⓁⓅ!

Q When I planted an azalea recently, I put pot shards in the bottom of the container because I'd always heard that they improved drainage. Now a neighbor just told me shards can actually prevent water from draining out of the hole. Is that true?

A *Yep, it's true, all right. My advice is to take that plant and the soil out of the pot and get rid of the shards. Then cover the drainage opening with a small square of plastic window screening or several layers of old panty hose. Either material will keep the soil in the pot while still allowing excess water to drain away.*

Life-Giving Liquid

When it comes to container-garden care, watering is your single most important chore. That's because potted plants can't send their roots deep into the ground in search of moisture, and depending on their location, rain may not even reach them. So how do you know when your charges need a drink? All you need to do is poke your finger into the top inch of soil. If it feels dry, it's time to water. But don't take chances: When you buy your plants, ask about their specific requirements, or consult a comprehensive gardening book.

Serve It the Right Way

Just as with inground plants, *how* you water your containers matters as much as *when* you water. So make sure you fully saturate the soil. If you moisten only the top few inches, you'll encourage the roots to stay there. Your proof of a job well done will be water running freely from the drainage hole. But just don't let that "badge of honor" stay in the saucer! Empty it right away if you can. If that's not possible, clear it out within 24 hours. Water that's allowed to stand much longer than that will keep the soil soggy, and that can lead to fungal diseases. (For pots that are too big to lift, siphon off the water with a turkey baster or sop it up with a sponge.)

Look Out Below!

Every once in a while, things can go haywire and container plants hand you a challenge in the form of a drainage malfunction. But they're easy to fix once you've diagnosed the problem.

No water drains out. Most likely, that means the opening is clogged. Just turn the container on its side (or as far over as you can) and shove a large nail or pointed stick into the hole until the blockage is cleared out.

The water drains out too fast. This happens when the soil has dried out so much that it's shrunk away from the container walls. If the pot is small enough, submerge it in a tub of water for half an hour or so. Otherwise, set a soaker hose on the soil surface near the plant's base and let the water run until the soil is saturated. No soaker hose on hand? Just use a regular version with an old sock over the end and the flow turned down to a trickle.

Eat Up!

Potted plants need exactly the same nutrients as their cousins in the ground. But, just as with watering, they must rely on you to provide their meals— their roots can't go foraging through the soil in search of snacks. The easiest way to satisfy your captive diners' appetites is to mix timed-release fertilizer

PORTABLE POSSIBILITIES

We all know that one of the most appealing aspects of container gardening is that you *can* move your plants around to give them the conditions they need. For instance, you can ferry sun lovers from one bright spot to another as Ol' Sol travels over your deck. Or you can rush extra-tender plants inside at the first hint of cold weather. The question is *will* you provide that kind of care and do it whenever it's called for? If the answer is "no," or even "well, maybe," then don't even think of bringing a "special needs" plant home from the nursery. At best, it will suffer undue stress, and stressed plants (like stressed people) tend to attract more than their fair share of trouble.

capsules into the potting mix at planting time. Then each time you water, they release small helpings of nutrients. Depending on the brand, the capsules remain active for about three to eight months, and when necessary, you just scratch more into the soil surface. If you prefer a more hands-on approach to feeding, mix up a batch of my Container Plant Feast (below), and use it every time you water throughout the growing season.

Acupuncture for *Plants*???

You betcha! Well, in a manner of speaking. Here's the scoop: Feeding and watering reduce the spaces between the soil particles in pots, and that in turn can drive air out of the soil, eventually suffocating the roots. But you can give your container plants quick relief by taking a screwdriver or large, long nail and gently working it down into the soil. Two or three holes are fine for a small pot; larger ones will obviously need more. And don't worry that you might poke more holes than you need—there's no such thing as too much aeration! For a longer-lasting fix, repot the plant(s) in fresh, high-quality potting mix with a big helping of compost added to it.

Container Plant Feast

This hearty meal will keep your potted plants well fed and growing strong all season long.

> **1 tbsp. of 15-30-13 fertilizer**
> **1/2 tsp. of corn syrup**
> **1/2 tsp. of unflavored gelatin**
> **1/2 tsp. of whiskey**
> **1/4 tsp. of instant tea granules**
> **Water**

Mix the first five ingredients in a 1-gallon milk jug, filling the balance of the jug with water. Then add 1/2 cup of this mixture to every gallon of H_2O you use to irrigate your container plants.

Say "Polymers, Please"

For impatient container gardeners, one of the greatest happenings in decades was the development of water-retaining gel crystals. When you mix them into the soil, these super-absorbent polymers hold on to both water and dissolved nutrients, keeping them readily available to plants' roots. That's a major time saver if you live in a hot, dry climate or have plants in exposed sites, where containers dry out in the blink of an eye. Some commercial potting mixes have the crystals already added, but it's quick and easy (and a lot cheaper) to do the job yourself. Here's all there is to it:

STEP 1. Start by pouring your potting mix into a large tub or wheelbarrow.

STEP 2. Add the water-retaining crystals to a bucket of water, and stir until they swell up to form a thick gel. (The directions on the package will tell you the correct proportion of crystals to water.)

STEP 3. Thoroughly combine the gel with your potting mix, using a trowel or your hands. (Again, follow the package directions for the ratio of polymers to soil.)

STEP 4. Put the soil-gel combo into your pots, and set in your plants.

One note of caution: Make sure you follow the package directions to the letter. No matter how dry or windy your site may be, an overdose of gel will keep the soil too wet, and that could kill your plants in a hurry.

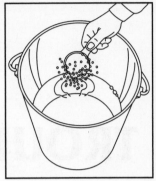

Add the crystals to water and mix to form a thick gel.

Thoroughly mix the gel and your potting soil.

Fill your pots with the gel-laced soil, and plant in the usual way.

TIMELY TROUBLESHOOTING

Winning the War on Pests and Diseases

No gardener—impatient or otherwise—likes to hear this, but regardless of what kind of plants you're growing or how well you take care of them, it's almost inevitable that some pest or disease will show up and start causing trouble. But don't worry! In this chapter, I'll share some of my favorite easy-does-it tricks for heading off a whole lot of time-consuming problems and minimizing the ones that can't be prevented.

Draw a map of your yard that shows fences, walkways, and your house. Also, mark which direction is north, so you'll know which areas will be shaded during the day. Jot down relevant details as you move along.

THE LAY OF THE LAND

I've already told you that taking the time to build strong, healthy soil can help you avoid a whole lot of hassle. Well, analyzing a few other factors in your yard is a big step on the road to happier and easier gardening. When you know what kinds of growing conditions you've got, you can select plants that will thrive in them. But if you ask a plant to accept surroundings that are not its cup of tea, it can't perform at its peak—no matter how much TLC you give it. And a plant that's struggling, or simply feeling a little under the weather, is a prime target for pests and diseases.

Pockets of Comfort

As we've discussed throughout this book, frost dates and zone numbers are important garden-variety guidelines, but many other factors, such as wind, rainfall, altitude, humidity, and even air quality, also affect a plant's health and well-being. Those details vary like night and day within both hardiness and heat zones. Even in your own yard, growing conditions are different from one place to the next. You'll find it well worth your time and effort to pinpoint these pockets, which gardeners call microclimates.

Places sheltered by walls or buildings. Most likely, they're warmer than the open space that is just around the corner.

Strips of ground beside busy streets. They'll receive more pollution than areas that are blocked by your house or a good sturdy fence.

Low spots where frost gathers. They'll get cold earlier in the fall and stay cold later in the spring. Low spots also tend to stay moist longer, even if the soil is well drained.

Areas that warm up early in the day. These spaces also tend to warm up early in the spring.

The direction of slopes. A north-facing slope gets less sunshine and, therefore, stays cooler than one that faces south.

ALL DECKED OUT

When you're outside exploring your yard's microclimates, don't overlook decks, porches, or patios where you might want to grow container plants. Even these outdoor living spaces have areas that get more wind or shade than those that are just a few feet away.

When the Wind Blows

A plant that's blowin' in the wind is a plant that's under stress. And a stressed-out plant is a prime target for every kind of trouble under the sun. But before you can put up an effective windbreak, or take advantage of an established structure, you need to know which way the wind generally blows. Here are two easy way to find out:

Quick Fix

- If you live in a cold-winter region, just look out the window during a snowstorm. Those blowing flakes will show you exactly which direction the wind is coming from, and what walls, fences, or other obstacles stop it in its tracks.

- When there is no snow, simply pound a few 3- to 4-foot stakes into the ground in your prospective planting area, and tie a banner, bandanna, or scrap of fabric to each one. Then keep an eye on those flapping flags, and take note of which way the breezes blow them.

Let There Be Light

The question is how much. Although a lot of plants need full sun, many others perform best in less light. How much less varies considerably, and in earlier chapters, we talked about some plants' individual preferences. With practice, you'll learn to tell various light levels at a glance. But in the meantime, here's how to decipher the wording you see in catalogs and on seed packets and plant tags.

One of the surest and most pleasant roads to easy-care gardening is making friends with the folks at your local top-notch garden centers. Get to know the salespeople who seem friendly and have the patience and ability to answer your questions. They are usually experienced gardeners themselves, and I've found that, time permitting, they're delighted to share their knowledge and enthusiasm. They can help you choose plants suited to your taste, budget, and growing conditions. They can also tell you when new shipments are due in, and sometimes even when a sale is coming up.

Dense shade. North-facing walls or the low, dense branches of evergreen trees cast dense shade. Very few plants will thrive in this situation, but don't despair—you will find a few winners (see "Made in the Shade" on page 330).

Dappled shade. This type of shade is what you get from large-leaved trees like oaks, maples, or elms. The foliage blocks the sun, but still lets in light.

As Grandma Putt knew well, partial shade is the trickiest kind to work with, but it can also be a lot of fun—at least if you like to experiment as she did. This is where practice and experience enter the picture because the effect of sunlight on plants depends not only on how long it lasts, but also on how intense it is. And that varies considerably, according to the time of day, the time of year, and where you live.

Grandma's GROW-HOW

Filtered light. This light falls through the openings in an arbor, the small leaves of trees such as willows or birches, or a translucent structure like a fiberglass overhang. A word to the wise: When catalogs say that a plant likes "shade," what they often mean is filtered light.

Bright light. In city gardens or on the north sides of houses, no direct sun reaches the site, but nothing blocks the sky. Bright light is magnified as it bounces off walls on its way to the ground.

Partial shade. Also known as part shade or part sun, partial shade means that a site gets direct sun for anywhere from two to five hours a day (six or more is generally described as "full sun").

More Light, Please!

Or maybe less. Unlike most of the growing conditions in your yard, the degree of shade can often be altered, at least to some extent. You can prune or remove trees and shrubs to let in more sun, or do several things to reflect more light on your plants. For instance, paint walls and fences white, choose paving materials that are very light in color, or hang mirrors in key areas. Water in any form also reflects and magnifies

Take 2

If you have an old wagon or wheeled tea cart taking up space in your attic or garage, haul the relic outside and use it to ferry your container plants into and out of the sun. Besides making the moving process faster and easier, the vehicle will add a decorative touch to your yard.

light. (Maybe this is the excuse you've been waiting for to install a fishpond or fountain—or even a swimming pool!)

When the problem is too much sun—a common fact of life in hot climates and at high altitudes—planting trees or erecting fences in strategic places can provide essential shelter for tender leaves and stems. When that's not possible, consider growing your more delicate plants in containers, so you can move them under cover during the hottest part of the day.

MADE IN THE SHADE

Some folks (especially those new to gardening) cringe at the mere mention of the word *shade*. But the fact is that for every degree of light you can name, there are plants that crave it. Here are some excellent examples.

DEGREE OF SHADE	SOME PLANTS THAT LOVE IT
Dense shade	Climbing hydrangea (*Hydrangea petiolaris*), Dutchman's pipe (*Aristolochia*), English ivy (*Hedera helix*), gladwin iris (*Iris foetidissima*)
Dappled shade	Bergenias, ferns, hostas, impatiens, wildflowers like jack-in-the-pulpit (*Arisaema*), and any early-blooming bulbs like crocuses and daffodils
Filtered light	Astilbes, bleeding hearts (*Dicentra*), Christmas fern (*Polystichum acrostichoides*), foxgloves (*Digitalis*), goatsbeard (*Aruncus*), hostas, spotted deadnettle (*Lamium maculatum*)
Bright light	Azaleas, camellias, candytuft (*Iberis saxatilis*), ferns, lungworts (*Pulmonaria*), rhododendrons, Solomon's seal (*Polygonatum odoratum*), violas
Partial shade	Columbines (*Aquilegia*), coral bells (*Heuchera sanguinea*), crested iris (*Iris cristata*), flowering tobacco (*Nicotiana*), foamflower (*Tiarella cordifolia*)

STANDING GUARD

In Mother Nature's scheme of things, there are no such things as "pests." All the members of the animal kingdom—from teeny-tiny spider mites to big, beautiful deer—are simply doin' what comes naturally (to quote Irving Berlin). The problem from a human point of view comes when they do it in our yards and gardens. Fortunately, there are a whole lot of ways to protect your plants from harm, while still letting the great wheel of life turn smoothly. And believe it or not, it's a lot easier than you might think!

If you want the most accurate take on the pest scene in your area, check with your neighbors rather than your local Cooperative Extension office. Most insects and bigger animals cause serious trouble only when they're present in large numbers, and the head count can vary greatly from one neighborhood to another.

Plant Wisely

After you've determined which plants will perform best in your growing conditions and you've learned what kinds of unwanted visitors to expect, there are some guidelines worth following:

- Plant what they don't care to eat. Most animals and a lot of insects have definite food preferences. So as much as you can, opt for their least favorite things or surround their food of choice with plants that are farther down on their wish list.

- Offer them a smorgasbord. Any insect or animal will zero in on a big expanse of its favorite food. But if it sees a whole crazy-quilt mixture of plants—some yummy, some so-so, and some that are frankly repulsive—it'll almost always head for tastier territory.

- Lay out the unwelcome mat. All plants give off chemicals from their roots, stems, and leaves. Many of these substances naturally repel a variety of insects and four-legged critters (yes, even deer!). So whenever you can, plant vegetation that will make your likely visitors turn and flee. For some of the most versatile repellent plants, see "Pest-Chasing Plants" on page 233 and "Scat!" on page 287.

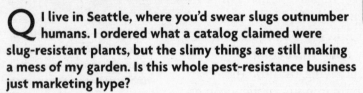

Q I live in Seattle, where you'd swear slugs outnumber humans. I ordered what a catalog claimed were slug-resistant plants, but the slimy things are still making a mess of my garden. Is this whole pest-resistance business just marketing hype?

A *No, it's not marketing hype, just a misunderstanding of the terminology. The word* resistant *simply means that a plant is less likely to fall victim to a particular pest (or disease) than its nonresistant counterparts are. But no plant is guaranteed to be completely immune to trouble. Also, the degree of resistance can vary greatly from one part of the country to another. In the Pacific Northwest, any plant will always be more prone to slug damage than the same variety would be in, say, Santa Fe or Las Vegas.*

Help Wanted

Of all the millions of insects in the world, the vast majority of them are entirely harmless. And many of them stand ready to keep the "bad" bug population in check. Some of the most prolific predators are assassin bugs, ground beetles, minute pirate bugs, and—of course—ladybugs. These pest-control workers will quickly find their way to any flowers that are rich in pollen and nectar. But the secret to keeping them on the job in your yard is to follow this recruitment policy.

Lay off pesticides. I know that's a frightening thought if you've been using them for a long time, but you can bet your bottom dollar that if you quit cold turkey, throngs of good guys will show up and start chowing down on the bad bugs in no time flat.

Give them a drink. All living things need water, but you don't have to install a fancy pond. Just sink plant saucers into the ground, set some pebbles inside (letting a few of them show above the surface), and pour in water. It gives insects—and insect eaters like toads, frogs, birds, and bats—a bar to belly up to and quench their thirst.

Mix it up. Plant a mixed bag of flowers, herbs, veggies, trees, and shrubs. The more menu and shelter options you offer up, the more kinds of helpers will come a callin'—and the more kinds of pests they'll polish off.

Go native. If you want a first-class dream team on your side, look for plants that are native to your neck of the woods. I guarantee that local heroes will flock to your doorstep!

If you're confused about exactly what kinds of flowers to use as recruitment bonuses, don't worry. Although a few bugs have very definite tastes, most are pleased as punch with any flower that's rich in pollen and nectar. But it's important to plant a mixture of flowers so that *something* will always be in bloom throughout the growing season. That way, you'll attract a variety of insects and they'll always have flowers to sip from. Surefire winners include asters, cosmos, mint, morning glories, and yarrow.

> ## DON'T PANIC!
>
> Or better yet: "Live and let live." Good-guy bugs can't stay around unless they have bad guys to munch on. So don't reach for your spray gun—or even your water hose—at the first sign of a slug or an aphid. Instead, think of them as lunch for your heroes. And even if you lose a tomato or tulip here and there, you'll still have a green scene full of flowers to smell, veggies and fruits to eat, and trees to hang your hammock from!

The Princes of Pest Control

Many critters feast on destructive insects, but two of them have truly monumental appetites for "bad" bugs. Who are these glorious gluttons? Bats and toads. And the good news is that it's easy to enlist their help:

- Every night, a single adult bat eats as many as 1,200 insects an *hour*, including mosquitoes, beetles, and the flying (and egg-laying) forms of cutworms, cabbage worms, and corn earworms. The simplest way to attract bats to your yard is to order ready-made houses, along with complete instructions for hanging them, from Bat Conservation International at www.batcon.org. For you do-it-yourselfers, this organization also offers simple building plans on its website.

Hummingbirds are famous as nectar sippers—and hovering showmen. But here's something you might not know: These colorful little guys and gals also eat hordes of insects. In fact, very often when they seem to be drinking nectar from a flower, they're really snatching up tiny bugs. To let the hummers know that you've got a pest-control position open, plant bright red flowers that are tubular or trumpet-shaped. Once the little guys take up residence, they'll go for other colors, too, but it's red that draws them in initially. Some of their favorite flowers are fuchsias, bee balms, daylilies, snapdragons, lilies, and trumpet vines.

The average toad consumes 15,000 destructive insects in a single year—and almost no beneficial ones. Their menu includes armyworms, gypsy moth larvae, mosquitoes, slugs, cutworms, and all kinds of beetles. Keep toads happy by providing some shallow water, like a birdbath sunk into the ground, and a place to hide from noise, predators, and the midday sun. You can buy "toad abodes" at garden centers, but an upside-down clay flowerpot with a gap broken out of the rim works just fine.

Wrens to the Rescue!

Little brown house wrens may not be as exciting to look at as more colorful birds are, but their pretty voices rival those of any flying songster you can name. What's even more important from an impatient gardener's standpoint is that each growing season, these diminutive dynamos eat thousands of insects. And a great way to lure a wren family to your turf is to hang up a few of these easy-to-make wren houses. Just follow this simple construction process:

Wrens are very territorial, so don't hang a wren house in your vegetable garden. If you do, the wrens will chase off other insect-eating birds that also protect your crops.

STEP 1. For each house, you'll need a half-gallon waxed cardboard milk carton that has been rinsed and dried thoroughly, a stapler, a roll of

1-inch-wide masking tape, a soft cloth, a small can of paste-type brown shoe polish, a penknife or box cutter, a ruler, a nail, a sturdy twig about 5 inches long, and some twine.

STEP 2. Staple the top of the carton securely, or if the carton has a plastic cap, screw it on tightly.

STEP 3. Tear off 1- to 2-inch pieces of masking tape, and stick them all over the carton until it's completely covered and the final texture resembles natural bark.

STEP 4. Using a soft cloth, rub the shoe polish all over the carton so that it covers the tape.

STEP 5. Cut a 1-inch-diameter entrance hole about 6 inches above the bottom of the carton.

STEP 6. Use the nail to poke a few drainage holes in the bottom of the carton. Also poke holes in the top of the carton, on each side, to ensure good ventilation.

STEP 7. Poke another hole in the box about 1 inch below the entrance hole. Insert the twig, leaving most of it outside as a perch.

STEP 8. Securely staple each end of a piece of twine to the top of the container to form a handle for hanging. Then hang the finished wren house in a sheltered location (under a porch roof is perfect), and wait for your pest-control squad to report for duty.

Cover the carton completely with strips of masking tape.

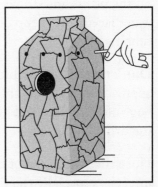

Poke holes in the carton to allow for drainage and ventilation.

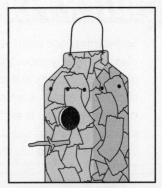

Hang your finished wren house in a sheltered location.

Hand-to-Hand Combat

Even if you have a lot of insect-eating helpers on the scene, there still may be times when the bad-bug population gets out of hand. But if you inspect your plants every day, or at least every couple of days, you can quickly deal with any little problems before they turn into big ones. Here are some simple ways to go about it.

Handpick them. This is the most effective way to deal with larger pests, such as slugs, snails, beetles, weevils, and caterpillars. Just pick them off the plants and drown them in a bucket of water laced with a cup of dishwashing liquid or rubbing alcohol.

Dunk them. If you'd prefer a less hands-on approach, hold a bowl of soapy water under a bug-infested plant and jostle the leaves; the pests will tumble down into the drink and drown.

Hose them off. One of the surest and easiest ways to get rid of many insects—especially the tiny, sucking kinds like aphids, thrips, mites,

The quickest way to get rid of large insects is to recruit a posse of young bounty hunters to handpick them for you. Just put a price on the buggy heads, hang up a few "Wanted" posters around the house (or neighborhood), organize the search, and the villains will soon be history!

Sometimes, one plant will be seriously infested while its neighbors are clean, or nearly so. In that case, simply throw an old sheet over the buggy plant, pull it up by the roots, and dump it into a tub of water laced with 2 cups or so of dishwashing liquid or rubbing alcohol. Leave it for a minute or two, then drop it in the trash. If any stragglers have found their way to nearby plants, just pluck them off, and get rid of them per the guidelines in "Hand-to-Hand Combat" (above).

and whiteflies—is to simply blast them off your plants with a strong spray from a garden hose.

Vacuum them up. Just put about 2 inches of soapy water into the reservoir of a wet/dry vacuum (a.k.a. Shop-Vac®), and suck up the culprits. Or use a regular handheld model and empty the contents into a bucket of soapy water. Vacuuming works especially well for insects that tend to scamper rather than fly, such as lace bugs, harlequin bugs, rose chafers, and carrot weevils.

Clip them off. When you find that a few leaves or stems are covered with bugs, just cut off the afflicted plant parts. Put them into a plastic bag, tie it closed, and toss it into the trash can.

In the Event of an All-Out Invasion . . .

Whip up one of the recipes you'll find throughout this book (like the versatile, potent, and food-safe Orange Aid on page 338). But when you do, or if you use even the "greenest" of commercial products, keep these points in mind:

- All insecticides—homemade or otherwise—will kill hero bugs right along with the "bad" ones. To make sure you've got the right target, aim your spray *very* carefully.

- Some plants are particulary sensitive to dishwashing liquid and rubbing alcohol, so when you use either one in a tonic,

Take 2

Anytime you prepare a tonic recipe that contains some solid ingredients (like citrus peels, chopped garlic, or even instant tea granules), it's important to strain the tonic before you pour it into a hose-end or handheld sprayer bottle. Otherwise, tiny bits of stuff could get caught in the sprayer head and spoil your chances for a successful delivery. So what's the strainer I recommend? You guessed it—a piece of old panty hose. It'll head off trouble every time!

Orange Aid

You'll love the aroma of this citrusy spray—and you'll love its firepower even more. It'll deliver a death blow to any caterpillar that comes within shooting range of your spray gun. It also works like a charm on other soft-bodied insects, including whiteflies and aphids.

1 cup of chopped orange peels*
¼ cup of boiling water

Put the orange peels in a blender or food processor, and pour the boiling water over them. Liquefy, then let the mixture sit overnight at room temperature. Strain the slurry, and pour the liquid into a handheld sprayer bottle. Fill the balance of the bottle with water, and spray your plants from top to bottom.

* Or substitute lemon, lime, or grapefruit peels.

test it on a few leaves before you spray the whole plant. And after you've completed your mission, hose off any residue because if it's left on, it could burn tender tissue.

Even though a potion may be lethal only to insects, ingesting it could harm humans or other animals. To be safe, keep all pest-control products in labeled containers, away from children and pets—preferably under lock and key.

NAMING NAMES

In earlier chapters, I talked about tactics for controlling the pests that most often target specific kinds of plants. But a great many insects and four-legged feasters have more wide-ranging appetites. When you're dealing with these gluttons, it pays to have some fast and sure good-riddance tricks up your sleeve. And you'll find a boatload of them right here.

Plants that get too much nitrogen are magnets for aphids and other sucking insects. So beware of a Big N overload! Avoid synthetic/chemical fertilizers, which deliver nutrients in highly concentrated form.

Aphids

These little sap suckers target every kind of plant under the sun. You'll generally find them clustered on new growth, draining out the fluids and leaving the plants wilted, discolored, and stunted—often infecting them with viruses to boot. Here are your best control measures:

- Pray for rain! A hard, driving downpour will kill a lot of aphids. And if the clouds aren't cooperating, give your plants a strong blast of water from the garden hose, making sure to spray the undersides of the leaves. Repeat two or three times, every other day.

- Repel them by laying banana peels on the ground under your plants—aphids can't stand bananas!

- Let em' have it with a blast of my Oil and Garlic Spray (see page 342).

Cutworms

Cutworms attack new seedlings and young transplants of all kinds, slicing them off at ground level. They strike in the dark, and they work fast. Because new batches of cutworms come along every few weeks, your garden is never really out of the woods during the growing season. Once plants are past the seedling stage, the culprits aren't likely to cause fatal damage, but they'll still make a nuisance of themselves. They'll also turn into moths and then lay next year's supply of cutworm eggs. The key to outwitting the rascals is persistence in following this three-step battle plan:

STEP 1. As soon as your seedlings appear, surround each one with a small barrier. Sink it into the soil so that 2 inches

CUTWORM COUNTDOWN

The parents of cutworms are dark-colored moths that will never win any beauty contests. Way back when, folks used to call 'em millers (maybe because of the flour-like dusting on their wings). They flit around after dark, and light draws them like a magnet. Old-timers lured them to their death with this age-old trick: Fill a wide, flat pan with milk and set it in the garden. Beside it, place a lighted lantern so that it shines on the milk. The moths will zero in on the glowing target, fall into the milk, and drown.

is belowground and about 3 inches is showing above. Good collar makings include aluminum foil, empty paper towel rolls, and tin cans with both ends removed. Whatever material you use, don't dawdle!

STEP 2. Once your seedlings have outgrown their collars, sprinkle a scratchy substance on the soil around each plant. The cutworms won't try to slink across anything that prickles their skin. Pine needles, coarse sand, and crushed eggshells all work well.

STEP 3. Every evening throughout the growing season, capture the worms when they come out to dine. Just set out boards, cabbage leaves, grapefruit halves, or potato chunks in your flower beds or vegetable garden. The next morning, the traps will be full of cutworms. What you do with them is your call. You can squash them, burn them, or dump them into a bucket of hot water laced with soap or alcohol.

Scale

Scale insects are notorious for sucking sap from plants in greenhouses and on windowsills, but they can get up to just as much mischief outdoors. When you see little waxy shells on stems and leaves, you'll know that these tiny insects are hard at work underneath their protective covers. As they progress, yellow spots will appear on foliage, and leaves may drop off. Eventually, the whole plant turns sickly and stunted.

If you catch a scale invasion in the *very* early stages, you can easily send the bugs to the great beyond by dipping a cotton ball or swab in 70% rubbing alcohol and dabbing each pest separately.

Like other sap suckers, scale insects leave an extra bit of nastiness behind: a sugary sap called honeydew that attracts nuisance pests like ants and bees. The sweet, sticky stuff is also a breeding ground for a fungus called sooty mold, which clogs plants' pores and prevents air and water from passing through. Left untreated, it can cause more damage than the pests themselves. Your best battle tactics depend on the kind of plant you need

Super Scale Scrub

This double-barreled potion works two ways: The soap kills the crawlers, a.k.a. unprotected scale babies, and the alcohol cuts right through the grown-ups' waxy shells.

1 cup of 70% rubbing alcohol
1 tbsp. of dishwashing liquid
1 qt. of water

Mix all of the ingredients in a handheld sprayer bottle, and apply to any scale-stricken plants every three days for two weeks. The scale invasion will soon sail off into the sunset!

Note: *Before you use this or any other alcohol spray on an entire plant, test it on a few leaves first. Then wait 24 hours, and check for any damage. Some plants are super-sensitive to dishwashing liquid and/or alcohol, and if you spray without testing, you could end up killing the pests* and *the victim!*

to protect. But act fast because a small scale invasion can beome a big one in the blink of an eye.

Annual flowers, herbs, and vegetables. Dig the plants out of the ground, or pull them out of their pots and destroy them—*yesterday*! Don't even think about throwing them on the compost pile. If you do, before you know it, your whole garden could wind up looking like a shell collection. Then just to be on the safe side, wash any containers the victims were growing in with a solution of 1 part household bleach to 8 parts hot water.

Trees, shrubs, bulbs, and perennials. Cut off infested stems (even if, in the case of bulbs and perennials, it means chopping the whole plant to the ground), and send the trimmings off with the trash. If parts of the plant seem unscathed by scale, it's okay to leave them, but hedge your bets by spraying the leaves and stems every three days for two weeks with my Super Scale Scrub (above). It'll quickly polish off any of the pests that you might have overlooked.

Two Tiny Terrors

Spider mites and thrips are so small, you can't see them without a strong magnifying glass, but they can cause major damage to every green, growing thing in your yard. Both pests suck the life-giving sap from plants, but the symptoms—and your best response—are different in each case.

Spider mites. When mites go on a sucking spree, plants look dull and unhealthy and lose their get-up-and-grow power. You'll see what looks like angel hair clinging to leaves and stems, and foliage will appear pale, wilted, or covered with yellowish specks. In the case of severe attacks, which usually occur in hot, dry weather, the victims often die.

If you want to confirm that mites or thrips have invaded your garden, pluck off a damaged leaf or flower, and shake it over a piece of white paper. If what looks like specks of dust or pepper rain down—and they hit the paper running—you've fingered the culprits.

Oil and Garlic Spray

This highly aromatic condiment is one of the most powerful tools in your plant-care pantry. It kills both soft-bodied insects of all kinds *and* nasty disease-causing fungi.

> **1 garlic bulb, minced**
> **1 cup of vegetable oil**
> **3 drops of dishwashing liquid**
> **1 qt. of water**

Mix the minced garlic and oil, and pour them into a glass jar with a tight-fitting lid. Put the jar in the refrigerator to steep for a day or two. To test the mixture for "doneness," open the lid and take a sniff. If the aroma is so strong that you step back, you're ready to roll. If the scent isn't so strong, mince half a garlic bulb, mix it into the oil, and wait another day. Then strain out the solids, and pour the oil into a fresh jar with a lid. When you're ready to use it, mix 1 tablespoon of the garlic oil with 3 drops of dishwashing liquid in 1 quart of water in a handheld sprayer bottle, and leap into action.

🄷🄴🄻🄿!

Q One day last summer, I found that spider mites had attacked several of my perennials. I sprayed the plants from top to bottom with an insecticide that contains parathion, but the problem just got worse! Is it because I didn't spray enough?

A *No, it's because you sprayed at all! First, these potent poisons can kill off a lot of the mites' natural enemies. Second, because spider mites are some of the most common garden pests in the world, they've long been bombarded with chemical pesticides. As a result, they've become immune to a whole host of them. What's more, scientific studies show that when they're exposed to some of these chemicals, including parathion (and carbaryl), they reproduce even faster than usual. Your best bet: Do everything you can to entice beneficial insects and other bad-bug predators into your garden.*

Once spider mites get a toehold, they can be the dickens to get rid of. So don't waste any time, depending upon the following:

- At the first sign of trouble, blast 'em off with a cold shower from your garden hose. (Do this early in the morning, before the sun has a chance to heat up the hose.) If your plants are small, just fill a handheld sprayer bottle with ice water, and let 'er rip.

- In later stages, mix 2 teaspoons of ammonia and 1 teaspoon of dishwashing liquid in 2 gallons of water. Pour the solution into a handheld sprayer bottle, and spray your plants from top to bottom every five days for three weeks.

- During dry spells, or if you live in an arid part of the country, sprinkle any bare ground to keep dust at a minimum. There's nothing spider mites like more than dry, dusty soil!

Thrips. These thugs scrape away a plant's tissue and then suck sap from the wound. Damaged leaves take on a silvery sheen. Afflicted flower buds either

343

never open or unfold covered with odd-colored streaks and speckles. Severe infestations weaken plants and stunt their growth. As thrips feed, some of them also spread viruses. Take action by:

- Clipping off the thrip-infested plant parts and dunking them in soapy water to kill the little suckers. Send any lingerers flying with a good blast from the garden hose (in this case, the water temperature doesn't matter).

- Filling blue margarine or chip-dip containers with soapy water, and setting them on the ground among your plants. The color blue draws thrips like a magnet, so they'll fly right in and drown.

Anytime thrips have been on the scene, it's likely that a virus outbreak will soon follow. So don't take chances: Once you've gotten rid of the thrips, spray your plants with a "flu shot" made from 2 cups of leaves from a healthy, sweet green pepper plant, 2 cups of water, and ½ teaspoon of dishwashing liquid. Liquefy the leaves and water in a blender, dilute the mixture with an equal amount of water, and add the dishwashing liquid. Pour the potion into a handheld sprayer bottle, and have at it! Something in the pepper leaves seems to protect other plants from viruses.

Slugs and Snails

Of course, slugs and snails are not insects—they're mollusks, closely related to shellfish like clams and oysters. But the damage they do puts them on par with the most destructive bugs in all creation. They chew ragged holes in leaves and flowers, often completely devouring seedlings and young transplants, while leaving behind disgusting trails of silvery slime. They can show up anywhere, but they appear most frequently and cause the most damage in cool, damp climates, and almost no plant is safe from their sharp jaws. Take your pick of these surefire slug-busting tactics:

- Go out after dusk when they're feeding, snatch them up with tongs, and drop

Studies have found that you can reduce slug damage by up to 80 percent simply by watering in the morning instead of the evening. The reason: It gives the soil time to dry out during the day, so the moisture-loving slimers can't eat as much when they mosey on out at night.

them into a bucket filled with water and a cup of vinegar, rubbing alcohol, or ammonia.

🌱 Trap them by setting citrus rinds, cabbage leaves, or potato chunks among your plants (again, wait until dusk). In the morning, scoop up the traps, slugs and all, and toss them into your bucket of doom.

🌱 Keep them away by surrounding their preferred plants with a scratchy substance, such as ground eggshells, sharp sand, diatomaceous earth, wood ashes, shredded oak leaves, pine needles, or coffee grounds.

Fence Out Four-Legged Friends and Foes

Insects are not the only creatures that help themselves to a backyard dinner at your expense. Plenty of larger animals—including some of your own best friends—also consider your yard fair game for fun and foraging. The quickest, easiest way to say, "Not here, my dear!" to dogs, cats, foxes, raccoons, armadillos, and rabbits (at least most of the time) is this simple trick: Surround your garden or beds with a strip of 2- to 4-foot-high chicken wire, hardware cloth, or similar material. Pull the top outward at a 45-degree angle. When the visitors get close to the fence, they'll feel trapped—and getting away will suddenly be a lot more appealing than the food that's waiting on the other side!

Take 2

There are plenty of good baits that will lure slugs and snails to their death, including beer, grape juice, and a half-and-half mixture of sugar and cider vinegar. But even if your bait of choice is harmless to children and pets, you don't want it disappearing into their mouths. To make sure that *only* slugs and snails can get to the stuff, round up some wide-mouthed pint bottles, like the kind many juices come in. Pour about an inch of bait into each bottle, then sink it into the ground so the top is just at ground level. The culprits will slither up to the edge and dive right in, but the beverage at the bottom will be beyond the reach of small, curious human hands and long canine tongues.

Soak It to 'Em

Even water-loving animals don't like it one bit when the stuff comes at them in a sudden blast. That's the secret behind a device that uses a motion detector to aim water at any varmints that are gunnin' for your plants, pest-controlling birds, or their feeder. It's not a cheap solution, but it *is* easy and effective. All you do is push a plastic stake into the ground, hook up a hose to the outlet, and attach the battery-powered sensor. When any invader wanders into its sights (so to speak), the gadget lets loose with a short burst of water. Then it turns itself off and resets to wait for the next invasion. A range of sensitivity settings lets you adjust the "fire" power to the size of the animal—so you can say "sayonara" to every trespasser from tiny chipmunks to great big bears.

Red Means Stop!

At least for a lot of squirrels it often does. Unlikely as it may sound, many of these mischief makers tend to avoid the color red. Scientists speculate the reason may be that, in many places, squirrels and certain redheaded woodpeckers compete head-to-head for the same resources. And the woodpeckers' sharp beaks may have taught the furry rascals not to be too pushy in claiming territory. Now I can't guarantee that the squirrels in your neighborhood are red-a-phobic, but it sure can't hurt to test the theory. So whether the little gluttons are dining on your flower bulbs, your fruit and nut harvest, or the contents of your bird

SCRAM!

If you want a repellent that's as good looking as it is effective, then *Coleus canina* is just the ticket. It gives off an aroma that humans can barely detect, but it sends cats, dogs, and rabbits running. What's more, this annual makes a fine addition to any yard. It grows to about 2 feet tall, with dark green foliage and spikes of blue flowers in summer. It's drought-tolerant and thrives in full sun to partial shade—unlike most coleus, which are definite shade lovers. Catalogs and garden centers sell it under the name of either *C. canina* 'Scaredy Cat', 'Bunnies Gone', or 'Dog Gone.' (Don't be fooled— they're all the same plant.)

feeders, try some of these simple ways to say to squirrels, "Restaurant closed":

- Set out red lawn furniture.

- Hang red balloons, banners, or ribbons in any troubled trees or bushes.

- Plant bright red flowers, or set containers of them among your vulnerable plants.

- Hang up a red bird feeder, or paint your current one a nice bright red.

Not sure what kind of critter is pulverizing your plants? In the evening, sprinkle white flour on the ground around the base of the victims. The next morning, look at the footprints. If you don't recognize them by sight, pull out your trusty Audubon field guide and make a positive ID.

That Is *Not* Your Litter Box!

All across the country these days, more and more folks are doing their gardening in containers. And judging from the letters in my mailbag, the vast majority of them share a common problem: cats that mistake the big pots for their own personal bathrooms. Well, here are four ways to say, "Take your potty break elsewhere":

- Plant low-growing groundcovers around the base of your potted trees and shrubs. You'll spiff up the container scheme and keep Fluffy out at the same time.

- Saturate cotton balls in lemon-oil furniture polish, and tuck them into the pots. Cats won't like the smell one bit! One ball will work for a small container; for larger ones, use two or three.

- Cover the soil surface with aluminum foil, and spread a thin layer of mulch on top. When Fluffy leaps into the pot to do her duty, the rustling sound and strange feel will make her hop right out again.

- Lay prickly branches—like ones you've pruned from roses, bramble fruits, or sharp-needled evergreens—on the soil. It's like posting a "Kitties Keep Out!" sign.

DASTARDLY DISEASES

Just like lawn and garden pests, the "germs" that cause plant diseases are living organisms. The only difference is that they're so tiny, we can't see them without a microscope. Most of the time you don't even notice them, but when the population gets out of hand, they can cause big trouble. So follow along for some simple secrets to keep your green scene out of sick bay.

Whenever you're working around your plants, be extra careful. Nicks and scrapes from lawn mowers, weed whackers, or wayward shovels, trowels, and pruners are open doors to all kinds of disease-causing organisms (and pests, too).

The Terrible Trio

Plant ailments are caused by three types of organisms: fungi, bacteria, and viruses. No matter which one you're dealing with, if the damage has gone very far, your only option is to pull up the victim and destroy it. But if you reach the scene early enough, you can often save the day by clipping off the affected plant parts and applying the appropriate tonic, based on the culprit.

Fungi. This type shows up more often than any other and can hit any part of a plant, making it wilt, rot, or get spots on its leaves. Fungi start life as spores, which multiply like crazy, especially on warm, wet leaves or stems. Fungi are responsible for two of the most common types of plant diseases,

Grandma's GROW-HOW

Whenever Grandma Putt's plants got sick for no apparent reason, she knew that they were most likely stressed out. Like people, plants tend to get out of sorts, or even fall ill when the weather turns sticky and sweltering or when a drought hits. What to do? Exactly what Grandma did: nothing! Don't spray, feed, or prune your plants, and don't pick any flowers or veggies unless they're about to go over the hill. Just give your garden a good drink of water and let it rest a spell.

molds and mildew. The spores sleep through the winter in the soil or in dead leaves or other plant debris until spring rains kick them into high gear. The good news is that most fungi spread slowly, so if you're quick on your feet, you stand a very good chance of heading off any serious damage.

Bacteria. These are smaller than fungi, and there are billions of them. Nearly all are harmless, and many are actually necessary to life. But the few real villains move fast and cause major problems, usually in the form of wilt or rot. There is no cure. Your only solution is to pull up the sick plants and destroy them. On the bright side, because most of the bacteria that attack plants can't live in frozen soil, they do the most damage in mild climates. However, up North, a few kinds spend the winter in the bodies of insects, which pass on the diseases to plants the following spring.

Viruses. These are the tiniest terrors, but only a few are true killers, causing plants to suddenly wilt and go belly-up. If your plants' leaves become twisted, crinkly, or mottled, chances are there's a virus at work. Viruses spend the winter in wild plants, and most of them are transmitted by insects, including aphids, whiteflies, thrips, leafhoppers, and cucumber beetles.

Quick Fix

One of the easiest ways to guard your plants against bacterial diseases—and other kinds, too—is to remember the old saying "Cleanliness is next to godliness." Every time you go out into your yard, take along a bag and a pair of pruners. Pick up debris as soon as you see it. And when you spot leaves, stems, flowers, or fruits that just don't look right somehow, clip them off and toss them in the bag. Then either burn it or seal it up and send it off with the trash. And do it quickly before trouble can set in.

An Ounce of Prevention

Many of the pest-prevention tactics I discussed earlier also help keep diseases at bay. In particular, choose disease-resistant varieties that are well suited to your growing conditions, encourage beneficial insects and other predators, and consistently give each plant the kind of TLC it needs to thrive—not simply survive. (Just like destructive insects, disease organisms zero in on plants that are weak or struggling.) In addition, these simple maintenance measures will go a long way toward protecting your green scene.

Aim low. When you water, point your hose at the ground. Better yet, install a drip irrigation system or a soaker hose. Wet foliage—especially after dark—is an open invitation to fungi.

Shun wet plants. Diseases can travel from plant to plant on tools, clothes, or hands—especially when foliage is wet. So after any kind of rain, wait until the plants are completely dry before you even touch them.

Keep it clean. Get rid of dead plant debris the minute you spot it, especially at the base of plants, where fungal spores thrive.

Mulch heavily. A thick blanket of fresh mulch will keep fungi in the soil from splashing up on your plants when it rains or when you water. It also controls weeds, which can spread both bacterial and fungal diseases.

Go on the offensive. Every week during warm, humid weather, spray your plants—especially prime targets like roses—with a good, healthy dose of my Fungus-Fighter Tonic (see page 223).

Even for experienced gardeners, some plant problems are hard to diagnose. If your plants show symptoms that aren't covered in this book, or you've tried the recommended treatment and it hasn't worked, then it's time to call in the pros. Clip off a few affected leaves, stems, or both, and send them to your closest Cooperative Extension Service. Include a note with as much information as you have about the problem, as well as the plant's location and growing conditions. And send along a snapshot of the plant if you can. Your friendly neighborhood scientists will examine the evidence and get back to you with a diagnosis and a prescription.

Let the Sun Fight Your Battles

One way to clear out any soil-dwelling fungi is to call on Ol' Sol to heat up your soil to 150°F or so. This trick is especially helpful if you live down South, where the climate is hot and humid, and you have more than your share of fungal woes. As a bonus (no matter where you live), this solarizing process will also eliminate pests like Colorado potato beetles and root-knot nematodes. For the process to work, however, you need to do the job during the hottest part of the year, which in most places is July and August. Here's the simple four-step routine:

STEP 1. Dig up a plot of soil that's about 10 feet square. Then spread a 1- to 2-inch layer of fresh manure on top and dig it in well.

STEP 2. Rake the soil into planting beds or rows (because you won't be able to cultivate after the soil has been solarized). Then water well, and let the ground settle overnight.

STEP 3. The next day, cover the plot with a sheet of clear, 3- to 6-mil plastic, and pile rocks or soil around the edges to keep it in place. Patch any holes or tears that you find. Make sure the plastic has some slack in it, so it can puff up (instead of blowing away or even bursting) when the heat starts rising.

STEP 4. Wait about six weeks—or longer if the weather's cool. Then take off the plastic, water the soil, and plant your crops. Don't dig any deeper than 6 inches, or you'll bring up untreated soil—fungi, nematodes, and all.

GO FOR THE GOOD GUYS

Don't confuse root-knot nematodes, which ransack the underground parts of many plants, with beneficial nematodes. Like their nasty cousins, the good guys are also parasites. But instead of setting up camp inside your plants, they move into the bodies of pests like cutworms, root maggots, and Japanese beetle grubs and polish them off. Most garden centers and seed catalogs sell beneficial nematodes. If you buy some, read the package instructions carefully and follow them to the letter. Good nematodes can't possibly harm your plants, but to get them to do their best work, you need to release them in your yard at just the right time.

More Ways to Nix Nematodes

Although solarizing your soil will get rid of root-knot nematodes temporarily, it's not a permanent fix. But fortunately, this simple strategy will say a loud and clear "No, no, nematodes!"

Feed their sweet tooth. Spread 5 pounds of sugar over every 50 square feet of planting area. The nematodes will choke to death on the stuff.

Bring on the enemy. Load your soil with things like eggshells, shrimp hulls, and seafood meal. They all contain chitin, which is what nematode eggs are covered with. Chitin eaters from near and far will show up to feast on the free lunch you've given them—and then start in on the nematode eggs.

Like many diseases, nematodes cause plants to become sickly, turn yellow, and wilt. To confirm the diagnosis, dig up a plant and look at the roots. If they're covered with galls that you can't break off, it means the N-squad is hard at work.

Give 'em a drink. Mix 1 can of beer and 1 cup of molasses in a 20 gallon hose-end sprayer, and thoroughly soak any area where nasty nematodes are doin' their dirty work. It'll deliver a knockout punch they won't soon forget.

Carry no passengers. Root-knot nematodes seldom travel more than a few feet from their hatching place—unless you give them a ride to a new home. After you've been digging around in a likely nematode stomping ground, hose off your shovels, rakes, the tines of your tiller, and even your gardening gloves if you've had your hands in the soil.

Grandma's GROW-HOW

If you love asparagus, as Grandma Putt did, you've got an A-1 nematode chaser close at hand. Every time you finish cooking some of the scrumptious spears, save the water you cooked them in, let the liquid cool down, then pour it onto the soil around any trouble-prone plants. Nematodes can't stand asparagus juice, so your problem is solved!

USDA
PLANT HARDINESS
ZONE MAP

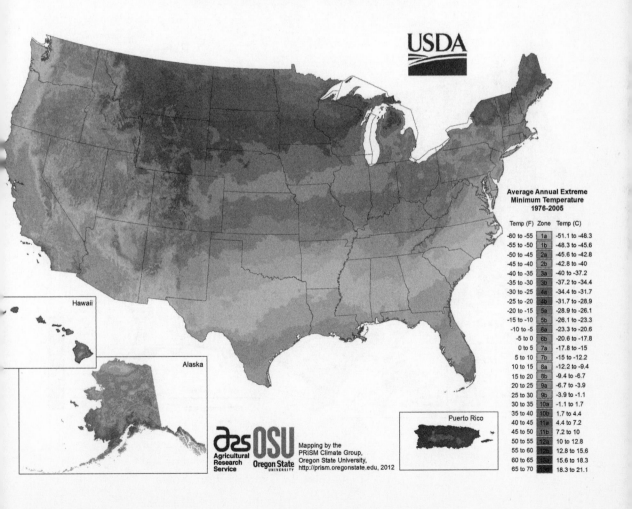

USDA

Average Annual Extreme Minimum Temperature 1976-2005

Temp (F)	Zone	Temp (C)
-60 to -55	1a	-51.1 to -48.3
-55 to -50	1b	-48.3 to -45.6
-50 to -45	2a	-45.6 to -42.8
-45 to -40	2b	-42.8 to -40
-40 to -35	3a	-40 to -37.2
-35 to -30	3b	-37.2 to -34.4
-30 to -25	4a	-34.4 to -31.7
-25 to -20	4b	-31.7 to -28.9
-20 to -15	5a	-28.9 to -26.1
-15 to -10	5b	-26.1 to -23.3
-10 to -5	6a	-23.3 to -20.6
-5 to 0	6b	-20.6 to -17.8
0 to 5	7a	-17.8 to -15
5 to 10	7b	-15 to -12.2
10 to 15	8a	-12.2 to -9.4
15 to 20	8b	-9.4 to -6.7
20 to 25	9a	-6.7 to -3.9
25 to 30	9b	-3.9 to -1.1
30 to 35	10a	-1.1 to 1.7
35 to 40	10b	1.7 to 4.4
40 to 45	11a	4.4 to 7.2
45 to 50	11b	7.2 to 10
50 to 55	12a	10 to 12.8
55 to 60	12b	12.8 to 15.6
60 to 65	13a	15.6 to 18.3
65 to 70	13b	18.3 to 21.1

Hawaii

Alaska

Puerto Rico

Agricultural Research Service

OSU Oregon State UNIVERSITY

Mapping by the
PRISM Climate Group,
Oregon State University,
http://prism.oregonstate.edu, 2012

AMERICAN HORTICULTURAL SOCIETY PLANT HEAT-ZONE MAP

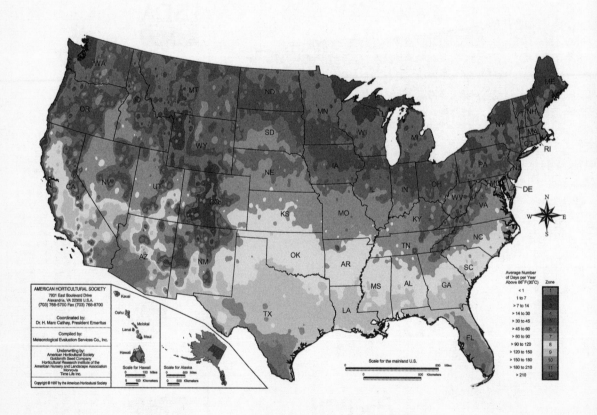

AMERICAN HORTICULTURAL SOCIETY
7931 East Boulevard Drive
Alexandria, VA 22308 U.S.A.
(703) 768-5700 Fax (703) 768-8700

Coordinated by:
Dr. H. Marc Cathey, President Emeritus

Compiled by:
Meteorological Evaluation Services Co., Inc.

Underwriting by:
American Horticultural Society
Goldsmith Seed Company
Horticultural Research Institute of the
American Nursery and Landscape Association
Monrovia
Time Life Inc.

Copyright © 1997 by the American Horticultural Society

Average Number of Days per Year Above 86°F (30°C)	Zone
< 1	1
1 to 7	2
> 7 to 14	3
> 14 to 30	4
> 30 to 45	5
> 45 to 60	6
> 60 to 90	7
> 90 to 120	8
> 120 to 150	9
> 150 to 180	10
> 180 to 210	11
> 210	12

Scale for the mainland U.S.

Scale for Hawaii

Scale for Alaska

INDEX

A

Aeration techniques, 30–32, 45, 324
Aeration Tonic, 31
Ageratum, 152
Ajuga, 183
Akebia, 172
Allergies, pollen, 76–77
All-Season Green-Up Tonic, 26
Aluminum foil uses
    cleaning tools, 234
    pest control, 232–234, 340, 347
    rose blooms, 157
    tomato yield, 211
American boxwood, 71
American Horticultural Society Plant Heat-Zone Map, 354
Ammonia
    in fertilizing tonics, 26, 38, 86, 118, 141, 279, 312
    in grass-clipping dissolving tonic, 48
    in lawn-saver tonic, 53
    for pest control, 229, 343
    in planting tonic, 122
    in thatch-control tonic, 33
    in tree wound tonic, 90
    for winter lawn care, 63
Anemones, 127
Angelica, 271
Angel's trumpet, 77
Animal pest control. *See also specific pests*

fences for, 345
for flower gardens, 149–152
herbs for, 282, 287
for lawns, 7, 51–54
pest identification, 347
plant choices for, 331, 346
for trees and shrubs, 96–99
for vegetable gardens, 228–233
water-spraying device for, 346
Anise hyssop, 119
Annuals
    in containers, 113–115
    deadheading, 111
    as deer deterrent, 152
    fertilizing, 139, 141
    in hanging baskets, 116
    pest control for, 341
    for privacy fence, 105
    from seed, 107–110
    self-sowing (perennial), 111
    transplants, 108–109
Antidesiccant spray, 102
Ants, 95–96, 287
Aphids
    aluminum foil for, 234
    ants and, 95
    best control strategies, 339
    companion planting and, 167
    herbs for, 287
    hosing off plants, 336

plant diseases and, 147
rose damage from, 170
traps for, 251
Apple juice, 149
Apple maggots, 248–249
Apples
    growing, 248
    storing, 245
    in topdressing tonic, 187
Apple trees, 245, 247
Armyworms, 14, 58, 334
Aroma, from trees, 74–75
Artichokes, 202
Asparagus, 202, 352
Asters, 127, 146
Astilbes, 121, 183, 330
Autumn eleagnus, 91
Avocado skins, as fertilizer, 162
Azaleas, 85, 330

B

Baby's breath, 108, 126
Baby shampoo
    for disease control, 207
    in fall cleanup tonic, 62
    in fertilizing tonics, 38, 211
    in pest-control tonics, 96, 132
    in planting tonics, 82, 122, 158
    in seed-starter tonic, 16

D

G

I